UNMAKING MIGRANTS

A volume in the series

Police/Worlds: Studies in Security, Crime, and Governance

Edited by Kevin Karpiak, Sameena Mulla, William Garriott, and Ilana Feldman

A list of titles in this series is available at cornellpress.cornell.edu

UNMAKING MIGRANTS

Nigeria's Campaign to End
Human Trafficking

Stacey Vanderhurst

CORNELL UNIVERSITY PRESS   ITHACA AND LONDON

First published 2022 by Cornell University Press

Library of Congress Cataloging-in-Publication Data

Names: Vanderhurst, Stacey, author.
Title: Unmaking migrants : Nigeria's campaign to end human trafficking / Stacey Vanderhurst.
Description: Ithaca [New York] : Cornell University Press, 2022. | Series: Police/ Worlds: studies in security, crime, and governance | Includes bibliographical references and index.
Identifiers: LCCN 2021040013 (print) | LCCN 2021040014 (ebook) | ISBN 9781501763526 (hardcover) | ISBN 9781501763533 (paperback) | ISBN 9781501763557 (ebook) | ISBN 9781501763540 (pdf)
Subjects: LCSH: Human trafficking—Social aspects—Nigeria. | Emigration and immigration—Social aspects. | Women—Nigeria—Social conditions.
Classification: LCC HQ281 .V375 2022 (print) | LCC HQ281 (ebook) | DDC 364.15/5109669—dc23
LC record available at https://lccn.loc.gov/2021040013
LC ebook record available at https://lccn.loc.gov/2021040014

For Florence

Contents

Acknowledgments

Most Nigerian names have a literal meaning. Some friends gave me mine on a Friday afternoon at a funeral celebration for my friend Adeola's late father. I had arrived wearing a dress tailored from the party's designated *aso ebi* cloth along with a big *gele* head tie, so it was decided that I should have a Yoruba name to match. When someone suggested Aduke, everyone at our table smiled and laughed, arguing over its exact translation but all agreeing that it was perfect. Some said it meant beloved; others said it meant spoiled. It is the one whom people love to look after, they finally decided. I had to admit that it was true.

Countless people have looked after me in the dozen or so trips I have made to Nigeria since 2008. Most important are those whose stories are found in these pages: the women I first met at the shelter who let me into their lives during a most difficult moment and for years after, the counselors and other staff who shared critical insights and candid conversations about a system they agreed was not working, and the administrators who opened their doors and offered introductions in a shared commitment to transparency and scholarly research. I thank them each sincerely and anonymously.

I have also been supported by a robust intellectual community at the University of Lagos, especially Prof. Franca Attoh, her colleagues in the Department of Sociology, and the entire Lagos Studies Association team. In 2015, colleagues at the Nigerian Institute of International Affairs (NIIA) helped me host a conference that let me connect more deeply with Nigeria-based scholars of trafficking, Profs. Clementina Osezua and Oluwakemi Adesina. The first chapter of this book is based on newspaper archives painstakingly organized in clippings at NIIA and at IFRA-Nigeria, the French Institute for Research in Africa at the University of Ibadan.

I began this project at Brown University in a cocoon of scholarly love and support that I only appreciate more as time passes. My colleagues Susan Ellison, Sohini Kar, Caitlin Walker, James Doyle, Láura Vares, and Colin Porter were invaluable to my growth as a scholar, as were many other fine mentors then and still today, most especially Katie Rhine. The Population Studies and Training Center at Brown University also provided key developmental support for early fieldwork trips, and the Center for Law, Society & Culture at the Michael Maurer School of Law at Indiana University, Bloomington, helped me expand the vision of this book for new audiences. I would also like to thank my colleagues at the University of Kansas in its Women's, Gender & Sexuality Studies Department, the Kansas African Studies Center, and the Gender Seminar at the Hall Center for the Humanities. All have been generous in their feedback and encouragement along the way, especially Nick Syrett, Katie Batza, Hannah Britton, and Ebenezer Obadare. I am grateful for Will Garriott's support in identifying this manuscript with the *Police/Worlds* series and in providing key developmental feedback throughout the publication and review process. Scott Jenkins also provided indefatigable copyediting support and general enthusiasm when it was most needed.

Finally, I would like to recognize all the other wonderful people who bring joy and meaning to my days beyond the work of academia—the friends who are now family and the family who are dear friends. They too have looked after me and made me feel connected to new worlds and possibilities. I am so very thankful for a life that includes all these many pieces, and I am so excited to finally share this book with you, too.

A previous version of chapter 6 appeared in *Political and Legal Anthropology Review*. My fieldwork was funded by the National Science Research Foundation (Doctoral Dissertation Improvement Grant #1021889), the Social Science Research Council, the Wenner Gren Foundation for Anthropological Research, the West African Research Association, and the American Council for Learned Societies.

UNMAKING MIGRANTS

INTRODUCTION

"I have nothing," Florence said to me often, "nothing going."[1] Sitting outside her family's small provisions shop, she did not mean that she lacked for food or shelter. She helped run this business from the front of her childhood home on the urban outskirts of Benin City in southern Nigeria, and her boyfriend traded car parts in a nearby market. Together, they rented a private room, ate well, and enjoyed small luxuries like a used smartphone and occasional generator power. By saying she had "nothing going," she meant that she lacked the opportunity to work for something better. The eldest daughter of a mechanic and his second wife, Florence had completed most of secondary school but fell short of graduating when an aging relative needed household assistance across town. "They are still quite small," she told me, gesturing to her three younger siblings as they ran between our flimsy plastic chairs outside the shop. "When I come to visit them, they are complaining, they are suffering. I am their elder and I wish I could give to them, but I cannot. I do not have. I have nothing."

While her younger brother attended a local university, Florence spent the first years of her twenties apprenticing to a hairdresser, only to struggle to find steady work with those skills when she was done training. "I want to be able to help, but there are too many salons in Benin. Too much. If you go on any street, let me say that you would find at least six of them. I trained for almost two years—so many months on Ghana weaving, on weave on, on spinning, and on others." Now she was helping out at her mother's shop, and she maintained occasionally lucrative relationships with successful men from the area, but Florence felt stagnant and frustrated with "nothing going" for herself.

1

FIGURE 1. "Learn Spanish, German, Italian." Women pass in front of an advertisement for foreign-language classes at an open-air market. Benin City, Edo State (photo by author).

"So I prayed to God for direction and I prayed for my helpers," she explained. "Finally the opportunity came."

Over the last three decades, Florence's hometown and the capital of Edo State, Benin City, has become notorious as a hub for migrant sex work, especially the so-called trafficking of young Nigerian women to Europe. Billboards offering language courses in Italian, Spanish, and German dot the landscape, and most young women have at least one aunt or cousin or childhood friend already abroad, working discretely in foreign sex industries (see figure 1).

As Florence struggled to find her way in various entrepreneurial schemes, she received letters and photographs from her boyfriend's mother in Italy, and she listened carefully to circulating stories of former classmates who had gone to "try their luck." Then, when Florence was twenty-five years old, a family friend offered to help her travel out, and she agreed. Within weeks, he had paired her with another woman from the same area and arranged their papers and tickets. Because flights from Nigeria to Italy and other parts of Europe were so heavily monitored for human trafficking, they would first fly to Gambia. From there, they would board another plane to Italy and work to pay off the travel debt.

Things did not go as planned.

On check-in at the Lagos airport, an immigration officer pulled Florence and her travel companion aside. Seeing two young women traveling together, the man demanded a bribe of 1,000 naira or about six US dollars. This kind of harassment from officials is common in Nigeria, but Florence refused to pay the bribe. "Why should I pay if my papers are real?" she would tell me later. The officer eventually turned them in, accusing them of being human trafficking victims. But it was a Friday evening and the counter-trafficking office was closed, so they spent the weekend at the airport in a holding cell. On Monday, both women were transferred to a shelter for trafficked women, still wearing the new clothes they had bought to travel in. That was where I met them—at the federally run center for human trafficking victims in Lagos, Nigeria, in 2010, where the fieldwork for this book began.

Florence was clearly upset. She spent much of her first several days at the shelter hanging her head low over her lap, praying in heavy whispers into folded hands. She repeated in pidgin English, "*I wan go, I wan go . . .*" (I want to go), over and over again, and she read aloud carefully marked passages from the Bible.[2] She would stay in the shelter for nearly two months, ostensibly for the purposes of "rehabilitation."

Rehabilitation—From What?

Most of the women I met at this shelter were, like Florence, stopped en route—at international airports, African land borders, and European points of entry—before ever reaching their destination. They had made the decision to travel out and had obtained a sponsor and travel agent to make the arrangements. Human trafficking is characterized by exploitation, so what starts as smuggling becomes trafficking when those agents deceive, coerce, or exploit their clients. This line between smuggling and trafficking is often difficult to distinguish in practice, but most of the women at the shelter were identified as victims and "rescued" before any abuse transpired.

Nigerian officials proudly framed this form of intervention as preemptive, agreeing that the women were yet unharmed while insisting their abuse was imminent. However, without any experience of injury or even danger, the so-called victims in these cases did not see their experiences as trafficking, and, like Florence, they adamantly protested their detention. Regardless of their wishes to be released, to be sent home, or to just be allowed to continue traveling, all intercepted women were repatriated back to Nigeria and taken to one of several state-run shelters for trafficked persons. Most went to the Lagos rehabilitation

center, the largest accommodation facility of the National Agency for the Prohibition on Trafficking in Persons and Other Related Matters (NAPTIP), because
of its proximity to the country's main international airport and nearby land
border.

This book describes what is at stake in this shelter for the women detained
there, and for the state agents, policies, and programs operating on them. It focuses on the shelter's rehabilitation program, which largely meets international
standards for anti-trafficking interventions, but also reflects particular social and
political concerns around women's migration and sexuality in Nigeria. Since
even the counselors at the shelter acknowledged that the women there had not
yet been abused, there was little sense that they would need help recovering from
trauma, integrating back into family life, or any other typical uses of therapy in
human trafficking rehabilitation projects. Rather, the purpose of rehabilitation,
as counselors often described it, was to convince the women of the danger of
their migration choices and to prevent them from making the same mistakes
again. This model of rehabilitation assumes that victims are complicit in being
trafficked, so they are the ones who must reform. Their desire to migrate and
willingness to take on debt to do so are treated as vulnerabilities that need to be
fixed. In short, this model equates human trafficking prevention with migration
prevention. It justifies campaigns against migration in the name of protecting
migrants, with little regard for what women like Florence could see or want for
themselves.

Reframing Rescue

This gap between migrants' goals and those of the agencies trying to help them
is documented across critical scholarship on campaigns against human trafficking and in activist work around the world. In popular media, human trafficking
is often discussed as a crime so abhorrent that it should crosscut conventional
political divisions.[3] The movement against human trafficking, however, is deeply
contested. Even feminists cannot agree on what should count as trafficking or
"modern-day slavery," and this disagreement has tremendous implications for
who we help and how we do it.

On one side of this debate are neo-abolitionists. They consider all forms of
commercial sex to be exploitative and therefore seek to abolish its practice worldwide. Drawing on the work of prominent feminist scholars like Kathleen Barry
and Sheila Jeffreys, these activists refer to commercial sex as prostitution and
argue that it inherently harms women, whether it is consensual or not.[4] By this
thinking, prostitution *is* human trafficking. Activists sharing this belief formed

the Coalition against Trafficking in Women (CATW) in 1988 to promote legislation that criminalizes the solicitation and facilitation of prostitution.

On the other side of this debate are labor rights feminists who organize in support of people in commercial sex industries—what they call sex work. Building from a sex-positive tradition of feminism, these groups see commercial sex as a legitimate form of labor that is deserving of the same protections offered to other workers. Rather than eliminate the sex industry altogether, they aim to address the problems sex workers face, such as stigma, violence, and financial exploitation, by framing sex workers' rights as a labor rights issue. Organized in part through the Global Alliance against Trafficking in Women (GAATW), they fight for the *de*criminalization of activities associated with sex work. They directly oppose the work of neo-abolitionist feminists, especially challenging the racist assumptions that third world women like Florence are incapable of choice and must be naive victims in need of rescue.[5]

Despite these differences, both neo-abolitionist and labor rights activists influenced the major international law that regulates human trafficking: the UN Protocol to Prevent, Suppress, and Punish Trafficking in Persons, Especially Women and Children.[6] Passed in December 2000 in Palermo, Italy, it is often referred to as the Palermo Protocol. It offers the following definition of human trafficking:

> "Trafficking in persons" shall mean the recruitment, transportation, transfer, harbouring or receipt of persons, by means of the threat or use of force or other forms of coercion, of abduction, of fraud, of deception, of the abuse of power or of a position of vulnerability or of the giving or receiving of payments or benefits to achieve the consent of a person having control over another person, for the purpose of exploitation.

What qualifies, however, as exploitation? This is where neo-abolitionists and labor rights activists disagree, and the Palermo Protocol does not clarify further. Although it addresses multiple forms of trafficking such as labor exploitation and organ trading, it gives particular emphasis to sexual exploitation, as indicated in its titular phrase "especially women and children."[7]

This ambiguity within the text of the Palermo Protocol has promoted ineffective and often counterproductive interventions around migration and sex work around the world. Activist organizations and governments interpret vague language to suit their own political agendas, or they reproduce this ambiguity in their own missions. Many agencies have tried to find common ground between the perspectives of neo-abolitionists and of labor rights feminists by committing to fight only *forced* sex work. However, these efforts still cast voluntary sex workers as "fallen women," undeserving of rights or legal protections, and therefore left without recourse in confronting other kinds of violence and ex-ploitation that sex workers face.[8] People working in sex industries, as a result, are left "running from rescuers."[9]

As an anthropologist, I regard people as experts on their own social worlds, and I distrust analyses that supersede a person's interpretation of their own life and work. The views of young, poor, African women, in particular, are too of-ten missing in conversations about their lives and well-being. For these reasons, I find the labor rights approach to human trafficking to be a more compelling framework for addressing the dangers that women like Florence might face. Nev-ertheless, in this book, I am less interested in advocating one framework over another. Rather, I approach human trafficking as a *discourse* or a way we have come to think and talk about a social problem. Instead of trying to choose or defend a single definition, this approach draws attention to all the messy con-tradictions that have become entangled in the idea of trafficking, including both neo-abolitionist and labor rights interpretations of anti-trafficking law.[10] With all this baggage, I do not find human trafficking to be a useful term by itself.[11] However, by studying critically how it gets used, we can see how this discourse is mobilized to police certain kinds of people and behavior, especially around sex, class, and gender.

From Liberation to Criminal Justice

To track these effects, we must step back from legal debates over definitions of trafficking to consider the role of the law in stopping human trafficking alto-gether. That is, we must examine the very notion that human trafficking is a criminal justice issue, best resolved by laws that criminalize sexual violence and labor exploitation.

This presumption can be traced to the 1970s with the movement to end vio-lence against women. In the United States, early women's liberation feminists wanted to end patriarchal violence in all corners of society, but they did not see the law as the primary tool for solving this problem. They favored community ac-countability over government intervention, or what they called the "prison/psy-chiatric state."[12] But when full social transformation stalled, criminal reforms were adopted instead, such as increasing prosecutions of sex crimes and eliminating the legal exemption for marital rape. Although received as victories for feminists, these reforms defined gender justice as criminal justice.[13] This move produced not only a narrower agenda but also a troubling one, given the racist history of US legal institutions, particularly prisons.[14] Critics call this shift *carceral feminism*—an unwelcome compromise of feminists' original vision for true liberation.[15]

The evolution of anti-trafficking discourses reflects a similar pattern on the global stage. In the 1970s and 80s, groups like the Third World Women's Alliance readily linked problems of sex work and sexual violence to global inequality, neocolonial development policies, and patriarchal gender norms, and they pushed for broad social change to address these problems. However, this vision was lost in the United Nations' shift to a "violence against women" framework for human trafficking in the 1990s. Rather than targeting systems of imperialism, sexism, and racism writ large, human trafficking was defined as a crime between individuals—thereby trading an examination of structural violence for a focus only on interpersonal violence.[16] Instead of challenging state power over women's lives, the role of the state expanded through new laws, agencies, and intervention mechanisms.

The shift to criminal justice changed not only how the state treated perpetrators but also how it treated its victims, codified in the three p's of anti-trafficking campaigns: prevention, protection, and prosecution. In terms of prevention, criminal definitions of trafficking hinge strictly on individual choice and consent, suggesting that anyone could be a victim. This focus symbolically isolates victims from social, political, and economic conditions that make them vulnerable to exploitation, and it directs prevention campaigns toward individual decision makers rather than the systems that could be improved. In protection efforts, the government co-optation of shelters and safe houses provides further administrative control over women's welfare, leveraging the provision of social services for other kinds of cooperation with the state, including cooperation in criminal prosecutions. Even when shelters are managed by nongovernmental organizations (NGOs), the mainstreaming of funding, standardization of services, and professionalization of care have still largely sterilized these spaces and separated them from their more radical political origins. In this manner, direct support for victims of trafficking, like that for other survivors of sexual violence, is subject to carceral logics rather than transformative politics. In her account of the US campaign against domestic minor sex trafficking, Jennifer Musto calls this trend *carceral protection*.[17]

This book builds on this analysis while exploring new questions raised by the Nigerian case. As in many African contexts, the Nigerian police force is corrupt, the welfare state is practically nonexistent, and women's rights advocacy has long been dominated by the charitable projects of elites. How is this expansion of state power received when the state is otherwise so absent from people's lives? What does it mean to adopt a carceral model of care as the only path to social services? How do women navigate this intervention in the context of other government abuses, and how do state agents defend it? Nigeria's own human trafficking crisis also happened to coincide with its most recent democratic transition in 1998,

closely followed by the global diffusion of anti-trafficking efforts after the signing of the Palermo Protocol in 2000. How then have ideas of democracy and citizenship been taken up in these campaigns, and how have women targeted by
these programs contested them? Ultimately, how do these carceral technologies
travel, and how are they resisted?

From Human Rights to Border Control

The global shift to carceral frameworks for addressing sexual violence coincided
with other important global shifts in migration policy. These changes helped el-
evate human trafficking from a niche women's rights issue to a global security
issue, again bolstering the power of the state along the way.

In a human rights approach to migrant welfare, trafficking can be understood
as a system of exploitation that is the *consequence* of strict border enforcement
and the legal vulnerability of undocumented migrants. If migrants were guar-
anteed the full protection of the law, they would not be vulnerable to the whims
of smugglers and debtors. Likewise, if the rights of sex workers were protected
like those in other industries, they would not rely on informal networks to do
their jobs. A human rights framework suggests that where trafficking thrives,
governments are *complicit* for rendering populations so exploitable.[18] However,
in the human rights campaign against trafficking throughout the 1990s, state
officials continually rejected any such responsibility.

In another shift, criminal law began merging with immigration law during
the 1980s—producing a legal infrastructure that attorneys and activists call *crimmigration*.[19] As the movement to end violence against women stoked racialized
fears of crime, anti-immigrant sentiment increased, and pressure mounted to
"stem the tide" of migration into the United States and Europe.[20] Debates over
a wall at the US southern border and imagery of "Fortress Europe" depicted land
borders as porous and unsafe. With migrants themselves framed as a threat, migration policies were debated in terms of crime and safety, rather than economics or social integration.[21] International borders were transformed into
police-security sites, with armed inspection and patrol forces. Individual violations of migration law were increasingly treated as criminal offenses, and criminal penalties for violations like unlawful entry grew tenfold.[22] Dedicated
immigrant detention centers proliferated to incarcerate unprecedented numbers
of migrant individuals and families, combining technologies of the refugee camp
with those of the prison. These facilities were often built from existing prisons.[23]

The emergence of crimmigration law and policy facilitated a different
approach to the problem of human trafficking. Rather than being developed

through the UN Human Rights Council, the Palermo Protocol was passed in 2000 by the UN Office on Drugs and Crime, alongside other protocols targeting transnational organized crime, such as smuggling and drug trafficking. It reframed human trafficking from a state-enforced system of vulnerability to a problem of individual crimes and criminal networks. As one state representative explained at a UN conference, "You have to understand . . . this is not like torture. It's not even about human rights. We governments are not the villains here. Traffickers are just criminals. We can't be responsible for what they are doing. In fact, if it wasn't that we needed the cooperation of other countries to catch them, I wouldn't be here."[24]

As with sexual violence, the criminal justice paradigm for migration law structured the standards not only for prosecuting traffickers but also for preventing trafficking and protecting victims. Instead of implementing interventions common to human rights and humanitarian projects, anti-trafficking campaigns quickly appropriated the same policing and detention technologies already in place for other forms of migration control. With the aim of catching both traffickers and their victims, signatories increased enforcement power at land borders and developed new patrol squads for immigrant crossing zones like the Mediterranean Sea.[25] Rather than making migrants safer, these security efforts have the opposite effect, driving illicit crossings into more hazardous parts of the desert and onto smaller, less reliable seacraft.[26] Fear of retribution also makes migrants less willing to turn to authorities for help along their journeys, even if they are subjected to the kinds of coercion or exploitation that characterize human trafficking.[27] Some anti-trafficking laws do incentivize cooperation with state programs by providing residency rights to undocumented migrants legally recognized as human trafficking victims, but these exceptional cases can serve as merely a "soft glove" to the "punishing fist" of otherwise severe immigration policy that makes all migrants' lives more precarious.[28] Rather than a regime of rights that confers obligations on the state, migrant vulnerability is recognized only through the arbitrary and self-congratulatory modes of pity and compassion, settling easily alongside regimes of repression and exclusion.[29]

Meanwhile, expanding networks of detention centers normalized the prolonged confinement of migrants at land borders and across the interior.[30] Whereas other victims of crime and survivors of sexual violence are not detained as a matter of policy, the regular detention of trafficking victims becomes thinkable within this landscape; they join the multitude of migrants and others interned for purposes of "not-punishment" by an expanding but hidden carceral state.[31] As this book will show, migrant women detained inside these facilities are subject to therapy that blurs the boundaries of protection, persuasion, and coercion. Counselors shift freely between the need to protect migrants from traffickers and the need to protect them from themselves, urging migrant women to personally re-form and to rethink their futures. These messages echo another arm of the global migration control apparatus—that which aims to "educate" and "enlighten" would-be migrants with information about the danger of illicit routes in order to persuade them not to migrate.[32]

Global anti-trafficking campaigns are often imagined to exist outside main-stream migration management politics, with their aim seen not as correcting criminal or disorderly modes of migration but as extracting unwilling victims from migration streams they did not intend to enter. This book suggests that this very assumption reflects the success of these campaigns, facilitating the percep-tion that trafficking victims are different from other kinds of migrants and that anti-trafficking is different from migration control. That distinction relies on the still fundamentally raced and gendered image of the trafficking victim as a pas-sive victim of abject suffering, incapable of forming or narrating her own de-sires. The history of anti-trafficking work in Nigeria reveals how effective that myth has been: state efforts to publicly shame deported women transform seam-lessly to lauded protection and enlightenment campaigns that further detain, renounce, and stigmatize women's migration, now sanctioned in the guise of vul-nerability reduction.[33] These ideological and technological continuities between migration control and anti-trafficking efforts expose the supposed exceptional-ism of the trafficking victim as unfounded.

Although these critiques of anti-trafficking campaigns are well established in both activist and scholarly circles, they are usually directed at migrant-receiving states in the global north, like the United States and United Kingdom, where racism and xenophobia have long motivated anti-migrant policies. These wealthy nations put significant pressure on migrant-sending states like Nigeria to reduce emigration, whether by strengthening border security or by adapting development programs to address the so-called root causes of emigration.[34] Con-sequently, when migrant-sending states participate in migration prevention campaigns, that participation is seen as a political concession to appease more powerful governments and to gain access to the valuable resources they control.[35] Anti-migration policies in the global south are rarely considered a reflection of internal political interests. This gap is more than an oversight. It reflects a set of implicit assumptions: that only migrant-receiving states are committed to pre-venting migration, that migrant-sending states generally cultivate good relation-ships with their emigrant diaspora, and that the interests of migrant-sending and migrant-receiving states are therefore opposed.

This book uses the case of Nigeria to better interrogate these assumptions. While not denying the power wielded by global north states, it suggests that we can better understand the mechanisms of migration control by paying attention to where these political agendas may align. It shows how officials from the Nigerian government have consistently blamed migrant sex workers for the country's poor reputation abroad, and it traces where these narratives have penetrated prevention and rehabilitation work in the region. What terms of citizenship and belonging are embedded in these programs, and how do they fix nationalist ideals of good and bad migrants? How do globally circulating anti-trafficking campaigns legitimize this stigma, and how do they reinforce other kinds of inequality, especially around class, education, and sexuality? What sense can we make of anti-migrant messaging within migrant-sending communities, where it cannot be explained using familiar frameworks of xenophobia and racism?

These questions are important when we consider the particular carceral technologies of migration control that are repurposed in anti-trafficking work. How do the different logics of immigrant detention translate to sites of origin and return? How are victim rehabilitation programs situated alongside other efforts to prevent emigration or to integrate returnees? How do migrant women understand these intervention efforts within their own country? Evidence from Nigeria demonstrates that anti-migration campaigns and border security mandates not merely imposed by rich nations but also taken up by elites elsewhere to support original political projects. Nigeria's anti-trafficking efforts thus provide an opportunity to examine the politics of migration and migration control in new contexts. By expanding our understanding in this way, this case shows how anti-migrant politics are not incidental but inherent to the structure of anti-trafficking work, embedded as a key piece in the global crimmigration apparatus.

Scope and Methods

To explore how these multiple carceral logics come together, this book focuses on a single shelter for human trafficking victims. Examining this site ethnographically provides insight into the practice and theory of intervention in real time: stopping migrants through interception and detention, dissuading them through therapy and reflection, and redirecting them through vocational training and sponsorship. These "arts of governance" are my main object of inquiry.[36] With this focus, the goal is not to determine the outcomes of these interventions (whether they "worked" or caused harm), but instead to understand how they came to be taken for granted as the most appropriate tools to address the dangers facing migrant women like Florence.

Feminists and anthropologists alike have long understood that people at the margins of society are best positioned to apprehend and appraise the social systems that marginalize them.[37] The women who were detained and declared victims at the shelter shared a special understanding of its logics, and I made myself a student of their insights, both in observation and in conversation. However, they themselves were not objects of this study; the origin of their desires to migrate, the agreements they brokered to pursue those choices, and their ordinary lives and livelihoods outside the shelter were ancillary to understanding the shelter itself.[38] Because I was less interested in the mechanisms of trafficking and smuggling, I did not spend significant time with women who evaded these barriers and successfully migrated to Europe. The women and men declared "traffickers" are absent from these pages as well; they appear only as they did at the shelter—as threats, as villains, or as specters.

In short, this book is an ethnography of intervention, examining a global system of anti-trafficking and migration control through the stories of one very particular shelter in Lagos. To that end, I spent twenty-four months conducting fieldwork on this project over the past ten years. That included one full year in Nigeria in 2010–2011 and five additional summers. In the early months of this project, a dozen women passed through the shelter whom I came to know particularly well, including Florence. They have stayed in touch with me in the years since, messaging over Facebook and hosting me on return visits to Nigeria. Theirs are the stories that fill these pages, put into context with conversations I held with approximately one hundred women who passed through NAPTIP rehabilitation programs and agreed to participate in this study.

During each phase of fieldwork, I visited the shelter daily, Monday to Friday, alternately shadowing staff and residents. Ethnographic research methods are half-jokingly referred to as "deep hanging out," and that describes much of my time there, lounging and *gisting* (chatting) with whomever was around. I stayed in shared, public areas within the building unless specifically invited into offices or bedrooms. Most days, people seemed to find my company an odd but welcome diversion in the face of so much waiting and boredom. I initiated early conversations by asking relatively benign questions about phrases I heard in Nigerian pidgin, the ubiquitous creole language I was slowly picking up.[39] I fielded residents' ready questions about "abroad," an umbrella term that seemed to capture anywhere worth going to. Regular viewings of Nigerian "Nollywood" films and local hip hop music videos also provided easy entertainment and good fodder for conversations about men, ambition, and travel.

Most of the women detained at the shelter already wanted to talk about their experiences independent of any prompting on my part. Idle and frustrated, they were eager to vent their complaints—to me, to the counselors, and to anyone else who might listen. Staff members, too, had strong feelings about what an outsider needed to understand about this space. To ensure informed consent, I always described my project to new arrivals, who were naturally curious about the *oyibo* (foreigner) lingering around the building, leather notebook in hand. This notebook was both a practical recording tool and a reminder of my researcher role; women sometimes asked me to put it away before sharing a story, and I obliged. At other times, invested in properly documenting the insights they were preparing to share, they demanded that I take it out. Counselors always respected these relationships and never pressured or even invited me to divulge what residents said in private.

As a condition of my access to NAPTIP facilities and consistent with their privacy policies, I did not take photographs of the women staying there. NAPTIP did permit me to record my conversations with residents, but I quickly found such devices both distracting and off-putting. All residents were still under investigation and trying to secure their own release from the shelter, and voice recorders lent an overly formal and interrogatory tone to our conversations. Instead, I took copious notes by hand during discussions, lectures, and meetings. Computers were likewise intrusive to use in real time, but I reconstructed all conversations into long-form narratives each day after leaving the shelter. Quotations and stories retold here are therefore approximations of what I observed, compiled to reproduce actual conversations and interactions at the shelter as closely as possible. Except in the cases of high-ranking public officials, all names are pseudonyms, and some women's stories are presented as composites to preserve their anonymity.

Silences and Ellipses

When I presented this research to academic, policy, and popular audiences over the last decade, one of the questions I heard most often is what the women at the shelter *really* knew about life in foreign sex industries. The answer to this question is key to legal designations that include deception as a means of trafficking: What did they know, and what did they consent to? Were they *really* victims at all?

I began this project five years after NAPTIP, Nigeria's federal anti-trafficking agency, was founded, and eight years after its first anti-trafficking NGOs were organized. By then, most scholars, counselors, and other stakeholders in the region were insisting that these campaigns had already been so effective that no woman could possibly accept a travel invitation without considering the likelihood that she would be expected to sell sex. NAPTIP officers boasted that their message was so pervasive in Benin—in effect, that their public campaign to restigmatize women's migration was so successful—that everyone knew the kind of work available to Nigerian women in Europe.

In my experience, there is some truth to this assumption. Women joke about "wanting to be trafficked," meaning they would welcome sponsorship or debt for the chance to go abroad. Yet only service providers talk about trafficking victims and survivors. That is, the word "trafficking" is used locally to talk not about exploitation but about opportunity. Meanwhile, Nigerians generally expect that most single, working-class, and poor women migrating abroad will sell sex. Would-be migrants might play along with other stories and readily relay them to officials and family members when they travel, all the while knowing the real work that awaits them.

Once inside the shelter, women often insisted that other residents must have known the truth of their arrangements, but they rarely admitted as much in their own case. Most women adopted a stance of denial and innocence—refusing to admit they would ever do such a thing. A few women were brought to the shelter directly from hotel raids inside Lagos, where they were actively working in local commercial sex industries and not merely traveling with the possibility of entering them, yet each still insisted she was just visiting friends there. Rarely did women openly identify as sex workers, and no one adopted any of the labor rights terms that have advanced sex workers' campaigns around the world, despite the growth of these movements in Nigeria and across Africa.[40] Instead, their stories were constantly shifting.

For some time, I found these denials around sex work frustrating. Even women I felt close to, who introduced me to their families and to their boyfriends, offered vague pretexts for their time in nightclubs when I saw them working there. I doubted my rapport with those who avoided discussing the nature of their relationships to different men, and I questioned my ability and authority to tell their stories if they refused to be candid about such a basic aspect of their lives. But my feelings were telling: the acknowledgment I sought was more about me than them—I wanted them to verify stories that they preferred to leave open to interpretation. By seeking firm confirmation of their intentions, I appropriated the same confessional mode that counselors at the shelter would demand. As in ordinary life, but especially in the context of the shelter rehabilitation program, the legal investigation process, and the post-shelter empowerment questions, women found power in discretion and deniability.[41] My role as an anthropologist was inevitably bound up in that, bolstered further by my status as an educated white foreigner, relating across significant class and cultural divides.

I do not venture to say, then, what most women *really* knew about their travel and work arrangements. I do not aim to uncover the truth of anyone's heart and mind when faced with the opportunity to go abroad. I have made this choice in part because they refused any such clarity with me—but also because, as best as

I could tell, they so rarely seemed to have resolved that question for themselves. I have come to believe that it is another important contribution of this text.

Critical studies of anti-trafficking campaigns have long drawn insight from the forceful resistance of sex workers and sex workers' rights advocates.[42] Other accounts build from the experiences of women who identify as trafficking victims, sharing direct accounts of violence and exploitation.[43] The women at this shelter provide a different kind of insight. Suspended in the pursuit of opportunities abroad and still unsure of what dangers that might have entailed, Florence identified neither as a victim nor as a sex worker. She and her peers expressed tremendous ambivalence about shelter interventions, regularly protesting their detention but also welcoming some conversation about difficult choices in their lives. With their travel interrupted, their stories offer no tidy conclusions about what they would have faced, how they would have felt, and how they would have fared. Instead, they ruminated in the shelter not knowing what would have happened, and they live with those questions unanswered still today.

NAPTIP's preemptive strategy for intervention acts on this uncertainty, asserting definitively that all migrant women should be detained because they would inevitably be trafficked if allowed to continue. By this sense, even if detention is unseemly, the horrors of trafficking would be worse: thus, the ends justify the means. Readers, too, may find this comparison relevant and seek details on the travel, labor, and debt conditions that Florence and others would have faced, to more confidently assess the merit of NAPTIP interventions.[44] However, this way of thinking reasserts the epistemic authority of outsiders to make these decisions on these women's behalf. Rather than evaluate the accuracy of NAPTIP's claims, I want to show the consequences of this paternalist reasoning within the shelter system. To do that, this text will analyze intervention justifications not just as facts to be checked but also as fables to be unraveled, revealing the underlying political and moral logics that sustain these projects.

Organization of the Argument

The first half of this book parses out the logics of intervention around women's migration, as articulated in the NAPTIP intervention program and the programs that came before it. The first chapter traces the immediate precedent for Nigeria's counter-trafficking campaign: the mass deportation of Nigerian women from Italy and the national panic that followed. It argues that evolving state efforts to control this migration, from public shaming to victim protection, reflect the global agenda of the Nigeria's new democratic republic. That government sought not only to modernize law enforcement and border security but also to more effectively police the country's most embarrassing emigrants, eventually leading to the establishment of Nigeria's federal anti-trafficking agency in 2003. The second chapter describes the practices of interception and detention that brought migrant women to the shelter despite their adamant protests, expressed in the Nigerian pidgin phrase *I wan go* (I want to go). It considers how women's resistance to intervention was both normalized and ignored in ways that are revealing of citizen–state encounters in Nigeria more broadly. The third chapter investigates the meaning of rehabilitation in this context, especially for women who were rescued preemptively and were not believed to have suffered trauma. I show how rehabilitation was not invoked as a psychological paradigm but as an institutionalized form of "personal development." In particular, this chapter examines how shelter programs aimed to discipline women's interior selves— the thoughts, desires, and dispositions that allegedly made them vulnerable to trafficking in the first place.

Chapters 4–6 explore the content of these arguments at the shelter, explicitly and implicitly prompted by the rehabilitation agenda. Chapter 4 describes the regular arguments between shelter staff and residents regarding the merits of migration. It recounts how they sparred over the appeals of traveling abroad, the kind of work they hoped to find there, and the risks they were willing to take. By situating ethnographic accounts from the shelter with NAPTIP's broader "enlightenment" materials, I show how ostensibly neutral information campaigns depict migrant women as naive and immoral, incapable of making decisions for themselves. To better understand how women understand these choices, chapter 5 describes how sex, money, and mobility are intertwined in Nigeria, how these issues were taken up within the rehabilitation agenda, and how they were discussed in counter-trafficking campaigns more broadly. It first explores the ambiguous categories of transactional sex that women navigate, and it situates these relationships vis-à-vis their expectations for work abroad. I show how counselors spurned residents' ambition as greedy and impatient, echoing broader discourses about the menacing sexual appetites of young unmarried women in Nigeria. Finally, chapter 6 discusses how heated theological arguments over different possible fates—what would have happened had these women not been intercepted while traveling, which path God had destined for them, and what they should do now—made each woman at the shelter contemplate, articulate, and defend her life choices. Here I show how state programs appropriated religious authority not by appealing to conservative moral codes but by facilitating sustained introspection and self-reflection.

Finally, the concluding chapter looks toward the future as women return home after rehabilitation and make their way in the world in the decade since this research began. It traces women through their final negotiations to leave the shelter, describing the arbitrary nature of decisions around release and vocational support, termed "empowerment." I then follow the women back to Benin City, where they slip back into old lives with barely a word to their friends or family about their experiences on the road or in the shelter. Many have since had children, gotten married, started and stopped new businesses. Here we turn to the real-world ramifications of these policies for a better understanding not only of governance and migration control but also of the well-being of women in Nigeria and beyond, whose precarious position in the global economy is ensured by demobilization programs offered ostensibly to help them.

The book closes with a discussion of the persistent themes of discipline and desire observed within the shelter. The epilogue explores the larger implications that these women's experiences have for our ideas about the national economy, global governance, and alternate visions of justice for migrant women. It ends with the proposition that these modes of intervention are not merely indicative of bad counter-trafficking programs but also typify some of the contradictions internal to the trafficking paradigm itself, as well as the complicated political-economic and moral landscapes that have shaped it. These contradictions suggest that we must consider not only how to better combat the exploitation of migrant women but also how to challenge the wider structures of governance, inequality, and exclusion that make such abuses possible.

Ultimately, this book aims not to expose the inadequacies or injustices of a single rehabilitation program but to explore the deeper questions it raises about women's agency, mobility, and empowerment in Nigeria and in a globalized world. Using the stories of Florence and dozens of others like her, it aims to re-humanize the figure of abject suffering that is evoked by the human trafficking victim. In its place, we can recognize the complex interplay of ambition, abuse, and acquiescence that shapes poor and marginalized women's attempts to make better lives for themselves and their families in a world that seems too often to have nothing left for them.

CRISIS

When the UN Office on Drugs and Crime (UNODC) passed the Palermo Protocol in December 2000, it consolidated a global mandate to end human trafficking. Participating governments around the world acted swiftly to comply with this mandate by legally prohibiting human trafficking and establishing the recommended prevention, protection, and prosecution programs. However, these states did not act in a vacuum. While referencing the Protocol as a common standard, every legislative action developed amongst specific legal, cultural, and moral frameworks for understanding and regulating migration, sex work, and sexual exploitation. For these reasons, the global proliferation of anti-trafficking laws after the Palermo Protocol cannot be understood strictly in top-down terms as a matter of replication or reproduction. By examining how the problem of migrant sex work was understood before the trafficking discourse came to dominate public policy, we can better understand the social dynamics of anti-trafficking programs that persisted across these frameworks.

In the decade before the Palermo Protocol was passed, migrant sex work was widely recognized as a problem in Nigeria, but it was not called trafficking and women were not seen as victims. The following national news story, published as the Palermo meetings were underway, was typical:

Up Against Sexport

Lagos—Nigerian professionals especially those in the health sciences, academia and other fields who departed the country in the wake of military misrule, left mostly because they felt undervalued. They also wanted more adventure and career fulfilment which the country could not provide at that time.

But more importantly, they had brains and whenever they arrived in a country, they just walked into the waiting hands of their expectant and obliging hosts. This, obviously was the greatest of Nigeria's export.

But, the new Nigerian professionals who are already practising in various parts of the world are completely different from their forerunners. All they have are mere sexual skills and sometimes, good bodies. . . . Once settled, they begin to repatriate illicit sex proceeds for one pressing family project or the other.

The commercial sex exports attained an unprecedented notoriety during the military regimes of Generals Ibrahim Babangida and Sani Abacha partly because they did not really take the country's image seriously. But since the return of democracy, a few states like Edo, which leads the pack of foreign-based prostitutes, is working very hard to see how young ladies will be discouraged from going abroad to work in brothels.[1]

This excerpt features three essential pieces of the historical puzzle that would determine how the global anti-trafficking paradigm was taken up in Nigeria. First, Nigerians saw migrant sex workers as willful, independent agents. Second, the primary harm of this migration was the embarrassment it brought to Nigeria—creating a blight on the national image—and not the harm it caused the women themselves. And third, the recent democratic transition lent new weight to the question of reputation and created new opportunities to do something about it.

Social scientists use the term "moral panic" to describe how specific people or issues come to be understood as a threat to society in ways that exceed the actual problem at hand.[2] This chapter presents the public concern around Nigeria's migrant sex workers as its own form of moral panic. That does not mean these problems were invented from nothing: significant numbers of Nigerian women did migrate to Europe throughout the decade. However, because these women were framed as a menace to the nation and their reform was the object of so much public scrutiny, they came to stand in for a range of other social anxieties around gender, citizenship, and nationhood that far surpassed the matter of migrant sex work alone.

These concerns focused specifically on women from the Edo ethnic group (also known as Bini), who are most associated with human trafficking and migration into sex work from Nigeria. Residing in a region just north of the oil-rich Niger Delta, Edo women are neither poorer nor richer than women from other parts of the country. So why would they constitute such a significant portion of this migration stream? Folk explanations abound, including societal decay, familial greed, and moral depravity. Many of these explanations reference the fall of the Benin kingdom, citing colonial destruction and occupation for the ongoing corruption of women's value systems. In order to better understand this legacy, we need to consider the historical tensions that shaped the positions of Benin and Nigeria in global politics and rendered Edo women migrants as political problems. The moral authority of the state evolved from the sacking of the Kingdom of Great Benin, through the British occupation of Nigeria, and within the military dictatorships that followed. From this evolution, we can trace the gendered institutions of coercion and care that would eventually address Nigeria's panic over migrant sex work.

Violent States and Benevolent Women

Originally known as Edo, Benin City has long been a hub of European contact in West Africa.[3] It was the urban center of the expansive Benin Empire beginning in the eleventh century and was home to the Oba (ruler) of Benin, whose elaborately decorated palace sat in the core of a planned city.[4] By the time the Portuguese arrived in 1485, the series of protective moats and walls surrounding the city were four times longer than the Great Wall of China. For centuries, the Obas of Benin welcomed contact with Portuguese, Dutch, and British envoys, controlling trade and maintaining the political independence of the kingdom. They cultivated exports in ivory, pepper, cloth, coral, and palm oil, charging significant levies to Europeans, and they profited significantly from participation in the transatlantic slave trade.

However, as the scramble to colonize Africa accelerated in the late nineteenth century, British traders grew impatient with Oba Ovonramwen's control over local markets. In late 1896, British general James Phillips staged an invasion of the city to unseat the Oba, promising his superiors that the value of the palace art would defray the cost of the mission. The Oba's army, however, surprised the invaders before they arrived in the city, killing hundreds and leaving only two survivors. Within days, the British organized "the Benin Punitive Expedition" and, on February 9, 1897, the military arrived to pillage the city and then burn it to the ground. Three thousand looted art pieces—known as the Benin Bronzes—remain in the British Museum and other American and European collections to this day.[5] Many of these pieces depict European traders as attendants to the Oba, referencing a more cooperative era.

After the invasion, the Kingdom of Great Benin was annexed to the British Empire, justified as a necessary civilizing response to what had become known in Britain as the "Benin Massacre." The Oba's heirs were no longer recognized as heads of state but instead as traditional rulers and cultural custodians, a practice that continues today. Remnants of the city wall and protective moats also remain on the Benin City landscape, skirting public marketplaces and dense residential districts. Warrior chiefs who resisted the British are now memorialized in statues along the ring road that passes in front of the Oba's rebuilt palace.

Nigeria spent nearly the entire twentieth century under colonial and military rule. It was granted independence from the British Empire in 1960, adopted a constitution declaring the First Republic in 1963, and operated as a democracy until 1966, when the government fell to a military coup and then civil war. A series of authoritarian regimes followed. Like the colonial occupation, each dictatorship asserted moral mandates for state violence, using security forces to impose their vision of social order, rather than the rule of law.[6] These patterns are relevant to understanding how police, border agents, and limited social service programs would eventually be used to combat migrant sex work and trafficking in the decades to follow.

For example, Major-General Muhamadu Buhari led a military coup ending Nigeria's Second Republic in 1983, premised on the need to reform not only the government but also the population itself. He initiated a concerted, dictatorial "War Against Indiscipline" to impose order on daily life in Nigeria. The wide-ranging campaign posted armed police to enforce bus queues in Lagos and imposed prison sentences on students who cheated on exams.[7] Women were targeted by a number of these initiatives, including prohibitions on teenage pregnancy, adolescent delinquency, and other sexual behaviors. Some states ordered "free women" (a euphemism for sex workers) to marry or risk losing their jobs or homes.[8] Buhari used explicit and spectacular forms of violence to enforce this agenda, common to the African "postcolony."[9] When he returned as head of state in 2015, this time as a democratically elected president, his success was widely credited to nostalgia for this aggressive social agenda.

In August 1985, Major General Ibrahim Babangida (known to most Nigerians by his initials IBB) staged a palace coup to unseat Buhari, installing a new regime that at least half-heartedly engaged international expectations for good governance. Historian Toyin Falola writes that "if Buhari was straightforward and sincere, Babangida was an evil genius—affable and cunning, he was a master of double-speak, deceit, and ambiguity."[10] IBB was president during the Western push for global economic reform implemented through Structural Adjustment Programs (SAPs). These reforms required massive reductions in already limited social services in poor countries around the world, especially disadvantaging poor women and families. IBB implemented these austerity measures to maintain access to international finance but defended his policies as "SAP with a Nigerian face."[11]

As structural adjustment mandates reduced spending in state programs, foreign aid and development organizations looked to find local NGOs to fill the gap in social services. Rather lose the opportunity to pilfer these funds, Nigerian politicians resourcefully adapted to these new revenue streams, creating what became known as GONGOs: government-organized NGOs.[12] One early example of IBB's quasi-governmental organizations was his wife Maryam Babangida's initiative "Better Life for Rural Women" (BLP), founded in 1987. In practice, BLP did little to combat the hardships felt by women and the rural poor that were created by the radical reduction of state services under IBB.[13] It was openly derided as a corrupt front for channeling money to politicians and for providing festive occasions for elite women to flaunt their fine cloth, earning the nicknames "Better Life for Rich Women" and "Bitter Life for Rural Women."[14] Still, the BLP exemplified an important shift in the logics of statecraft that underlined IBB's regime. In contrast to Buhari's ruthlessness, these programs pretended to serve Nigeria's neediest women on behalf of IBB's administration, staging spectacular displays of personal and institutional benevolence in the process. This model was so successful that, after BLP, every politician's wife would go on to found organizations to serve women's interests. Because they are more known in Nigeria for providing access to money and prestige than for their charity work, critics of the government call this phenomenon "First Ladies' Syndrome."[15]

In 1993, IBB hosted elections for a democratic transition but ultimately nullified the results in anticipation of another military coup. He was succeeded by General Sani Abacha who ruled ruthlessly with a flagrant disregard for human rights and the rule of law, generating international outcry at the execution of environmental activist Ken Saro-Wiwa. Meanwhile, his wife Maryam Abacha founded her own women's projects. Her "family" programming mainly promoted income-generating activities and credit schemes, but she declared them part of a "social crusade" for discipline and morality. These projects thus catered simultaneously to international financial markets eager to incorporate marginal communities while further relieving the government of responsibilities to provide a social safety net to the poor.[16]

These tensions between coercive and often violent uses of state power, on the one hand, and the benevolent, moral guidance of elite women, on the other, would come to characterize Nigeria's response to migrant sex work and sex trafficking. First Ladies' projects developed models for moral interventions that were gendered in their leadership, in their goals, and—importantly—in their methods of intervention. They shared sentiments with other state crusades against women's indiscipline, but they favored social services over police harassment. Even where their impact was limited, the shift represented an important opportunity for elite women to consolidate material and symbolic power, positioning themselves as guardians of women's virtue and national honor, while ordinary Nigerians struggled to make ends meet in an ever more dire political and economic landscape.

Exile and Opportunity

With the national economy, government services, and private savings all in shambles, millions of Nigerians looked to leave in the decades following independence. They sought opportunities in wealthier countries around the world, including the in United States, Europe, and the Middle East. Those with education and contacts abroad sought visas to migrate legally. Those without legal options used whatever resources they had available. For example, since Edo rites require coral beads for use in traditional dress, networks for trading Mediterranean coral between Benin and Italy date back to the late fifteenth century.[17] Perhaps building on these relationships, men and women from Benin City traveled to northern Italy to pick tomatoes and do other menial labor starting in the 1980s.[18] That cohort initiated the pattern of chain migration that persists today.

Italian agriculture stagnated in the early 1990s. Some Nigerians returned home, some traveled elsewhere, and some sought other work in the region. With limited access to legal employment, many women entered the lucrative local sex industry.[19] In a significant display of entrepreneurial skill, cross-cultural dexterity, and community alliances, Edo women quickly dominated the market of street prostitution throughout much of Italy. These founding madams generally managed their own careers and turned significant profits. They sent money home, financed new building projects, and sponsored important rites and parties, displaying their success in Nigeria and motivating successive waves of women to "try their luck" abroad.[20] The established madams invested some of their profits in sponsoring that travel, generating debts with the new arrivals. Eventually, the successful madams moved into other industries as well, especially commercial import–export schemes that sent goods back to Africa. Many married Italians and gained full residency rights in Italy. By the year 2000, Italy was the only European country with more legally resident women than men among its Nigerian population.[21]

Nigerians were not the only group looking to migrate during this period. Structural adjustment programs of the 1980s imposed austere fiscal reforms not only on Nigeria but also on developing countries around the world—devastating national economies, curbing already limited social services, and pushing out waves of migrants from across the Global South. The fall of the Soviet Union in 1991 triggered flows from the east as well, including a number of streams that are still associated with human trafficking.[22] Although poverty and political instability can accelerate migration, these migrants were motivated most by a demand for cheap labor in destination countries, including in sex industries.[23]

Despite this demand for cheap labor—or perhaps because of it—growing flows of migrants into rich economies prompted efforts by destination governments to regulate that movement. When the European Union was formally established in 1992, it opened borders within the continent but increasingly closed borders on the periphery, a phenomenon called "Fortress Europe."[24] At the Tampere summit of EU member states in 1999, these efforts culminated in a shared commitment to harmonize immigration policy and fight irregular migration. To address similar concerns, the United States expanded the population of undocumented migrants targeted for deportation and increased enforcement on its southern border.[25] International law is also built in response to political goals, and this growing global effort to "secure borders" eventually helped motivate passage of the Palermo Protocol, along with two other UNODC protocols—one addressing the smuggling of migrants and the other targeting the illegal arms trade.

Sharing these concerns, Italy, throughout the 1990s, accelerated its own border enforcement and removal programs, leading to the deportation of undocumented Nigerian women accused of doing sex work in Italy. In local memory, these women were deported "by the planeload," but most newspapers report groups of a few dozen at a time.[26] Altogether, approximately 800 Nigerian women were deported from Italy from 1999 to 2001. Of these women, 86 percent were from Edo State, and another 7 percent came from the neighboring Delta State, accounting for 93 percent of total deportees.[27] Border security measures are often defended as protecting migrants and trafficking victims, and even absent the language of rescue, removal is sometimes framed as a benevolent form of repatriation. In reality, deportation tears migrants from their homes, networks, savings, and sources of income, often after lengthy imprisonment and police harassment.[28] As the Italian government imposed harsher penalties for migration offenses, Nigerian migrant women became more fearful of removal and therefore more dependent on their sponsors. They acquired higher debts, traveled on more dangerous routes, and took greater risks to avoid the police once they had arrived. Thus, deportation not only presents a problem for those forcibly removed from the country; just living with the *risk* of deportation increases the vulnerability of undocumented migrants.[29] Nigerian women living in Italy understood this crisis as a threat to their livelihood. But in Nigeria, many people saw that problem quite differently.

Reputation Redemption

General Sani Abacha died in office as military head of state in 1998, prompting Nigeria's transition to the Fourth Republic in 1999. His eventual successor, Olusegun Obasanjo, had served as military head of state from 1976-1979, when he relinquished power to democratically elected Shehu Shagari. He was a vocal opponent of Abacha's dictatorship and was imprisoned for allegedly organizing a coup to remove him from office. After Abacha's death, he was released and became the dominant political party's candidate for president. He was elected in February and sworn into office in May 1999, just as deportations of women from Italy accelerated.

Obasanjo was the first civilian president in nearly two decades, and he made foreign relations a central point of his presidency, expressly aiming to repair Nigeria's reputation abroad. For example, after years of Abacha's open hostility to international organizations, Obasanjo earned praise for welcoming the world's public health experts to help address the country's expanding HIV epidemic. He supported popular joint peacekeeping missions in Liberia and Sierra Leone, and he spent much of his two terms traveling abroad. He understood the deportation crisis within this diplomatic frame, declaring migrant sex workers to have dishonored the country.

This national shame over certain emigrant groups predated Obasanjo but expanded under his leadership. Exiled Nigerian players in the international drug trade were infamous during the military regimes of the 1980s, with thousands of worldwide arrests of Nigerians reported regularly in local newspapers.[30] Nigeria's ambassador to Italy, Judith Attah, first warned the country about the problem of migrant sex work through this comparison, insisting in 1994 that "if urgent steps are not taken to arrest the situation, women-trafficking would be more devastating in Nigeria than drug trafficking." The ambassador's emphasis on the devastation *in* Nigeria reveals the impact that concerned her the most: not the well-being of these migrants but the threat they posed to the nation.[31] When Italy began deporting migrant women a few years later, the Nigerian news media treated the deportees as they had treated drug traffickers—as criminals damaging the country's international reputation abroad. "Prostitution: The Scourge of a Nation," one typical headline read, placed over a photo of women slouching in rows with their arms behind their backs. The text followed: "Nigerian ladies have taken Europe by storm with their bizarre sexcapades. For a fee, they sleep with all manners of men and animals and do other sodomic things. Thus, the nation's image is further rubbished."[32] Nigeria's next ambassador to Italy, Chief Etim Jack Oboyo, followed his predecessor's lead, insisting that "the new democratic dispensation in Nigeria imposes on us a duty as joint stakeholders to join hands together in the fight to totally redeem our image."[33]

It is useful here to consider exactly how migrant sex work and mass deportation are imagined to disgrace the national image. Migration alone might be construed as embarrassing where it is seen as evidence that the country itself is no longer habitable. A Nigerian parable that evokes both historic and modern-day slavery suggests as much: "Nigeria is the only country where exile, even if it means enslavement, is now preferred to life at home. A common joke in Lagos is, that a slave-ship from America, anchored off the shores of the ex-capital city, will be so overfilled with elated candidates, that it will sink right there, before setting sail for the New World."[34] Nigerian political humor often makes light of dire conditions and points out the structural causes of these ills, as this story does.[35] One may find the "elated candidates" to be laughable in their naivety, but the joke rests on the relatability of that desire and desperation. It does not insinuate that the emigrants themselves are personally immoral or corrupt—they are just determined to seek something better. Any embarrassment is a collective one, shared as the plight of the community as a whole.[36]

Contrast this sense of shared recognition with a similar story of women seeking passage to work abroad. Although the format here is different—a news report versus a popular anecdote—the editorial tone still guides the reader's sympathies:

> In the face of such embarrassing statistics [of the high numbers of local women working in prostitution abroad], Edo girls are unrelenting in their search for the "golden fleece" through prostitution. As some are getting deported home, others are moving out of their homes en route [to] Spain and Algeria.
>
> Recently, travelers up north in Benin were . . . humiliated when 20 of the commuters were asked to disembark from the bus they had earlier boarded because "some people have chartered it." Those people turned out to be young girls of between 16 and 18 who were being piloted to Kano from where they [could find] their way abroad through the trans-Sahara route. The 60 young girls were soon herded into the luxury bus.
>
> On another day, passengers who usually wait for three hours [for a bus to fill and depart] were surprised to see the bus filled up in 30 minutes. A surprised broadcast-journalist who inquired about the magic was told about the presence of some 40 "ambassadors"—prostitutes.[37]

During the 1990s, after decades of kleptocratic military rule, fleeting democratic regimes, and brutal structural adjustment programs, Nigeria's social safety net was in tatters. Yet, the ambitions of the young women on the bus are presented as neither reasonable nor relatable. Rather, they are stubborn and foolhardy, "unrelenting in their search for the golden fleece." They "humiliate" others by making use of a luxury bus service, presenting themselves as a legitimate chartered group to the dismay of those around them. But their fellow passengers are not the only ones disgraced by the encounter. As they choose en masse to rush toward this life, these women are deemed bad "ambassadors" for the entire nation, flooding out at an unmanageable rate. Nationalism is often bound up in women's honor, and women are punished harshly when they disgrace not only themselves but also the collective.[38] Migrant sex workers in this telling are embarrassing not because they are beacons of structural problems but because they are corrupt and immoral individuals, failed emissaries for the nation.[39]

This distinction is important, because by locating the true source of national embarrassment within individual moral failures, Nigeria becomes the victim of migrant women's wrongdoing rather than the cause of it. Even within a democracy, this framework absolves the state of any direct responsibility for the conditions that might motivate women to seek high-risk migration projects and work in foreign sex industries. The problem is not systemic poverty, political neglect, or global inequality, but the women themselves.

A Threat to Be Contained

As established in the decades previous, two key technologies were available to address this problem. First, Nigeria's security and police forces had for decades been used to impose moral order on groups deemed deviant or unpatriotic. Second, civil society organizations could promote social reform, especially those led by elite women with a focus on gender issues. Ultimately, the two projects would be closely tied.

As a part of his diplomatic focus, Obasanjo worked directly with the Italian government to coordinate the return of migrant sex workers—more than one thousand in the first three years of his term—and to combat this problem within Nigeria. When he took office in 1999, Italy was deporting dozens of Nigerian women every few weeks, and Obasanjo created a ten-person police task force to manage their return. The Italian police escorted deportees in chartered flights and then turned the women over to the police task force at the international airport in Lagos.[40] The task force then took them to the national Force Criminal Investigation Department, the Nigerian equivalent of the FBI, which deposited them in a nearby detention facility described in newspapers at the time as a "permanent transit camp for whores."[41] Even as adults, deportees were never simply "released" from these camps but were turned over to parents and other guardians. Police at the time argued that "the law does not allow them to release the girls without the consent of their parents," leaving some deportees "stranded" (detained longer) when they either refused to provide family contacts or the family members refused to collect them. Through national news media, the police "appealed to parents and guardians of the deportees to come for their wards."[42] When a group of pregnant deportees "ironically" refused to provide contact information for their families, the police reported having "no other option than to send them to the police hospital" until they gave birth.[43] In this manner, deported women were presented as a threat that the government tried to contain with whatever legal tools were available (see figure 2).

One reason offered for detaining deportees was that their assumed involvement in sex work had made them likely vectors of contagion for HIV. As one newspaper reported, "Most of the deportees are said to have contracted the HIV virus, necessitating their being quarantined by police authorities."[44] Even without evidence of medical need, deportation announcements often reported that women were detained "pending examination," further stigmatizing these women, as well as others living with HIV. The police task force forcibly tested all returnees for HIV and encouraged journalists to publicize the results. These tests and the public references to them capitalized on widespread fear during the peak of Africa's AIDS crisis—a concurrent moral panic around women's sexuality during this period.[45] Public statements by officials emphasized the hidden dangers these women posed, as if even their apparent good health was a malicious form of deceit. "We have seven of them looking as healthy as everybody but HIV positive," one official told journalists. "We can't hold them from going back into the society because there's no law they have broken," he added, hinting at the risks they posed to the community and the state's need for further detention options.[46]

Other reports suggest emphasized dangers beyond mere biological or epidemiological conditions—what one official called "the mentality within them." With the announcement that 350 migrant women sex workers had been deported in the first ten months of 1999, the *P.M. News* reported the following:

> These girls he said are the pretty ones who leave their country and their family in the quest for survival in another country but on getting there turn to slaves to their host citizens. "Nigerian girls are slaves to the foreigners," he said.

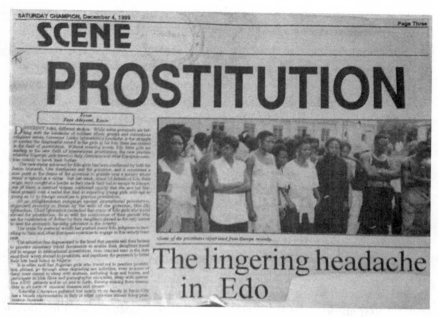

SATURDAY CHAMPION, December 4, 1999   Page Three

SCENE

PROSTITUTION

From
Toys Abejomi, Benin

Some of the prostitutes repatriated from Europe recently.

The lingering headache in Edo

FIGURE 2. "Prostitution: The lingering headache in Edo." Newspaper coverage of deportees publicly shames a crowd of women returnees with the caption, "Some of the prostitutes repatriated from Europe recently." Archives of the Nigerian Institute for International Affairs, Lagos.

The ambassador explained that the girls who are between 18 and 25 years are identified and subsequently repatriated through their indecent mode of dressing, behaviour and their penchant for sex in open places.

An official of the Italian Embassy in Nigeria said the girls look beautiful and of unquestionable character when you see them but what "resides" inside them is quite different.

"Their idea about freedom, their idea about fulfilling the desire of their heart is quite different from ours. The mentality inside them is wrong and that is how and why even their mothers who should love them and love their destiny are busy planning how they could go back and continue their job," the official said.

The official therefore urged everyone to be concerned about these Nigerians, know why they do what they are doing and the means of stopping them in order to save them and save the country's image . . .

Funso Alabi, actor and crusader whose six minutes dramatic presentation centered on help from within, brought the message even more poignantly: "Sew your dresses well and always close your legs."[47]

Although the ambassador's description of the women as "slaves of foreigners" evokes the language of trafficking, he still ultimately blames them for the "the mentality inside them," the inner corruption of their moral character hidden behind the external beauty of their bodies. He faults their ideas of freedom, desire, and destiny and urges officials to find additional means of stopping these women for the betterment of the nation. The story also points to a larger social divide between "their ideas" and "ours." In these statements, members of the elite class such as politicians and actors position themselves as "crusaders," siding with foreign officials and against migrant women and their families. "Even their mothers who should love them," he describes, are busy plotting their return to Italy.

Adopting a role similar to the first wives of previous heads of state, the wife of the governor of Edo state, Eki Igbinedion, regularly echoed this sentiment in establishing herself as a local leader in this fight against migrant sex work. Although she is often credited with founding the local opposition to trafficking in Edo state, this early activism positioned her against these women rather than with them. She worked with her husband, Governor Lucky Igbinedion, to expand state reach into the problem, advocating to criminalize all prostitution, prohibit all sponsorship of foreign travel, and forcibly repatriate all Bini women abroad. She used public speaking occasions to decry the evident failure of various social intuitions in Benin. For example, she demonized Edo mothers for supporting their daughters' travel, as described in the news magazine *Tempo*:

> According to her, mothers as custodians of culture must take the blame for the increasing involvement of their daughters in prostitution. She noted that many mothers actually encourage their daughters, withdraw them from school and sell their properties to put up the huge sum needed by the so-called sponsors to ferry their unsuspecting daughters to Italy.[48]

Mothers likely did facilitate their daughters' journeys, but there is little evidence that they did so coercively. Poor families across the region depended on the remittances sent by women abroad for basic needs and other comforts. Women who remained behind especially benefited from a direct source of foreign income, more so than from the money earned and managed by male household heads. Women rarely inherited property in the Bini tradition, and migrant sex work opened new opportunities for both daughters and their mothers to accumulate wealth directly. As one mother observed, "My husband is irresponsible. My daughter in Italy built this house and bought this small car. If not for her, I wonder what my fate could have been in this world. [She begins to pray for her]."[49] In this way, migrant sex work and associated remittances *did* threaten the traditional family structure—by challenging male authority and providing women greater financial independence.

Other social intuitions were also imagined as corrupt forces in this moral crisis. Christian churches were perceived as supporting women's migration by encouraging the pursuit of wealth and Western goods, facilitating connections for recruitment, and benefiting from remittances. Benin remains a center of Pentecostal Christianity in Nigeria, and churches in the city helped the popularize the "prosperity gospel," an interpretation of biblical texts that validates wealth as a sign of God's favor. Even if churches did not openly condone sex work, they helped legitimize the popular sentiment that absolved successful migrants for the work that made their income. Migrants who returned without significant profits—including deportees—were stigmatized as failures, but those who displayed their success in acts of conspicuous consumption and public generosity were "deified," both within the church and outside of it.[50]

Religious leaders from outside the Christian church were directly implicated in migration schemes. Migrant women often committed to their travel sponsors through an oath ceremony led by a traditional priest. Oaths are commonly used to solemnize a range of debts and contracts and are recognized as legally binding in Nigerian courts of law.[51] However, stories of sacrificed animals and pubic hair used in these rituals scandalized the international NGO community. People unfamiliar with the practice became further convinced that women could not share their true stories for fear of *juju* punishments.[52] By this construction, migrant women would eventually be framed as victims not only of traffickers but also of their own culture and beliefs.[53]

Altogether, migrant sex work appeared as the cumulative failure of what would otherwise serve as the moral pillars of society: personal morality, familial protection, and religious leadership. In the popular understanding, these were not innocent girls stolen in the night, leaving fearful parents with lost daughters. Instead, they were members of corrupt and greedy families, scheming to profit from sexual promiscuity despite the clear harm to their community and country. Because they blamed personal and cultural corruption for Nigeria's migrant sex work problem, campaigners expected to find resistance among the communities they targeted, especially amongst poor and working-class families who depended on migrant remittances.

Resisting Intervention

These social divisions between elite crusaders and migrant communities appeared in formal intervention schemes and in resistance to them. For example, people accused Eki Igbinedion of discouraging migrant sex work to defend her own class privilege. As one mother of a migrant daughter reported:

> She (Mrs. Igbinedion) would continue to get such treatments from people, because she does not know what it means to be poor. Now that people can build houses, eat, and send their children to schools, she has said those children who have been assisting their parents, should be deported. You know rich people do not like competition; they want to be the only ones who can travel abroad. She wants to take away peoples happiness and means of livelihood.[54]

In talking about access to family support, travel, and happiness, this mother recognizes that migrant sex work is not merely a sustained by economic desperation, but instead reflects deeply contested assumptions about what constitutes opportunity and well-being, and who belongs in different, desirable spaces.

These divisions are further exemplified in the symbols selected to designate Eki Igbinedion's organization, Idia Renaissance. Queen Idia is an iconic historic figure of the ancient Benin Kingdom, known as a great warrior who rushed to the defense of her son Esigie, the Oba of Benin, who ruled from 1504 to 1550. Her visage is preserved in ivory masks maintained in the British Museum and the Metropolitan Museum in New York. Each mask features the heads of miniature Portuguese traders, referencing the kingdom's historic power over Europeans (see figure 3). The mask served as the emblem for FESTAC '77, a pan-African festival celebrated at the peak of Nigeria's oil wealth.[55] As the namesake of Igbinedion's organization, Idia represents the pride of the Edo people not only within Benin but also across Nigeria and the rest of the continent. She is an icon of African art and African achievement in the global imagination. As described in Idia Renaissance's website, Idia "symbolize[s] dignified womanhood and courage in daunting circumstances," and "from this history Idia Renaissance draws inspiration, moral energy and cultural originality to prosecute its campaign for cultural reawakening."[56]

A closer reading of the story of Queen Idia, however, reveals as many points of contention as it does points of pride. The war she famously helped win began when her son tried to prove the corruptibility of all women by luring a supposedly honest woman into adultery. Women in contemporary Benin recognized the hypocrisy of the elite class, rejecting the supposed benevolence of these institutions:

> Why would she invoke the name Idia and think it will help her cause? Idia is like her (Eki Igbinedion). Idia was not a poor woman searching for a means of livelihood. She only needed to tap her fingers for yams and it would be laid at her feet. Idia did what she had to do, to save her son's life and his throne. Those who have children abroad, either for

FIGURE 3. "Edo Culture is Against Human Trafficking." The Queen Mother pendant mask, stolen from Benin City in 1897, symbolizes the lost dignity of Bini women. Poster produced by the UNODC/UNICRI NGO Coalition Against Human Trafficking.

prostitution or anything else they do there, have also done so to look after their children and better their lives.[57]

Idia Renaissance would go on to enjoy great popularity with international donors as a partner in anti-trafficking campaigns, but its unpopularity with many Edo families suggests that its "local" designation obscures significant differences between the NGO leadership and the community it targets.

These social divides were apparent in the state's hostile reintegration schemes for deported migrant women. Without legal grounds on which to formally arrest the deportees or to stop them from trying to return to Italy, the police task force was reportedly left with "only" the option to publicly shame them.[58] They presented deported women to news journalists at the airport, at the detention site, and upon their return to Benin City, to humiliate them and discourage others from attempting similar paths. There is little evidence that these parades prevented other women's migration into sex work. As newspapers reported with astonishment, "Even though many of the deported women have been paraded publicly, it has not deterred those willing to travel out of the country for prostitution."[59] However ineffective the parades may have been as deterrents, they succeeded in pitting migrant women against the public, both in the parades themselves and in the salaciously narrated media stories they produced. One account from 1999 is typical:

> On 30 April, a thick crowd of residents which gathered at the state police headquarters to witness the display of Italian returnees who were forced to swallow their shameful spits as the returnees turned the heat on them all.
>
> They made everyone feel stupid for leaving their homes to witness the hurriedly announced "show of shame."
>
> The crowd started converging at 3 p.m. that Friday once news broke out that the deported prostitutes had arrived in Benin and were to be paraded by the police.
>
> At 5.20 p.m. when the 74 deportees filed out of their police cells, they betrayed no remorse. They barked at the crowd, including journalists and policemen for wasting their time to "come and look." There they inflicted a big defeat for the police's original agenda.
>
> Their being paraded in Benin where most of them lived before finding their way outside the country was meant to be a psychological war. It backfired.[60]

Like other forms of public punishment, the spectacle of the parade is meant to put shame on the deported women and restore the moral order that they had so threatened.[61] However, in this story, that effort is sabotaged when the deportees fight back and shame those around them. The sense of crisis is magnified by the brazenness of these travelers, their gleeful departures, their purportedly flagrant work practices (a "penchant" for sex outdoors, noted elsewhere), and ultimately their refusal to demonstrate remorse on their return. The article goes on to describe an eleven-point remedy proposed by the traditional leaders of Benin, including wider publicization of migrant women's deaths, police vigilance around illicit migration, and the creation of a department of "social security" that would deal with problems arising from cases of youths traveling abroad for prostitution.

Obasanjo's government did expand their efforts significantly over time. By 2001, the efforts to stop migrant sex work had grown from a single ten-man task police force to twelve regional police units, fourteen dedicated teams from the Nigeria Immigration Service, a special presidential adviser, and a presidential task force led by the Minister of State for Justice. Even as the work expanded into new bureaucratic sectors, each agency still framed their work as stopping dangerous women, for the protection of society. The Federal Health Department had created a section in Benin City specifically to treat women returning from Europe, in which HIV-positive deportees were reportedly "quarantined and their movement restricted."[62] One newspaper even expressed concern for "the safety of policemen" charged with detaining the women on arrival. The officers were framed as potential victims of the women's wiles, "moved by [their] seductive attraction [to make] advances at the teenage girls." Imprisoned young women were framed as infiltrators, "rattling" the country's highest criminal investigatory arm and threatening society at large.

The conventional tools of law enforcement and civil society were doing little to deter subsequent cohorts of migrant women, who brazenly continued to seek opportunities abroad. If they were to succeed in this fight, Nigerian politicians would need more effective strategies for the psychological and social battle they had declared. As symbolic advocates for social services and moral integrity, elite women would soon provide this leadership.

Titi Abubakar's "Amazing Crusade"

As president-elect, Obasanjo rejected "First Ladies' Syndrome" as a phenomenon of prior corrupt regimes: when reporters asked what role his wife Stella would play in the new administration, he quipped, "She will simply be my wife."[63] Nevertheless, she assumed the staff and office of the First Lady and soon thereafter established the Child Care Trust (CCT), a charitable foundation to support children with disabilities in Nigeria. She also became the international spokesperson for a previously local campaign against female genital mutilation (FGM), touring neighboring African countries to raise awareness for the cause. In a nod to democratic transparency and the consolidation of the NGO era, these organizations were more formally separated from the federal government than were previous First Ladies' projects, although they still thrived on "donations" that were understood as political favors and were likely pilfered from other state budgets.

These choices to address FGM and children with disabilities were politically astute in several ways. Neither represented particularly popular social issues within Nigeria, but instead capitalized on broader trends in international aid and development.[64] Generic campaigns for poor women and children did little to galvanize interest in a growing landscape of specialized organizations, and they also emphasized the persistent unreliability of Nigeria's welfare state. Rather than a universal right to basic services for women, families, or the poor, both projects leveraged what Jean Comaroff has characterized as "claims to entitlement based on suffering and injury."[65] FGM, in particular, was and continues to be a politically potent issue in African politics more widely.[66] FGM was also a common ground for asylum applications in Europe, which was considered embarrassing for the Nigerian government and a burden on European governments.[67] Positioning Stella Obasanjo as a (rather effective) international spokesperson against this practice thereby captured international political attention while reclaiming Nigeria's position as a moral leader among African nations.

The wife of Vice President Atiku Abubakar, Titi Abubakar, needed her own project as well. Like Stella Obasanjo, she would seek a cause that could position her as a leader of women's issues on a global stage. Such a cause should merit significant political and financial support within Nigeria and internationally. It would affirm her status as the protector of Nigeria's honor and values in a time of national pride and possibility. With drafting meetings underway for the Palermo Protocol and with the deportation of migrant women ongoing, human trafficking would fit this bill.

Titi Abubakar reports first learning of Nigeria's migrant sex workers when she was a master's student in hotel management in Italy in 1986–1987. "I saw what our Nigerian girls did to themselves," she would later describe. "I was so disgusted with the way our girls sold their bodies for money. . . . So when we came into office in [May] 1999, I said to myself the time has come for me to use all my God-given energy to help these girls."[68] Her initial public statements focused on the problem of prostitution writ large, publicly blaming women's organizations, mothers, and sex workers themselves for promoting moral decay and decadence.[69] She regularly expressed disdain for transactional sex and general promiscuity, arguing that "most female [university] students now thrive in greed, uncontrollable desires and insatiable lust for materialism to violate the much-cherished dignity of our womanhood."[70] Like many Nigerians at the time, and many others around the world, she saw "prostitution" as a problem and immoral women as the culprits.

Early in her term as Second Lady, Abubakar also began to use the language of trafficking. In October 1999, she hosted a three-day national workshop on "Women Trafficking and Child Labour." The following April, she registered an NGO based on that mandate, known as WOTCLEF, or Women Trafficking and Child Labour Eradication Foundation. In addition to honoring her personal moral commitments, this effort capitalized on themes that were pressing at the time of Nigeria's democratic transition—the widespread concern for migrant sex work, especially insofar as it reflected Nigeria's international reputation, the role of state authority, and the benevolence of the new regime.

In December 2000, Abubakar attended the signing convention for the Palermo Protocol and reportedly was only one of two Africans invited to speak. She delivered a paper on the rule of law subtitled "Controlling the Global Sex Trade," insisting that the Protocol would "stem the tide of the pro-sex-industry lobby." Specifically, she argued that it affirmed that women's consent could *not* be used to defend against accusations of trafficking.[71] Although her interpretations largely differed from the Protocol's text and its applications since then, the celebratory speech affirmed her support for the abolition of sex work, using the terms trafficking and prostitution interchangeably and working to criminalize the entire global sex industry.

When she returned to Nigeria, Abubakar used WOTCLEF to reframe the national problem of migrant prostitution as one of trafficking—a mission she calls as her "amazing crusade."[72] She made frequent speeches condemning the scourge of human trafficking, which were covered widely in the national media. WOTCLEF sponsored "brigades" in local schools to further educate youth about the harms of trafficking. It organized a series of sensitization workshops, teaching law enforcement personnel and the National Immigration Service to better identify traffickers and trafficking victims. The NGO also hosted single-day rehabilitation and orientation programs for "deported victims," claiming to have counseled more than one thousand women by mid-2001.

From Deportees to VIPs

Other earlier First Ladies' projects had focused on public education and narrowly defined charitable programs, which easily could have been adapted as interventions against human trafficking for the purposes of Abubakar's organization. However, the Palermo Protocol had set a criminal justice framework for trafficking, specifically mandating legal prohibition and criminal prosecution. Under Abubakar's direction, WOTCLEF prepared a bill that would incorporate the Palermo Protocol definitions of trafficking into Nigerian law. She presented the bill to President Obasanjo in November 2000 and to the national legislature in February 2001. According to WOTCLEF press releases, Abubakar was the first civilian in Nigerian history to put forward a draft of legislation, and she used frequent public speaking engagements to urge the nation into action.

At one such event in August 2001, Titi Abubakar publicly presented thirty-three migrant women to President Obasanjo. They had been en route to Europe but were intercepted at Nigeria's border and then flown on a military plane to the capital Abuja. Journalists invited to the affair described the women with a tenuous attachment to Abubakar's language, suggesting both pity and suspicion of them as "repatriated victims" and as "innocent (?) girls." Ultimately, they declared that it was "indeed a sorrowful moment" for the president, who was forced to confront this shame upon the nation.[73] In photographs posed for the media, Abubakar stands amidst the deportees alongside other administration officials. The migrant women all look down and avert their eyes, while the officials look straight into the camera. This parade was different from the rituals of public humiliation through the streets of Benin, but it was a parade nonetheless. "With these victims, Mr. President," Abubakar declared, "your government can demonstrate to the whole world that you are actually and truly determined to put a stop to trafficking."[74]

Obasanjo vowed that day to repatriate and rehabilitate all Nigerians trafficked abroad for prostitution. However, by that time Italy's mass deportations were largely slowing down, and NGOs like WOTCLEF and Idia Renaissance were already providing direct assistance to existing deportees. To fulfill his promise, the administration focused instead on border security and policing. As described in the previous chapter, this focus is consistent with the impact of the Palermo Protocol, which shifted anti-trafficking work from a human rights to criminal justice framework and from an approach that checks state power to one that strengthens it. The Nigerian government secured a grant from the United States worth $3.3 million to support law enforcement efforts around drug trafficking and human trafficking, including specific programs to train and equip the dedicated police anti-trafficking units. It created five new dedicated units within the Nigeria Immigration Service (NIS), supported by equipment from the Italian government worth $2.5 million. Anti-trafficking measures thereby bolstered Obasanjo's government not only by expanding state agencies and budgets but also by increasing its legitimacy through international partnerships to support those efforts.[75]

Earlier efforts to sensitize border agents and other task force teams had introduced agents to the language of trafficking but still encouraged harassment and public shaming. In 2002, the NIS announced a new policy to "treat deportees as VIPs," boasting that it "now conveys the deportees in luxurious buses provided by the Italian government, counsels and makes them have [a] sense of belonging, unlike before."[76] This shift marked the end of open hostility toward migrant women.

The implementation of globally accepted anti-trafficking rhetoric both sustained and transformed existing state intervention schemes in Nigeria. First, the anti-trafficking framework legitimized the state's efforts to stop migrant women, defining those actions not as arrests but as rescue. Second, it justified additional detention, defined not as punishment but as protection. However, a commitment to more humane and internationally sanctioned treatment of deported women did not at all require supporting their efforts to migrate. Like Titi Abubakar, the NIS still conflated the fight against human trafficking with "waging war against our young girls going out for prostitution." It demanded increasing funding to interrogate the passport requests of every girl from Benin and to more effectively intercept women at Nigeria's porous land borders.[77] Anti-trafficking efforts were still fundamentally designed to oppose the efforts of migrant women, but the state was learning to present its efforts in new ways.

In July 2003, the national legislature finally passed Titi Abubakar's bill to formally prohibit human trafficking in Nigeria. The law transferred responsibilities for Nigeria's anti-trafficking campaigns from a dozen task force teams within the Nigerian police and immigration services to a new dedicated federal agency. NAPTIP, the National Agency for the Prohibition of Trafficking in Persons (and Other Related Matters), grew to have a staff of more than 200 people and annual operating budgets reported in the millions. With separate administrative departments for investigation, prosecution, victim protection, and public enlightenment, its founding completed the government's shift from a victim-shaming to a victim-empowering approach.

As we will see in the next chapter, these departments are largely consistent with global intervention standards, as set by the Palermo Protocol and assessed annually by the US Department of State. But they remain grounded in popular logics that blame migrant sex workers and "the mentality inside them" for bringing shame upon the nation. If Nigeria needed to engage in "psychological warfare," therapy would be a more effective tool than public humiliation—while also replacing images of state violence with reports attesting to the quality of narrowly focused state services.

After its founding, with help from international donors and local collaborators, NAPTIP's Department of Public Enlightenment led a massive education campaign that introduced "trafficking" into the national lexicon. Teams from the National Youth Service Corps went to secondary schools, universities, and public markets to perform skits to raise awareness about sex trafficking. Radio jingles, billboards, and airport banners broadcast the dangers of migration and the real nature of the work waiting for women abroad. These materials reframed the problem of prostitution into one of trafficking. However, they still described *all* migrant sex work as trafficking, urging women to resist its lures (see figure 4). Even in the guise of trafficking, migrant women—the would-be victims—were still the ones deemed morally and socially responsible for these choices.

By 2008, when I first traveled to Nigeria, no matter where I went in the country everyone seemed to have had heard of human trafficking, knew specifically

FIGURE 4. "UniBen Rejects Prostitution and Human Trafficking." NAPTIP billboard posted inside a central roundabout at the Univeristy of Benin. Benin City, Edo State (photo by author).

about the Benin–Italy link, and, for better or worse, assumed most young Nigerian women traveling to Europe would eventually enter the sex industry. Today, this warning—along with the stereotypes and stigmas associated with it—has so permeated public consciousness that people believe anyone traveling from Benin *must* know, on some level, what she is going to be up against. She may trust her travel broker (often a family friend) to look for any available alternatives, and she may hope that her case could be the exception to the rule. But there is a sense that she has been warned and that most women will agree to any story the agent offers, while knowing with a wink and nod that there is still no real money in hairdressing, even in Europe.

These women—mostly in their early twenties, from Edo State and the surrounding region, all eager to migrate and most prepared to enter the sex industry—would be profiled and intercepted at Nigerian and foreign border points in the state campaign against human trafficking, before eventually being sent to the federally-run shelter where this research is based.

DETENTION

Like many of the other shelter residents, Florence was referred to Nigeria's anti-trafficking agency, NAPTIP, after refusing to pay a bribe to a Nigerian immigration officer at the Lagos international airport while she was trying to travel to Italy. NAPTIP officials brought her to the shelter, where she did not say much. Her head hung down over the Bible that she had carried on her journey, and she looked up occasionally to bellow in protest the same words: "*I wan goooo*," she moaned, echoing down the dim cement hallways for hours. "*I wan go!*"

The 2003 legislation founding NAPTIP avows, "The Agency shall ensure that . . . a trafficked person is able to return home safely, if he so wishes and when he is able to do so," and that "where the circumstances so justify, a trafficked person shall not be detained, imprisoned or prosecuted for offenses relating to being a victim of trafficking, including non-possession of valid travel stay or use of a false travel or other documents."[1] This same language is reproduced in the 2015 law, affirming that victims should not be held against their will. However, neither piece of legislation explains what it means to be "able" to return home or what "circumstances so justify" detaining them further.[2]

In practice, nearly every woman at the shelter was detained against her will, and their protests were neither nuanced nor discreet. Women demanded constantly to be released, insisting in Nigerian pidgin English, *I wan go, I wan go*—I want to go. This phrase provided the script for nearly every interaction that residents experienced. To visiting aid organizations who asked their name and age, *I wan go*. To empty rooms in moments of frustration and exhaustion, *I wan go*. And of course, to the earnest staff counselors and interested anthropologists who

asked what was wrong or did they have comments after group counseling or anything else really, *I wan go, I wan go, I wan go.*

Staff at the shelter rarely acknowledged these demands directly but instead
urged women to be patient with the process. They would insist that everyone was
essentially free to go, or nearly free to go, or soon to be free to go, all while lock-
ing the padlock on the building's security gate at the close of every business day.
But while they denied or obscured the fact of detention in conversations with
those detained, it was acknowledged openly by administrators and other stakeholders. In one of the agency's glossy promotional magazines, NAPTIP's director of rehabilitation boasted, "We thank God that we put in an effort and that is
why we insist that victims that come back must stay for at least six weeks in our
shelters whether they like or not." Here, de facto detention is a feature and not a
flaw of the system: it is an "extra "effort" that is ostensibly indicative of the agency's
commitment to helping these women.[3]

Protective housing facilities that prohibit residents' movement are called
"closed shelters," and they are a common feature of women's services around the
world, found in Bangladesh, Central and Eastern Europe, Cambodia, India, Is-
rael, Malaysia, Nepal, the Russian Federation, Sri Lanka, Taiwan, and Thailand.[4]
Like a range of facilities from humanitarian safe houses to immigrant detention centers, these closed shelters are semi-carceral institutions.[5] Activists and
advocates largely denounce their security policies as unnecessary, paternalistic,
and harmful to women. Still, they persist as a regular feature of public services,
allowed and even incentivized by global anti-trafficking standards and monitoring mechanisms that reward consistent occupancy rates and disregard residents' resistance to these restrictions.[6]

The simultaneous denunciation and embrace of detention within NAPTIP is
therefore not merely an aberration or corruption of global norms: instead, they
mirror a wider ambivalence around the issue of detention, made possible by the
obfuscation of detention itself. Therefore, this chapter asks readers to spend time
with migrant women's lived experiences of confinement within the shelter—not
only their suffering but also their ready recognition of and resistance to this system, as well as their reasons for acquiescing to it. It examines the contours of
detention's enforcement, materially and rhetorically, from barbed wire on the
walls to passing comments over mealtime. The thick description of detention
from inside the shelter walls shows how contradictions between policy prohibitions are normalized in the day-to-day functioning of carceral care. By situating these stories in both the political-moral universe of global anti-trafficking
mandates and the wake of Nigeria's deportation crisis, this chapter explains how
the systematic detention of migrant women could be made to feel mundane, benevolent, or not there at all, despite residents' constant vocal demands to go.

Security Forces

After NAPTIP was founded in 2003, its Lagos shelter opened in a massive, non-descript five-story office building, tucked off a major city thoroughfare in the corner of a large federal ministry complex, a remnant from the city's days as the capital of Nigeria. Steady streams of bureaucrats and politicians enter the adjacent government offices, heralded by the names of the anti-corruption offices and paramilitary insignia stickered across cracking plastic signs at the gate. The NAPTIP building, in contrast, bears no indication of its occupants, its function concealed to prevent traffickers from finding the women held inside.

The other government agencies employ a half-dozen guards to stand watch over the narrow driveway access to the compound; all wear bulletproof vests, with firearms strapped casually behind their shoulders. Military checkpoints and elaborate police escorts are common in Nigeria, so these security measures are relatively normal for most guests to the shelter. Whether I arrived by motorcycle taxi or a friend's luxury SUV, the guards invariably waved me, a young white woman, through the checkpoint without trouble. By contrast, these guards likely seemed foreboding for the residents watching the comings and goings of cars from behind the shelter's barred windows. The counselors blamed the shelter security measures entirely on the nearness of the government agencies: "You are all free," they declared, "This place is not a prison. The only freedom you don't have is to go outside. And the only reason you can't go out there is because of the other agencies. If not for them you can go around the compound. So please, you are free." Of course, the residents wanted more than fresh air. They wanted to be free to leave entirely, and they understood the security spectacle as deterrent to their escape. When a child being held at the shelter once fantasized about escaping, Florence warned her, half-seriously, "Well, don't go that way. At that gate, is the police. They will shoot you when they see you. And the other way, is more government. They will shoot you. And the other way too is guards. So you have to be careful, but if you run quickly, you can do it."

Outside, the only clue to the building's purpose is a small plaque near the main entrance, thanking the United States Agency for International Development (USAID) and the Italian government for their help in renovating the space in 2003.[7] The entrance by the plaque, however, is no longer in use; like several other sections of the building, it has been lost to perpetually postponed maintenance. A few years after the facility opened, a tree fell through part of the foyer roof, and the money never materialized to repair it. Instead, everyone uses the access point on the rear side of the building, against the compound wall, hidden behind two mango trees and a dilapidated IOM-branded passenger van, also nonfunctional.

Two men sit guard outside this side entrance, unarmed and wearing plain-clothes and flip-flops at a heavy wooden-laminate desk, weathered from rainy seasons spent partially exposed under the veranda. A stack of large worn ledgers sit atop the desk, each tracking the movements of different sets of people who come in and out of the shelter. With my daily visits, my name quickly came to dominate the pages of the guest log, alongside those of the other regulars—nuns from charity organizations, political officers from nearby consulates, local and international journalists, and the occasional fellow academic researcher. Once every couple of weeks, higher-ranking administrators shuttled from the zonal headquarters office across town to offer tours to especially important donors and stakeholders. The staff psychologist would visit occasionally as well. Their visits are all tracked in the NAPTIP staff log.

A third ledger tracks the movements of the shelter residents. After the women's paperwork is processed at the NAPTIP headquarters, their custody is formally handed over to the shelter manager, and they are taken to a nearby military hospital for an initial medical evaluation. They are then taken to the shelter, where for the next six weeks they are only permitted to go to agency headquarters or, as their cases advanced, to testify in court. Otherwise, they are not allowed to leave the building.

In Nigerian jails, prisoners regularly rely on the contributions of family and friends for basic provisions, but women at the shelter are not allowed contact with the outside world, neither to supplement their care nor to let their family know they are safe. Their phones are confiscated until their case has been investigated, for fear that they would try to contact their traffickers. "You are not given phones for your own safety and protection," a counselor explained once to Florence soon after she arrived, "and you were even lucky you were allowed to make calls." Counseling staff and NAPTIP administrators consistently emphasize that these precautions are necessary for security reasons. These policies that protect possible victims from traffickers serve to isolate them as well.

Staff and Residents

Navigating the building reveals further histories of investment and divestment from NAPTIP's rehabilitation mandate. Behind the guards' desk, an uneven cement staircase leads past locked residential floors and up to the counseling staff offices, with two vacant floors of office space above that. NAPTIP is organized into seven zones across the country, and the top floor of the shelter building was once headquarters for the entire Lagos zone, including those staffing NAPTIP departments for investigation and monitoring, legal prosecution, public enlightenment, and research and program development. A few years after the agency was founded, the zonal headquarters moved into a new building across town in the quiet tree-lined streets of the Government Reserve Area, leaving only the Department of Counseling and Rehabilitation in the original facility. Many of the offices they left behind have since suffered storm damage. Some were used to store old bunk beds and broken plastic chairs, but most sat empty. The other floor was vacated by the IOM in late 2010, when it moved to a chic remodeled office building down the street, replete with floor-to-ceiling glass walls and regular generator power. Even though the shelter building is in a federal compound on a major commercial thoroughfare in an affluent district, it rarely received electricity from the city grid—perhaps an hour or two per day, on average. Especially after the relocation of the administrative staff, there was no budget to supply fuel for a generator on a regular basis.

NAPTIP counselors are the primary employees still based at the shelter, and their offices are off a long, dim, and damp hallway, lit only by light passing through a single window on either end; these two windows' glass panes have long been broken, their iron bars rusting in the humid air. Counselors mention casually that the windows had been smashed by residents in angry fits of vandalism and attempts at escape; others were surely casualties of the same storms that had put the corners of the rest of the building in shambles. Of the three dozen offices lining each side of the corridor, one-third are occupied. Staff counselors keep desks there to process paperwork and host private counseling sessions. Each office houses two counselors and contains identical heavy, modular wood-laminate desks, warped with humidity, beneath walls covered in sun-bleached posters from the NAPTIP Public Enlightenment office, the IOM, and local women's shelters.

A part-time nurse occupies another office; she is a recent nursing school graduate who provides pregnancy and HIV tests to all newly arrived residents—remnant practices of the forced medical inspection of deportees in the late 1990s. Next are the residential quarters of "Mommy Matron," who manages the day-to-day logistics of the space, supervising the two cooks, as well as the supplies, cleaning, and maintenance of the facility. There is always one counselor on twenty-four-hour duty as well, who uses a sparse but neat bedroom adjacent to the matron's office for overnight shifts. Together, they sustain the gendered form of detention and care specific to the shelter, characterized by maternal figures, sexual health inspections, and supervised reflection.

Below the staff floor, accessible through another cement staircase, were the dormitories and recreation spaces for residents of the shelter. In addition to migrant women like Florence, NAPTIP hosted several types of trafficking victims, largely distinguished by gender and age. The residents themselves often contested these labels, raising questions about who "counts" as trafficking victims, what kind of help they might need or deserve, and who should get to decide those terms.

The youngest children at the shelter were boys and girls, ages five to ten, who had been identified as victims of domestic trafficking while serving in roles known locally as "house help." They came from small villages to stay with distant relatives in Lagos or neighboring cities, with promises of better schooling in exchange for help with domestic chores. This long-standing cultural practice has been critiqued for exploiting children by blurring kinship and labor roles.[8] However, the children typically resisted NAPTIP's intervention efforts, asking only to be returned to their work.[9] Although an important element of NAPTIP's anti-trafficking agenda and an important case to assess critically, these children were outside the scope of this project.[10]

Not many boys older than age ten passed through the shelter, but the few who did were teenagers and young adults identified as victims of international labor trafficking. They came from neighboring countries of Togo and Benin to work in mining or construction industries, doing manual jobs with irregular pay and serious risks of physical injury. Although West Africans all ostensibly enjoy freedom of movement within the ECOWAS (Economic Community of West African States) region, migrants are still subject to border and identity card regulations that can forcibly return them to their countries of origin.[11] These young men also resisted the trafficking label, arguing explicitly for the right to engage in this work.[12] As we see in the next chapter, they were offered a different set of services at the shelter, without mandatory "rehabilitation." They only ever stayed a couple days, usually confined to a makeshift men's dorm in the dining room on a separate floor from the dormitories for women and children.

Migrant women comprised the third and largest population of victims at the shelter. They ranged from seventeen to forty years old, with the majority in their early to mid-twenties. Most were literate and finished at least middle school; many had graduated secondary school, and some had even attended university. Most of these women had also already completed some type of vocational training and apprenticeship but said they could not make a sufficient income using those skills. Every one of them sought to migrate out of Nigeria and was eventually identified as a victim of international trafficking.

All the women brought to NAPTIP were made to stay in the shelter for six weeks of investigation. They slept in communal bedrooms furnished with bunk-beds, mosquito nets, and buckets for the water fetched each morning and night from the borehole outside. Although no one was especially pleased with these conditions, the relative comforts of the space were not much different from the home environment of many residents, whom I would later visit after they left the shelter. Sharing rooms, carrying water, managing for days without electricity—these are normal parts of life for most people in Nigeria. What was most frustrating for residents, then, was not the conditions of the shelter space but the injustice of being trapped idle within it.

Finding Women

As NAPTIP's flagship shelter, the Lagos facility listed an official capacity of up to 120 victims, but in the decade I spent studying the shelter, I never saw occupancy rise much above 30.[13] These figures fluctuated from week to week, dropping off completely every month or so. During those times, the counseling staff would catch up on paperwork and watch movies on phones and laptop computers. They often attributed these drops in occupancy to the success of prevention and awareness programs, suggesting that there were fewer victims who needed NAPTIP's assistance. However, no one would say that human trafficking had been eliminated in Nigeria. These discrepancies are good reminders that trafficking victims do not just exist as such, out there in the world, but must be *produced*: they must be socially recognized as victims, identified by bureaucratic norms, and collected by agents in the field. That process started with Titi Abubakar's reclamation of deportees as victims of human trafficking in 1999, described in chapter 1, and it has continued to evolve in the decades since.

Single women have faced harassment at Nigeria's borders since the colonial era, including dubious concerns about their own virtue and well-being.[14] During the deportation crisis, the dedicated task-force teams from the Nigeria Immigration Service (NIS) and the Nigerian police force formalized and accelerated these efforts, systematically arresting women who were trying to leave Nigeria in the "new war on Sexport."[15] When the deportation crisis subsided after 2001, the Obasanjo administration focused its efforts on law enforcement and border security, supported by equipment worth $2.5 million donated by the Italian government.[16] During this period there was a shift from targeting returnees to targeting aspiring migrant women who had not yet left the country. The punitive language of arrest also evolved to the more neutral language of interception. These efforts were reported at length in local news media to underscore the increasing reach and vigilance of the state: "In Katsina State, 20 were intercepted between March and June while nine were intercepted in Borno State between March and August. A total of 65 were intercepted in Ogun State between July and September; 57 were stopped in Kano State in March while Zone A intercepted 38 between March and June."[17] But although the language and strategies changed, the goal was the same: to stop women from migrating.

With the NAPTIP legislation passed in 2003, the government framed inter-vention as prevention, rescue, and protection, while still betraying contempt or suspicion of migrant women themselves. Under a 2010 headline "Teenagers from Edo State Rescued from Slavery in Mali," one article describes the interception of four women and one man, all adults aged eighteen to twenty-one, who were stopped when young, unrelated women of the same age bracket, traveling with-out documents, aroused suspicion of human trafficking. The journalist's narra-tive blurs any boundaries between naive, innocent victim and reckless, unruly youth, while still validating the authority of the state to intervene:

> In what appears like a recurrent cycle of shame, the men of Nigeria Immigration Services have foiled an attempt to export five Edo girls into slavery . . .
>
> The girls, Blessing, Abigael, Ella Ojo, Faith and Isabella and Lucky, the only boy, (other names withheld) had quietly absconded with [sus-pected human trafficker Stella] Daniel to chase the proverbial Golden Fleece in Mali. They all claimed ignorance of the civil war in the coun-try of their destination. For them, the attraction to work in a bar abroad was too tempting to ignore.
>
> The promise of ₦30,000 CFA, equivalent of ₦10,000 monthly [$60], was more than enough consideration to "escape" from the allure of love and care of their parents. They confessed to have sworn to on oath with their madam not to run away until they have fully refunded her through services to customers. However, the alertness of the eagle eyes men of Nigeria Immigration Service at the border post saved them from what appears like exportation into sex slavery in foreign land.[18]

Here, the "eagle eyes" and protective instincts of the men of the NIS contrast with the willful ignorance and deception of the "girls," who "escape" the tender care of their parents only to "chase the proverbial Golden Fleece" through res-taurant work in Mali.

The sensationalist editorial tone here is common to Nigerian news writing. It also appears in the more technical description of expertise offered by the Comptroller of Immigration Services at the border, Julius Ogbu, who was in-terviewed for the same article:

> They said that were going to work in a restaurant for the trafficker. She said she recruited them from Nigeria. Incidentally, neither the traf-ficker nor any of the girls had traveling documents. More curious was the fact that none of their parents was aware they were traveling out-side the country. That was why we had to detain them and conducted

further interrogation. By the time we put our facts together, we came to a conclusion that it was actually a case of human trafficking. Number one, no traveling document; number two, their parents and relatives were not aware that they were leaving the shore of this country.

And their age is between 18 and 20. Only one of them is 22. That is the age they gave us in our records. They all claimed they were from Edo State. By virtue of our training: you are trained to be a border patrol officer and patrol prepares you for jobs in mega routes while control officers are those you see in the main borders. You're also trained to be very vigilant so that any movement that is suspicious, you apprehend, and interrogate and then you refer [to NAPTIP].[19]

Although all these women meet the age of legal adulthood in Nigeria, they are apprehended on suspicion of betraying their parents. Ogbu later clarifies that NAPTIP would have the mandate to investigate the case fully to ascertain whether it is truly human trafficking, but in the interim, he emphasizes suspicion both of the "trafficker" and the women themselves. Even the image accompanying the article, a photo of their blurred, downturned faces, represents the women as repentant delinquents: while framing them as victims, they are also understood to have eagerly consented to traveling. The NIS is trained to patrol and be vigilant not only of "traffickers" but also of all the kinds of unauthorized travel, collapsing missing permission from the state ("no traveling document") with missing permission from the family.

These strategies filled the shelter with women who did not think of their own experiences as trafficking but instead understood that the state was punishing them for trying to migrate illicitly. Although this was not a formally articulated policy of NAPTIP or of the global anti-trafficking apparatus, it is integral to the practices of victim care and protection at the shelter.

Minimum Standards

The formal definitions of human trafficking and expectations for appropriate interventions were set in the Palermo Protocol, passed by the United Nations Office of Drugs and Crime (UNODC) in 2000. Unique in the conventions of criminal law, it established a victim-centered approach to human trafficking that called on governments not only to pursue criminal prosecutions but also to provide protection and assistance to all victims, including housing, counseling, and vocational training.

Although the Palermo Protocol provided legal standards for signatory countries to implement, the primary mode of enforcing international norms has come from the US State Department. The US Congress passed the Trafficking Victims Protection Act (TVPA) in 2000, the same year as the Palermo Protocol. It prohibited trafficking within the United States and also established a sanctions regime to impose "minimum standards" for anti-trafficking efforts around the world.[20] Enforcement of those sanctions would require close review of every foreign government's efforts to stop human trafficking, which is provided in the State Department's annual Trafficking in Persons (TIP) Report.[21] This report describes countries' anti-trafficking efforts, assigns them a ranking based on a three-tier system, and offers policy recommendations to improve their score.

The TIP Report's ranking system aims to produce consistent, comparable, empirical data for every country in the world. However, this emphasis on fixed indicators has been widely criticized for collapsing the range of complex social problems that get labeled as human trafficking and for discouraging more holistic, innovative, or contextually appropriate forms of intervention.[22] By establishing a priori measures for government efforts, the TIP Report incentivizes the same narrow, quantifiable interventions, such as the total numbers of victims identified, sheltered, or rehabilitated. Such measures are most efficiently met through aggressive forms of state interventions that ignore the wishes or well-being of the victims themselves and cater instead to the strong external pressures to be seen as "doing something."[23] Instead of choosing the best intervention and support strategies for the types of violence or exploitation present in the region, the TIP Report incentivizes strategies that will be legible in annual reports, especially producing metrics that can be counted.

The State Department has done little to address these incentives in the way it reviews data or makes recommendations. For example, in 2008, Nigeria earned a second-tier ranking, and the TIP Report recommended that the Nigerian government increase occupancy at the shelters, noting that on one visit the Lagos unit housed only 15 victims, despite having space for 120. Then, in 2009, the report noted approvingly the increased number of housed victims, averaging between thirty and forty people. With this evidence of an intensified effort to fight human trafficking, Nigeria earned its first top-tier ranking. The same report, however, simultaneously recommended that the government "ensure that victims' rights are respected and that they are not detained involuntarily in shelters." That is to say, the TIP Report cited increased numbers of victims at the shelter as a reason for improving the overall score while recognizing that at least some of these victims might be there involuntarily. These contradictions suggest that the State Department does little to evaluate or consider this aspect of

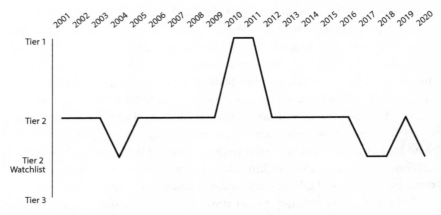

FIGURE 5.   Nigeria Country Rankings in the US Trafficking in Persons Report, 2001–2020.

counter-trafficking programs in their rankings. Indeed, Nigeria appears to be the only country to even be obliquely reproached for practices of involuntary detention in the TIP Report, despite the State Department's official condemnation of such policies elsewhere.[24]

I began fieldwork at the shelter during the year that Nigeria was awarded its first Tier One ranking, meaning the US State Department believed it "fully complies with the minimum standards for the elimination of trafficking." Since then, it has returned to Tier Two and Tier Two-Watchlist status, announced each June along with a list of recommendations to improve Nigeria's prevention, prosecution, and protection efforts (see figure 5). As part of their explanations for these rankings, the US TIP Reports critique law enforcement agencies as complicit in human trafficking—arranging false documents, border passage, and administrative sanction to supposed criminal enterprises. Yet despite this evidence of corruption, they urge the government to further invest in these offices and promote sensitization to identify more vulnerable migrant women. As consistent within the TIP Report and the criminal model of anti-trafficking more broadly, schemes to strengthen state intervention appear as the only and inevitable solutions, regardless of the wishes and well-being of migrants themselves.

Preemptive Interception

This disregard for women's own intentions and preferences was evident at the shelter, where the residents actively protested the intervention of the state. All the women I met there had wanted to travel out and had arranged for a broker to help facilitate the journey.[25] Air travel offered the safest way to move from Nigeria to Europe, but it was closely monitored for trafficking, so most took the initial part of the journey by land, risking dangerous desert and ocean crossings. They moved in small groups of two to five women through different parts of West Africa on their way to Italy or, less often, Spain, Belgium, or the Netherlands. Legally, human trafficking is characterized by exploitation, so what starts as smuggling becomes trafficking when travel brokers abuse, coerce, deceive, or exploit their clients. But these women were identified as victims not for anything that the "trafficker" did to them but merely on the expectation that such exploitation was imminent. I call this "preemptive interception" because women were targeted based not on what has happened to them but on expected future harms.[26]

A preemptive model for intervention does not require migrant women to attest to experiences of exploitation or even to agree to the merits of intervention. Border officials manipulated this opportunity, threatening to turn women over to NAPTIP unless they paid a bribe. They knew that these women were not seeking help and would especially not want to entangle themselves in state investigations. Like so many other women I met at the shelter, Florence framed her own experiences in these terms.

"I wanted to travel, but there was no help. So, I tried to help myself, and the opportunity came," she explained. This comment emphasized that she thought of the choice to leave Nigeria as an act of self-determination. "I waited four months after talking to the man," she recalled. "Then finally, we would go to Gambia and then to Italy." Such patience challenged assumptions that women in her position had been rash or naive. "They said it would be easy, but then they asked me at the airport, what am I going to do there? I said I want to go out." She had not anticipated the interrogation and shook her head as she remembered the moment. "But why they really stopped me is because I did not give the man bribe," she insisted, turning her gaze up to meet my eyes. "I said I don't have money. I don't bribe anyone. So that is why they came to take me to NAPTIP." In this narrative, Florence regrets her unpreparedness at the airport and expresses disappointment that her agents had not better prepared her to navigate questions at the airport. Still, she does not hold them responsible for the corrupt officials who halted her journey. Like many aspiring migrants, she understands that states close borders to people like her and brokers try to open them—to "help" and, with some luck, provide the opportunity she sought.[27] She was frustrated when the scheme did not work but did not see herself as a victim.

The rational for detaining Florence bears some resemblance with neo-abolitionism—the division of anti-trafficking activism that maintains that all prostitution (as they call it) is exploitive and therefore that all forms of migrant prostitution should count as trafficking, whether a woman says she consents to it or not. Like Titi Abubakar, neo-abolitionists interpret the Palermo Protocol and laws based on its definitions as supporting their position to "disallow a consent defense for traffickers."[28] However, NAPTIP's position is more nuanced.

Neither Nigeria's anti-trafficking legislation nor other federal regulations formally prohibit voluntary commercial sex work in or outside the country, as neo-abolitionists desire.[29] The NAPTIP Act does criminalize associated activities, including the "promotion of foreign travel that promotes prostitution," and so it has been broadly interpreted as a mandate to stop all forms of migrant sex work—consistent with previous prevention efforts during the deportation crisis. As Victoria Nwogu explains, the Palermo Protocol encourages states to criminalize not only the act of trafficking but also attempts to commit this act—language that the NAPTIP Act reproduces.[30] This mandate licenses law enforcement to intervene where trafficking is suspected but has not yet transpired, thereby impeding lawful activities like migration and effectively leaving law enforcement agents to prove that "there will be actual exploitation of the intercepted 'victims' upon arrival at their destination"—NAPTIP Act's definition of human trafficking.[31] But although criminal prosecutions have formalized standards of proof for attempted and suspected crimes, no such standards exist to justify victim protection, even when it is forcibly imposed.

Neo-abolitionists justify any interventions as necessary because they insist that a woman cannot consent to her own exploitation in sex work. In justifying these detentions, NAPTIP asserts only that abuse and exploitation are so consistently built into this *particular* migration stream that their occurrence is essentially inevitable, rendering aspiring migrants' initial consent irrelevant. I once asked the counselor Fred if any of the women he had met at the shelter ever actually wanted to do sex work, and he said no, emphatically. But then he went on to describe how some people come to the shelter and do not want any help, and eventually they leave to go do more prostitution. "So they want to do it, then?" I asked. "No, no," he insisted. "They just don't know." This distinction matters because it allows NAPTIP to intervene unilaterally to stop all migrant sex workers while still claiming to observe international norms that identify trafficking only as *involuntary* sex work. I witnessed exactly this debate again while presenting Florence's story at an anti-trafficking stakeholders' workshop in Lagos in 2015. Officials from the US Embassy, who were responsible for compiling Nigeria's country profile for the TIP Report, kept insisting that the intercepted women we were discussing were not victims because they had consented to migrant sex work. In response, the NAPTIP officials kept insisting that they could not stand by and wait for women to suffer before they helped them. The US officers left the workshop early, seemingly in a fit of exasperation.

Mandatory Detention

A select few of the women I met at the shelter themselves asked for help from border agents while traveling. They variously lost trust in their travel brokers or otherwise changed their minds about going and welcomed some initial assistance, but still did not consent to the long-term detention in the shelter that followed. Understanding these cases shows how detention was built into the intervention process, the condition for any support that NAPTIP might offer.

For example, Rose told me that after she had left Nigeria and was passing through Burkina Faso, her travel mates worried that their broker could not keep them safe on the journey, so they decided to turn back. "We told [officials at the next border check] what happened—that this woman was taking us abroad. Immigration then restrained the woman and said she did a big crime." At that point, the broker was being held for illegal smuggling, and the women were free to return to Nigeria, but there was a problem. "We didn't have our passports, because the woman said she'd take care of everything," Rose recalled. "So, they called the Nigerian embassy and gave us a free pass to go back to Nigeria. The embassy also gave us money for the return and a hotline number if anything else happened."

With this support, the Burkinabe officials released them to return home on their own. "We came through all the countries with no problem, just showing our free pass to get through. But then we came to the Nigerian border, and they gave us trouble." Ironically, it was entry into their own country that raised alarm. Rose speculated, "If we would have passed through the bush it would have been no problem and we would not have come to NAPTIP. Instead we were feeling free with our pass, so we went through immigrations." It is common for all kinds of people in West Africa, not just illicit migrants, to avoid the hassle and corruption of formal border checkpoints and instead "pass through the bush." In this case, the stakes of that encounter escalated because border officers had been trained to identify and detain human trafficking victims.

"That's when they stopped us and put us in that cell," Rose described. "In the cell, we met [three other women also staying at the shelter]. They had already been there three weeks." Her wide eyes recalled the shock she had felt at this discovery. "But they let us out to get food and things and so we called the hotline number the embassy gave us," she continued. "NAPTIP then called and said to them that we had done nothing wrong and they should let us be free. Can you imagine—all other countries we were fine, and here we were trying to do the right thing and return to our own country and they try to punish us!" By "doing the right thing," I took her to mean rejecting the opportunity to migrate illegally, possibly into sex work. She framed their return as a virtuous choice, and certainly one the government should support. But even NAPTIP appears ambivalent in the story. "NAPTIP corrected them," she explained, "but brought us all to [the zonal headquarters in] Ikeja and then to the shelter." The agency affirmed their innocence and right to liberty while scolding the border agents, but still referred them for rehabilitation at the shelter where they would all stay for the next six weeks.

Another woman, Osas, was intercepted under similar circumstances, after growing distrustful of her guide and seeking help from border agents. But inside the shelter, she expressed great frustration with NAPTIP, both for her detention and the moralizing rhetoric of rehabilitation. "That *oga* [NAPTIP boss] still blames me for what happened," she said to me, exasperated. "He says since I am better learned, I should have known better to believe the man and to go along with the plan to travel." She seemed unpersuaded by this logic. "Do you know that I speak five languages? English, Yoruba, Igbo, and my parents' languages. That *oga* even said he would hire me because I speak so many languages. I have a certificate in information technology, so maybe I will do that. But instead I am here"—stuck inside the shelter.

"Maybe I should have known better," she conceded briefly, "but as soon as I saw that mistake I fixed it. I was the one to make us stop at that last check, the one between Burkina Faso and Mali." She took ownership for the choice and then explained how she made it.

"We had traveled by car to there, but then they put us on a public transport bus and told us to find so-and-so person at the next place. But when other people on that bus said that the man was deceiving us, I knew I don't want to do prostitution, so I made them turn around to come back to Nigeria." Again she emphasized her self-determination and responsibility for her actions. "I fixed my mistake," she insisted, "but *no bi pikin.*" In pidgin, this means "I am not a child." "This shelter—it's like a jail. See me here." She gestured to the metal bars over the windows and around the room crowded with bunk beds. "*I wan go.*"

Even when women professed wrongdoing and remorse, they were still required to stay in the shelter. No one was released immediately, whether they understood their experience as trafficking, supported further investigation of their travel broker, or accepted the other interventions of the government.

Normalizing Resistance

These standards of intervention normalize the expectation that migrant women need not experience abuse, understand their own circumstances as trafficking, nor welcome state intervention to be identified as victims. NAPTIP staff did more than just ignore or deny women's resistance to the rehabilitation program: they recognized it as an inevitable part of the intervention process, priding themselves on their persistence despite such obstacles to care.

During one visit from a team of European officials on a "fact-finding mission," one of the delegates asked the staff directly, "So what do you do if someone wants to leave?" As was common for these visits, several NAPTIP administrators had shuttled into the shelter from the regional headquarters across town and were leading the tour. The counselors present nodded knowingly at the question, affirming how relevant it was to their work, as an administrator took the opportunity to answer.

"If someone wants to go, we will not just open the door for them. We cannot just let them leave," he explained. "That is part of counseling. We tell them the things that we can do; we convince them until they see it is better to stay. We must do social inquiry, family linking, and investigation. They cannot just go out on their own. We will never do that. We will not just open the door and give them money or take them to the [car] park and let them go. No, we will not."

This response illustrates how de facto policies that keep women in the shelter, although they may formally conflict with Nigeria's anti-trafficking laws, are presented as a point of pride within the agency and explained with conviction to visiting international delegates who are inspecting the quality of victim protection programs.

Kenny, one of the counselors, stepped in to clarify the administrator's comment: "Unless they are a voluntary return person. That is different. Then they can come and go as they please, and we will have some that like being here; that tell us they are not ready to go to see their family yet. Those can just come and go."

These efforts to explain actions that the staff take "to convince them [that] it is better to stay" were evident each day I spent at the shelter. Heated arguments and desperate pleas were an ordinary part of the job, and counselors responded—sincerely, as far as I could tell—with patient assurances, explaining the process and the necessary steps to release. For example, one woman, Cynthia, was still visibly upset and barely speaking to staff after spending three days in the shelter when Kenny approached her in the dormitory after lunch. "So, I hear you were crying earlier, *abi* [right]?" she asked. "I understand your plight," Kenny continued, "but I have to tell you, crying will not get you home. If it did, you'd be there by now. Please, have patience. Have patience with us." Cynthia barely responded, and Kenny continued. "We have our own supervisors, our own people to report to. They are the ones who make the final decisions and we are doing everything we can to help you with that. We just need to wait a couple days now." For a state agent charged with enforcing NAPTIP's detention policy, Kenny also distances herself from it as much as possible, adopting a tone of personal sympathy. "We will find out what will happen next week," she assured, "but until then, just be happy, and don't cry. And you should eat; you haven't eaten. I promise that I would be upset too if I were in this situation. Even more upset, maybe. But there is nothing we can do now." In this exchange, Kenny directly affirms Cynthia's feelings and even puts herself in her shoes.

Other times counselors and residents engaged in more confrontational debates about the terms of their condition, such as the time Kenny was rushing down a hallway with folders in her arms and Yemi saw her pass by the doorway in a whir. "*I wan goooo,*" Yemi began hollering after her, surprised to see Kenny stop and return to the small room where I was sitting with a group of women as they tailored some donated clothes. Kenny smiled at first and teasingly chastised her for not greeting her properly, joking that Yemi would never see progress on her case with this attitude.

"Ah, this place is a *prison!* NAPTIP is a *prison!*" Yemi declared in response. "You shouldn't keep us here, locked up, with no phone, no way to go outside."

The accusation that the shelter was a prison surprised me at the time, but Kenny seemed more annoyed than disturbed. "We must do investigation," she explained simply, shaking her head. "So we cannot just let you go. We first must do our work. And are you even made to work here? What work have you done?" she demanded. Yemi was twenty-one years old with a daughter of her own, whom she had left behind with her mother to better support her financially from abroad. She wanted to work; that was why she traveled. Still, she said nothing, and Kenny continued, "No, you are just to sleep and eat and that is it, so you cannot call this place like that [a prison]." She paused. "If God wants you to go today, you will go," Kenny said finally. "And if God wants you to go next week, no amount of shouting or crying or talking will change the day."

Governing Forces

Built into these logics of detention was the supposition that, whether or not the women appreciated it, the shelter provided needed protection to migrant women, so part of the work that counselors did was to convince women of these dangers. They painted gruesome pictures of the risks women faced as (would-be) human trafficking victims, warranting not only immediate interception but also ongoing protective custody at the shelter. They warned women of the potential aggressiveness and violence of traffickers who had been foiled by the NAPTIP intervention and may now face criminal charges. When one resident, Rose, asked why she was not allowed to cross the compound to buy grilled corn or plantains from the woman on the street, Ben explained that people could want to poison them, especially if they could be witnesses in a criminal investigation or prosecution, so they had to be very careful. "It might not be safe even if you don't know it," he insisted, a story I heard repeated by others as well. Ben recognized Rose's incredulity: "Even this girl who used to stay in this shelter," he told me, "she has been calling me, telling me that this guy—Mister California, the trafficker, the recruiter—he is bothering her family. Her mother is not even staying in her own place, because of his harassment. That is why we at NAPTIP must do our jobs very well. To protect you." Stories like this emphasized that these women were vulnerable not only while traveling but also throughout the investigation process and that the six weeks to confirm these accusations was a worthwhile sacrifice in case the fears of violence were well founded.

Although I have no reason to believe that Ben's story was fabricated, its frequent circulation as the lone story of long-term harassment may reflect how rare these kinds of reprisals really were. None of the women I knew ever mentioned such fears, even though they had taken out significant debt to fund their journeys. Travel brokers are aware of how often journeys can be interrupted, whether through failed border crossings, visa problems, or deportation, so they build into repayment schemes the costs of failed trips.[32] Outstanding debts, even in the tens of thousands of dollars, are not always collected. Sine Plambech makes the same observation of travel brokers in this region: "because the traffickers had so many women going to Europe, they did not turn to violent means to collect the unpaid debt of the deported women."[33]

Even where risks of retaliation are real, counter-trafficking advocates and scholars argue that they should be balanced against the loss of freedom of mobility on a case-by-case basis.[34] The formal commitments *not* to detain victims of human trafficking in the TIP Report and NAPTIP laws suggest that this balance should be weighed heavily in favor of the victim's liberty. Instead, counselors here understood that their job is to convince women of the need for protection in the first place.

This process of persuasion was sometimes effective, but some women still did try to escape. While I was away one week, a new resident tried to jump from the second-floor veranda rooftop, injuring her ankle when she fell short of the adjacent cement wall topped with barbed wire. Kenny told me the story later in hushed tones, shaking her head in disappointment. I asked if many residents had tried to leave, and Ben pulled out his cell phone to scroll through old photographs. He found one showing a small group of women who a few years earlier had broken bathroom mirrors into shards to use as weapons and then tried to melt the padlock with matches to escape. I had heard him mention this escape attempt before. When repeated at the shelter, these rumors could sound like threats. As Kenny exclaimed to a resident who had been whining I wan go, "You think you are the only one frustrated here? See these windows. They were broken by people very angry, I would say even more than you. In fact, you are not the worst; many are worse. They broke these and the mirror upstairs. So do not think you are alone. We know you are not happy here."

Yet, to understand women's endurance in the shelter as imposed entirely by force of violence or the threat of violence—by padlocks and barbed wires and fears of reprisal at home—misses its deeper relationship to the state at work: people expect government officials to wield power arbitrarily in Nigeria; they expect the state to provide barriers and not services; and they expect, in the end, for it to be irrational. In pointing to policies and procedures as external reasons for women's detention ("we must do investigation," "we must do our work"), Kenny appeals to the virtue of a bureaucracy that will not take shortcuts by personal request or bribery. But at the same time, these are the same references to vague bureaucratic obligations that are often used to obscure work that could quickly be expedited.[35] For people without connections in Nigeria, bureaucracy remains impenetrable. As author Chimamanda Ngozi Adichie commented in a national newspaper interview, "Ours is a country in which the individual is abused and made to feel helpless by the state."[36]

Women at the shelter would carry these expectations into all of their interactions with the Nigerian government, including their detention at the NAPTIP shelter. They ultimately knew that, in practice, arbitrary forms of intervention were within the state's prerogative, however unfair.[37] As Ruth Marshall describes, "The lawless arbitrariness of a state where policeman are thieves, legislators are criminal predators, and the common man has no hope for any form of redress renders overwhelming the urge to move from the plane of immanence to transcendence in the quest for certainty and understanding."[38] For all their protesting I wan go, I wan go, no one ever demanded to see a lawyer, judge, or even a parent. They certainly did not invoke a language of rights or due process that one might expect, for example, in the United States. There were no such cries of dismay, of "You can't do this to me" or "I have rights."

In short, Nigerians take for granted that the state will not only neglect but also abuse its citizens—from bribe-seeking airport officials to the seemingly indefinite detention policies of the shelter itself—and the women at the shelter navigated NAPTIP intervention based on these expectations. As a result, women at the shelter at least partly yielded to their detention there, biding their time until release, despite the frustrations they expressed along the way.

Conclusion

Aspiring migrants across the global south experience staying in place not as root-edness but as being stuck, as enforced immobility that bars personal fulfillment.[39] Migration thereby presents not only an economic opportunity but an existential one—a chance to live by one's own choices. Understood in this frame, the regular protestations at the shelter, "*I wan go, I wan go*," were more than a plea to leave the building—to enjoy the sun or get fresh air—or to leave NAPTIP's custody. In try-ing to leave the country, the women detained at the shelter were taking control of their own lives, ceding the certainty of stagnation for the possibility of travel. *I wan go* was a protest not only of the shelter but also of Nigeria, of being stuck again in more ways than one. Nigeria's anti-trafficking scheme, building on the earlier deportation panic, consolidated efforts to stop migrants at the borders and detain them for weeks afterward. While many migrants experience this closure abstractly as they hustle for papers or wait in border camps, women intercepted in these pro-grams experienced the same forces up close, in airport cells, in padlocked shelters, and direct counseling from the state.

The shelter thereby provides a space to observe more than the simple fact of detention, its legal inconsistencies, or its moral objections. It reveals the work required to normalize these practices in historical context, amid regulatory scru-tiny and nationalist fervor. An ethnography of detention reveals conceptions of governance operating in real time, from how shelter staff assert the power and authority of the state, to how to women navigate these assertions, yielding and protesting at once. Evidence from these encounters supports a more complicated view of NAPTIP's detention practices than simple political expediency or cor-ruption: state officials appear earnest in their intentions to help women and they seem proud of the results. Still, their personal sensibilities around women's well-being chafe against the pragmatic constraints of migrant women's choices.

Interception and detention, then, were only the beginning. The real work of rehabilitation would tackle this incongruity head-on, challenging counselors to not only stop migrant women but to change the way they think altogether.

VULNERABILITY REDUCTION

When I first started visiting the shelter, I could not make sense of its seemingly contradictory rehabilitation policies. On the one hand, NAPTIP boasted of rescuing migrant women preemptively, before they had experienced the bodily or psychological harms of trafficking. On the other hand, NAPTIP law and policy mandated that the agency provide protection and trauma therapy to all victims of human trafficking. These service programs were consistent with international norms set by the Palermo Protocol and US TIP Reports, which assumed victims would want and need help recovering from sexual abuse and exploitation. But what did that look like for women who were intercepted without those experiences? Most had barely left the country. Few reported incidents of violence or sexual exploitation during their journey. Even those who had lost trust in their brokers and turned back home on their own accord were openly resistant to intervention, but they were still mandated to stay for rehabilitation. Why?

I asked the counselor Ben for help understanding this contradiction: "So, if they want to go home, can they?"

"Well, if they keep saying that, *I wan go*, eventually we will refer them to the zonal director, and he will listen to them. He has the authority to decide, but ultimately he too wants to see a happy ending." A happy ending for the director, however, did not require allowing women to be released on demand. Ben continued, "So he will ask them, do you want to go to school? And the person might say that they do but only if their school fees are paid, so he will agree: if you go to school NAPTIP will pay your school fee. But that means they have to stay and cooperate."

I had seen women communicating clearly, consistently, *I wan go, I wan go*, with no incentives offered in exchange for their cooperation. I asked him again, "But what if they still really want to go? Will you just let them?"

Probably misreading my own sympathies, he insisted, "We will not just let them go," shaking his head as if almost offended by the insinuation. He did not want the agency to look negligent, as if it would be giving up on those women too easily. "It is our job to convince them," he clarified.

I tried to ask once again. "So, you cannot force them to stay here? Or you can only force the young ones?"

"No, no, we do not force them," he repeated. "It is no use to force anyone; our job is to convince them that this is for the best."

Ben's comments exemplify how involuntary detention is both obscured by *and imperative to* the kind of rehabilitation offered to women at the shelter. He insists simultaneously that no one will be released on demand, but also that no one will be made to stay, and that this is for everyone's benefit—it leads to "a happy ending." The purpose of rehabilitation is to get victims to share this vision, to agree that NAPTIP's interventions are "for the best"—justified by the danger of trafficking and morally righteous in helping women change their path. I never saw women successfully negotiate their way out of the shelter, but the counselors worked constantly to *convince* them to stay and cooperate. These conversations constituted the majority of Ben's job: engaging the protests of resistant women and counseling them to think differently.

Rehabilitation services are an essential part of anti-trafficking programs, mandated in the United Nations' Palermo Protocol, in the US TVPA and TIP Reports, and in Nigeria's own anti-trafficking legislation. They typically include safe residential spaces to help women transition to independent living, talk therapy to treat the mental trauma of trafficking, and vocational training to develop alternative career paths. However, women intercepted preemptively did not have these needs. They had left their homes just days before, and many had decided to migrate only after failing to find work in the fields they had trained for. Most importantly, they had not experienced abuse or exploitation, and at least on a case-by-case basis, the staff realized this too. Not only did those women not see their experiences as trafficking but also the counselors did not see them as traumatized. The premise for their early interception was that these women were in the process of being trafficked and would have later suffered abuses if not for the state's intervention. Regardless, counseling remained a primary component of the shelter program.

This chapter shows how counselors adapted the therapeutic elements of rehabilitation to suit the women they saw as victims. Specifically, it argues that NAPTIP designed therapy to *convince* migrant women to change their minds and cooperate with the anti-trafficking agenda. This is important because it locates the source of women's vulnerability to trafficking within their own ambition and worldviews, rendering them culpable for their own trafficking. The language of rehabilitation and vulnerability thereby facilitates and legitimizes the evolving state project to govern women's migration, not only through detention but also through the personal reform projects that counselors facilitated.

Therapeutic Standards

Article 6 of the Palermo Protocol requires governments to "consider implementing measures to provide for the physical, psychological and social recovery of victims of trafficking in persons." The US TIP Reports have also required evidence of formal trauma therapy services for countries to earn top tier rankings. But Nigeria does not train enough mental health professionals to provide this kind of treatment, nor do Nigerians necessarily think about victim support in these terms.[1] Even when the global aid industry placed increasing attention on treating trauma worldwide, Africa was largely left out.[2] Many Nigerians—including Nigerian physicians—think the common terms of mental health just do not apply to them, observing matter-of-factly that "people don't get depressed in Nigeria."[3]

Of the dozen or so counselors based at the shelter who interacted with residents on a day-to-day basis, only two were formally educated as social workers. The rest boasted various university degrees with majors like business, math, and economics. As is typical for salaried positions with the federal government, all were hired through political connections and nepotism at the main headquarters: an uncle who got someone's application in front of the right eyes, a cousin who had lived near NAPTIP's executive secretary years earlier, and so on. There was a single trained psychologist on the NAPTIP staff in Lagos, but he was only brought in to counsel the most "severe" cases.[4] His offices were located in the zonal headquarters across town, and in my experience, he more often visited the shelter with other high-ranking agency officials to tour the space with important donors and international stakeholders. Counselors participated in occasional workshops on trauma care but rarely applied this framework to their work. For example, when discussing issues of older children at the shelter wetting the bed or sobbing in fits, no one offered a psychological interpretation of these behaviors as symptoms of trauma. Instead, counselors dismissed them as acts of attention seeking and misbehavior. No one considered whether the process of interception and detention itself inflicted trauma on shelter residents.

In the decade after NAPTIP was founded, several US TIP Reports noted the lack of proper trauma treatment skills among NAPTIP staff, recommending improved training for everyone who interacted with victims. NAPTIP obligingly convened several workshops to this effect, but the agenda and program notes from one such event suggest that much of the actual training offered was irrelevant at best. A four-day workshop on "stress and trauma management for victims of human trafficking" was organized by NAPTIP in collaboration with the UNODC in September 2010 at one of the major state universities near Lagos. Each day consisted of morning and afternoon sessions, addressing a total of eight separate topics. Four appear to have been recycled from corporate human resources lectures: "Developing a positive attitude to work," "Why employees resist change," "Health and stress management in the workplace," and "Emotional intelligence / well-being." As is common in conferences in Nigeria, the first and last sessions were reserved for opening and closing ceremonies. Only one-quarter of the time was dedicated to teaching counselors and other stakeholders how to better deal with victims of trauma and human trafficking. Still, the effort was noted approvingly in the next annual US TIP Report, alongside the recommendation for additional trainings.

Global development and aid incentive programs are rife with training mandates, where the quality or effectiveness of the training matters less than its ability to be counted and tracked by the systems controlled by the global north.[5] Andrew Jefferson describes such a pattern in the human rights workshops for Nigerian prison staff that followed Nigeria's democratic transition, noting that "the logic seems to be that training is good because it is training." However, the content of globally circulating workshops often fails to resonate with meaning specific communities find in their work. In the case of Nigerian prison reform, the externally imposed trainings disregarded prison officers' own ideas of reform and responsibility and thereby proved ineffective.[6] Although these failures may be noted in assessment reports, compliance and competency are still imagined as a binary or at best a linear scale, progressively imposing external, universal standards for "correct" behavior. These systems not only ignore local understandings of care but also frame local practices exclusively in terms of deficiency and deviance. They situate Western norms as the ideal to which all other nations must aspire while obscuring the structural inequalities that perpetuate those differences. As Jefferson notes, the diagnostic model—"description wrapped in approbation and denunciation"—manages to "*keep accounts of* (bad) practices" without "*accounting for*" their cause or content.[7]

Likewise, merely tracking the lack of formal psychiatric services in the shelter or the inconsistent application of therapeutic language reinforces normative and evaluative reporting frameworks—deficit models of corruption or incompetence—that validate the expertise and authority of wealthy nations that control reporting mechanisms. To "account for" these practices and not just keep accounts of them, this chapter examines how counselors themselves understood the work of therapy and rehabilitation.

Improving Yourself

When counselors talked about the purpose of rehabilitation, they described urging residents to use their time for reflection and reform. Ben liked to compare the shelter to a training ground. One afternoon, he came to talk to a resident named Victoria who had been upset all morning, repeating *I wan go, I wan go,* and complaining, among other things, that she was not able to manage her normal personal care routines. Ben interrupted her objections to share a long story about his NAPTIP training with other paramilitary agencies. For six months, he was not allowed to do his own personal care routine either. He described getting up by 5 a.m. every morning, running until 6, exercising for another half-hour, and following orders the entire day, explaining that the trainees had no time of their own to go into town or to do what they wanted.

"All that," he concluded, "is to say that I know how it feels, to be living under regimen." A few other women had been lingering in the room after lunch and joined Victoria to protest that it was not at all the same, but he continued. "I know what it is like, but I also knew I was there for training. I was able to prepare myself mentally. If you don't see this place as training, you will have a problem. So, what is next? That is the question."

"*I wan go,*" Victoria repeated.

"Yes, yes," Ben conceded. "Of course everybody *wan go,* so that is not the question. The question is, What you are going to do when you get there? You have to have a plan."

"Me, I will go to US! Follow my friend," Victoria declared half-jokingly as she gestured toward me.

"Be serious and think about what you would like to do," he insisted in a somber tone. "You can use this place to improve yourself."

In interactions like these, Ben locates the work of rehabilitation in individual reform, but not in a medical model of trauma recovery. Instead, he compares it to professional training, mental preparation, and personal improvement. This emphasis is consistent with NAPTIP'S 2008 National Policy on Protection and Assistance to Trafficked Persons in Nigeria. It ordered shelters to provide "psychosocial services"; "cultural, spiritual, and vocational guidance"; and a "warm, protective and supportive environment for personal development." Studies of other counter-trafficking programs suggest that this disciplinary ethos is common in intervention programs around the world. Research in shelters in Southern and Eastern Europe shows similarly that "to be a good victim . . . is not to be too assertive, to be malleable, to change and 'to learn,'" including acquiring a professed aversion to migration.[8] In Serbia and Moldova, rehabilitation is perceived as a "transformation of deviant identities" or a "correction of personalities," such that shelter beneficiaries were expected to reflect on their own values and priorities.[9] More than providing economic support or healing, these rehabilitation programs promise to make participants better people. Or, as one of the counselors once put it to a frustrated resident in her second week with NAPTIP, "OK, so we at the shelter, we are not just here to tell you, no you cannot travel. We want to make sure you are learning things while you are here, so that when you leave, you will be improved. You will go back to your place, and your mother will say, 'Who is this girl, who is doing this thing?'" It was a project of transformation—a transformation so thorough that even a mother would not recognize her own daughter. This concept of transformation is important because it identifies the "victim" herself as needing to change for rehabilitation to be successful. For women intercepted preemptively, rehabilitation does not act on the trauma caused by trafficking but on the range of dispositions and desires that (are imagined to) make her trafficking possible.[10]

Although this reform effort was a concerted one, it was far from the regimented lifestyle of Ben's paramilitary training. On the wall of one of the counseling offices was a weekly calendar of shelter programming, a relic from when the shelter funding was more generous and programming more rigorous. The chart dictated a full daily schedule with activities from morning to night, including recreational and vocational training in photography, beading, catering, hairdressing, tailoring, and even computer skills. By the time I began fieldwork in 2008, however, the calendar was much less crowded; only a few of the listed activities were still available, and even those were sparsely attended. A teacher still came in to provide informal education twice a week based on a UNICEF curriculum for children. Participation was required for all residents, but the adults quickly became bored with the literacy and arithmetic lessons that were far beneath their skill level. Of the many vocational training classes originally offered, only hairdressing and tailoring remained, and the level of instruction seemed just as ill-suited. Many of the women at the shelter had already completed training in these areas and had decided to travel only after failing to find satisfactory work in their chosen fields.

The scarcity of formal programing, however, did not necessarily detract from the mission of the shelter, given its specific goals of achieving personal reform. When counselors urged residents to "use their time in the shelter well," as Ben did earlier, they meant not to learn a skill but to think. To use time wisely was to examine the choices that got them to the shelter and reconsider the plans they will make once they leave. If idleness can be an impetus for such reflection, then the unstructured time was conducive to the work counselors believed women needed to do. The few consistent weekly activities supported this effort as well, in mandatory group therapy sessions and ecumenical worship led by counselors on themes like patience, faith, and direction. Informally, counselors also prompted this work as they walked through the halls of the shelter, weighing in on conversations amongst different residents and prompting new ones. By encouraging this introspection, staff members deflected the many protestations women made about their detention and suggested that each woman was individually responsible for making her time there worthwhile.

Culpability and Vulnerability

When I asked counselors at the shelter why women there needed to change, they would explain that since the women had been vulnerable to trafficking before they came to the shelter, they would also be vulnerable to retrafficking upon their release, unless something was done to intervene. This rationale again suggests that vulnerability to trafficking is not related to the behavior of traffickers or even to the structural conditions of poverty and opportunity that these women face. Rather, it derived directly from the women's desire to migrate, as well as their willingness to take on debt and engage in sex work to do so. NAPTIP officials reported the risk of retrafficking as the motivation for intervention, and counselors regarded a woman's commitment not to migrate again as the mark of successful rehabilitation.

In this way, the rehabilitation program pathologizes women's ambitions to migrate, framing their determination to leave as the problem to be fixed. This thinking reflects earlier moral panics around the deportation crisis. As the Italian ambassador to Nigeria remarked at the time, "Their idea about freedom, their idea about fulfilling the desire of their heart is quite different from ours. The mentality inside them is wrong." Rehabilitation offers a therapeutic paradigm to intervene on that mentality, to provide a psychosocial services, to *convince* these women to see the world another way. It rhetorically transforms moral culpability into humanitarian vulnerability. Both locate the object of intervention in women's interior selves or subjectivities—the thoughts, desires, and dispositions that made them want to migrate in the first place.

This usage is not inherent to the concept of vulnerability. When vulnerability emphasizes conditions of risk over individual behavior, the term facilitates the analysis of social structures rather than individual behavior, supporting more systemic solutions to problems of inequality. However, as a diagnostic and technocratic term in global aid and development, "vulnerability" too often has the effect of naturalizing those conditions as permanent or inevitable.[11] In anti-trafficking campaigns, the term specifically has been used to silence third world sex workers as hapless victims.[12] In the shelter, talk of vulnerability directs blame away from global disparities in capital and opportunity, away from security regimes that enforce those borders, and away from the failure of state education, labor, and social welfare systems to provide meaningful alternatives within Nigeria. It obscures structural causes of vulnerability to exploitation and instead holds ambitious women responsible for their own supposed trafficking.[13]

Because it is located within their own ambition, this usage of vulnerability also suggests culpability. Women's desires to migrate are dismissed as naive and misdirected, warranting exactly the kind of paternalistic intervention NAPTIP provides. As a result, the rehabilitation process sustains prior suspicions toward migrant women, cloaking them now in the guise of victimhood and vulnerability. This ambivalence is consistent with prevailing attitudes toward sex workers elsewhere around the world, as objects of both pity and disdain, as both victim and whore.[14] Women at the shelter are seen both as victims—passive, naive, too vulnerable be able to consent to these choices—and as culprits who are responsible for their own vulnerabilities and require intensive intervention in order to achieve personal reform. As such, it is their own desires and inclinations that are most in need of change.

This reasoning is gendered, as Ben made clear to a visiting team of trafficking awareness volunteers, organized through Nigeria's national youth service program.[15] Noting that all the residents at the time were female, one visitor asked if it was an all-female shelter or whether there was another shelter for male victims. "Most victims are female," Ben responded, "so we don't want to put male victims of this age with these girls, especially since most of them are abused in different ways. So, we will just put the younger boys in this place." The visitor repeated her question, asking if there was a different shelter for trafficked men then. "No, not really . . ." Ben said, trailing off. He continued,

> It's more like a different package. Male victims are more easily resettled with their families, so usually we can just do that quickly, whereas with the girls, it is more complicated. We can usually just hand the boys over to their families to be reunited. Males will just want to hustle, so we have to respect that. But with females we have to develop a business plan, do all these things. There is more risk with females because they are more vulnerable to attack. So we have to do what we call social inquiry, to

inspect the family because we have had some cases where the trafficker harassed the family so we have to make sure that thing has died down before we return the victim there.

There are good reasons to provide different services for different kinds of exploitation that get labeled as trafficking. Within West Africa, men are more likely to be recognized as victims of trafficking for labor abuses and not for sexual exploitation; they also often travel only a bus ride or two away from their hometown, rather than across many land and sea borders. It is possible that these men do not face the same level of harassment or retaliation from their traffickers, and therefore require fewer protection measures, when compared to those traveling to Europe at much higher costs. Without a known risk of sexual exploitation, counselors would also be less likely to understand them as benefiting from the psychological services ostensibly tied to rehabilitation.

However, from Ben's explanation and others like it, that logic was not operating at the shelter. He simply asserted that women were "more vulnerable to attack" without further elaboration, implying that a "business plan" should somehow arm women against these vulnerabilities.[16] Ben, along with the rest of the counseling staff, willfully relinquished male victims to high-risk lifestyles of crime and "hustling," while urging personal reform for women making similar choices. These gendered discrepancies thereby suggest a deeper difference in approach between male and female victims, motivated by more than their need for physical protection. Whereas Ben reluctantly accepts men's hustling, the "different package" of rehabilitation services for women refuses their pursuit of equivalent options. Time at the shelter is used to try to prevent them from hustling in the first place.

Reforming Resistance

Implicit in this model of intervention is the idea that the women who resist rehabilitation the most are also the ones who need it the most. Their protests are not just incidental inconveniences but signs of their persistent vulnerability to being trafficked again. Repeated demands to be released—*I wan go, I wan go*—indicate something still aberrant within them, rather than standing as the legitimate demands of responsible adults. Gallagher and Pearson suggest that shelter staff around the world often deny the existence of de facto detention practices when they focus on ultimately serving the victim's needs.[17] The counselor Ben demonstrates this leap in the opening vignette—"No, no, we do not force them," he insisted. He does not see the shelter as coercive, but as patient.

Although Ben was uneasy with the idea of involuntary rehabilitation ("it's no use to force anyone"), other counselors at the shelter took this line of thought a step further, insisting that no women should ever be able to refuse their services. These counselors expected that residents would want to leave the shelter. If the staff's job was to convince them to change their own goals and priorities, it made sense that the women would never volunteer to engage in this process. Counselors sometimes referred to these residents as "brainwashed" by their circumstances: they just could not see the harm of their own choices.

NAPTIP official Lily Oguejiofor emphasized this responsibility when she was interviewed in the agency's glossy internal promotional magazine about the difficulties in working with the women residents She described her approach as follows:

> *As Director of Counseling and Rehabilitation, what challenges do you face dealing with TIP victims?*
>
> Like every other aspect of life, rehabilitation has its own challenges. It is more challenging because we are dealing with trafficked persons. I am sorry to say it, but trafficked persons are really very difficult people to deal with. These are people who have gone through trauma. They have been deceived and have experienced a lot of hardship. Here they are with us, some of the trafficked victims have not really reached their destination and were still hoping to get to their destinations, and they take it out on us, the rehabilitation officers. They feel you have stopped them from reaching the promise[d] land and we have serious difficulties settling them down. Then, even those that are deported come back angry because while there, they were serving their madam, hoping to be free soon and then begin to make money themselves. And then, suddenly they are brought back. When coming back, they are furious, lots of them, very furious. Most of the victims that we receive are people [who] think we are meddling into their lives. Just a handful of them come back sober. So, what you experience is that you are working for people who think you are trying to help but they end up fighting with you.
>
> I remember my first experience going to receive victims from the airport in Lagos. It is a story that I've never stopped telling. They came back challenging everybody and angry at being brought back. So, it is like a thankless job and by the time they get into the shelter, it takes a lot of time to calm them down. It takes time, efforts, and skills from the Counselors to do this and to tell them alternative means of livelihood. In spite of the fact that counselors are trained not to be [empathetic], not to get involved and so on, they are human beings and at a

point, their patience is tasked to the limits. So, it is a big challenge that you are trying to help people and they feel you are disturbing them.

We thank God that we put in an effort and that is why we insist that victims that come back must stay for at least six weeks in our shelters whether they like [it] or not.[18]

Here, Oguejiofor notes that women are primarily angry because they wanted to leave the country and were not allowed to continue on their journey. Some, she recognizes, would prefer to stay "serving their madam." But rather than question whether they ought to be designated as victims, she frames this resistance only as evidence of the trauma and hardship they have suffered. By describing the few who are not resistant as "sober," she suggests the rest are simply not capable of understanding their own lives. That is, to be a victim of trafficking is to lose these capacities, and the purpose of NAPTIP's rehabilitation is to restore them.

Although involuntary detention is formally prohibited by NAPTIP law and policies, Oguejiofor says publicly that "we insist that victims that come back must stay for at least six weeks in our shelters whether they like [it] or not." This interview was published in the agency's own magazine, between reports of successful prosecutions and color photos of NAPTIP staff posing with international donors. It was edited and reproduced to publicize what the agency's public relations team saw as NAPTIP's achievements. Where resistance here provides the reason for rehabilitation, detention is the method. That their resistance to detention is so adamant only makes their work all the more commendable, highlighting the staff members' earnest commitment to their work as they use their "time, efforts, and skills" to work with such difficult clients.

Much anthropological work in recent years has explored the strategic performance of trauma in order to access public services, especially in refugee and humanitarian programs.[19] In those cases, migrants must present authorities with signs of their personal trauma histories, often written on the body or psyche, to support legal claims to residency papers and other resources. These stakes are inverted at the shelter. There, the *authorities* try to convince the *migrants* that they have been abused, or that such abuse was imminent. At the shelter, the state is the one that needs alleged victims to see their experiences as dangerous and warranting extreme intervention, a recognition that would retroactively justify their involuntary interception and detention. This logic also inverts the common critique of human trafficking interventions that define the "worthy" victims as those innocent and naive women forced into prostitution and so on.[20] While NAPTIP's distribution of reintegration resources sometimes replicated this scheme (see the conclusion), the approach within the shelter is different. It assumes that women who are apparently complicit in their own trafficking are those most in need of attention.

During a decade of fieldwork in these centers, I did meet a few women whom Oguejiofor would describe as already "sober." They had stories more closely resembling the archetypical trafficking cases of forced prostitution, and some really could not return home: they blamed relatives for sending them abroad, or they were orphans who had been exploited by foster relationships. However, the few residents I met of this sort were also exceptional in that they did not vocally object to their confinement within the shelter. All the restrictions and discomforts of daily life notwithstanding, they exhibited patience as the counselors processed their case, and they complied eagerly with daily activities. Yet, by the same token, this group did not receive same level of attention given to other residents. By Oguejiofor's logic, they did not need the same kind of counseling, the same kind of *convincing*, that the others required. Indeed, they enjoyed praise amongst the counseling staff, who described them as well behaved and level-headed. They were invited to speak to guests and reporters at the shelter more often, and they readily cooperated with such requests.[21]

The residents who resisted, by contrast—those who wanted to resume traveling or even just to go home—they were the ones who needed rehabilitation. Their protests were considered direct evidence of an impatience with life's challenges, a refusal of NAPTIP's generosity, and the senseless embrace of choices that would harm them and their country. They were the ones who needed to be convinced.

Opening Up

An important step in this process of rehabilitation was for women to "open up" to the counseling staff—to be honest about their original intentions, to consider the alternatives that NAPTIP presented, and to cooperate in any ongoing investigation of their case. Victim cooperation was essential to the few successful convictions that NAPTIP achieved, but most women did not think of their travel brokers as traffickers. When NAPTIP investigators and counselors asked them about their travel arrangements, they faithfully repeated the stories their sponsors had provided, aiming to protect everyone involved from accusations of wrongdoing. Nearly all the women denied that they had wanted to enter foreign sex industries, and many denied wanting to go to Europe. Still, counselors always assumed otherwise.

Faced with this challenge, members of the counseling staff used a combination of individual rapport and purported agency incentives to urge women to disclose their real plans. Many flatly refused to believe the stories women told them, shaking their heads, and promising that the residents would only be released from the shelter once they cooperated. "You say you *wan go*," counselors regularly admonished, "but you've not even talked." Ben once explained on behalf of his colleagues, "It's really important to open up to your counselor. I am not anyone's [assigned] counselor here, but I can tell you that if you open up to them, they might just go the extra mile on the matter. But if you are just quiet, then no one will know what is on your mind."

Counselors sometimes exaggerated these claims, suggesting that full disclosure was the primary prerequisite for their release. For example, in the first group counseling session for a newly arrived group of women, many kept demanding to know how long they would have to stay at the shelter. Ben then explained their detention as follows: "You are not meant to stay here more than six weeks. But it could be that the office asked for some papers, and by law then you are technically free but you are holding yourself. Some people are here to try your case. They are holding someone in a cell to prosecute. . . . But that is why you must be open with your counselor. Don't hide your story. Tell the truth." In more intense moments of argument and frustration on this issue, counselors' tones went from friendly or pleading to threatening. Another counselor once admonished Florence this way, insisting, "If you just laugh, you will laugh with your counselor all the way through New Year's. If you don't talk, you will see Christmas in this shelter I promise you. You think all these people who are going, you think they are just picking them and taking them? No, they have a file, and that file has to be complete. If you do not talk for that file you will stay for shelter."

Women being held at the shelter understood that giving information about their travel plans advanced the investigation against their sponsors and alleged traffickers, and so many actively resisted the efforts. During their first week in the shelter, when away from the counselors and NAPTIP staff, Florence and Blessing joked often about staying quiet. In a particularly macabre quip, Blessing joked that she wanted to cut her lips or just sew them shut so that she could not talk at all. She imitated how people would call after her—"Blessing, would you like to eat?"—and then pinched her lips closed, muffled her speech, and bobbed her head in response. The visual effect was quite funny, and everybody laughed at the charade. We took turns asking her other questions—"Blessing, do you have water? Blessing, do you want plantain?"—until Florence asked, "What of, Blessing, you *wan go*?" "YES!" she blurted out, breaking the vow of silence.

Even as only offered as a diversion, these jokes suggested that women opposed not only their own detention at the shelter but also the entire investigation being launched ostensibly on their behalf. The counseling staff was administratively separated from the department responsible for criminal prosecution, and their proximity in the shelter allowed counselors to build closer personal relationships with residents. However, when counselors allied themselves with the prosecution process by admonishing women to cooperate, those relationships were tested. Once Florence rushed out of a meeting with the investigation staff, who had traveled across town to talk to her about her file.[22] I was sitting with two counselors and several other residents in an informal education class session when she burst into the room, shouting, "I didn't know the girl! I don't know her!"

"For the third time today," Ben declared solemnly, looking up from the arithmetic workbook, "it's just time to tell the truth about all of it, and stop denying everything."

"Which truth do they want to hear?" Florence demanded, "Which truth?? I gave them my brother's number. Me, *I wan go!*" She was exasperated.

"You want to go? But you've not talked, Florence," another counselor interjected.

"What do you want me to say?" she pleaded.

"What did I tell you the day that I took you, when we were in the van?" he said, gesturing toward Blessing, her travel companion, to remind her.

Florence shrugged that she did not know. Ben looked expectantly at Blessing for the answer. "He said that we were lying," she said.

Growing angry again, Florence repeated herself once more: "I never met that woman before, and she does not know about me. I didn't know her before. We just met at the airport, where I saw her. I didn't go follow her—when we reach the [destination] airport my brother was to come pick me."

"*Na lie*," the counselor replied flatly in pidgin—it's a lie.

Florence groaned and spun around. She left the room muttering, "They are investigating, *abi*? Please, let me investigate too."

Florence did not know at the time that Blessing had already "opened up" to the counselors about the real plans a travel broker had arranged for them to reach Italy, undermining the account they had originally offered together. Blessing never told Florence what she had said, but she complained privately to the counselors that they did not hold up their end of the bargain. She was frustrated that she had not already been released, even though she had told them what they wanted to hear. Ben explained frankly to her, "Okay, fine, but the stories still have to match up. Even if you have said everything, there are two others, and their stories have to match up too. And right now your own matches with one, but not the other . . ." He trailed off for a moment before saying directly what he had been implying: "If that girl Florence doesn't tell the truth, it will remain stuck, because the stories will not match." Promising release from the shelter in exchange for a revised statement is extortive, especially given the importance of the statements for meeting agency prosecution goals. But in his pleas, Ben still seemed to me to be reaching for something more than that.[23]

"Opening up" was an important step not only in the ongoing criminal investigation but also in the rehabilitation process. Changing a story demonstrated clear reform of the supposedly rebellious mindset that made each woman vulnerable to trafficking. It served both the prosecutor's interest in obtaining the truth of the act and the counselor's interest in finding the truth of the person. Like political prisoners before them, "to say yes is to be transformed, saved even. But to say no is to hold 'submissive acquiescence' at bay."[24] "Opening up" thereby advanced both the rehabilitative and prosecutorial arms of the NAPTIP agenda at the same time, while silence and denial were interpreted as stubborn resistance.[25]

Changing Methods for Changing Minds

In sum, NAPTIP's rehabilitation program did not replicate medical models of talk therapy for trauma victims, nor was it intended to. These differences were due in part to the scarcity of psychiatric services in Nigeria and in part to their incompatibility with the kinds of "victims" NAPTIP targeted, who were not seen as traumatized. International monitoring mechanisms, from the US TIP Report to European fact-finding missions and UN briefs, necessarily assess these efforts according to universal, international norms. By those standards, the shelter rehabilitation efforts might look like a tepid imitation, a spectacle created for donor audiences, an effort to simply "summon the state into being."[26] However, evaluations built from a deficit or developmental scale miss what else is going on in this space. In place of that medical model, counselors shared a different sensibility about what the women there needed. The shelter program was not simply providing "bad" therapy but rather fulfilling another vision altogether.[27]

This distinction in analytical frames is important to our reading of African political projects in general, which are too often situated along linear measures of good and bad governance, as if all relevant insight can be gained from knowing whether a state is weak, corrupt, or inept. This is especially true where governmental services like health care and community projects are outsourced to local and international NGOs, leaving few opportunities to observe the content of governmental practices in real time. The disciplinary functions of rehabilitation at the NAPTIP shelter challenge us to interrogate the violence of detention, the appropriation of psychiatry, and the neglect of women's wishes, not just as failures of the state but also as productive political projects.

These intervention tools transformed the moral panic around migrant sex work in the 1990s to fit within the global anti-trafficking apparatus. They moved the "psychological warfare" out of public streets and mass media and into an enclosed facility for "psychosocial support," but the goals remained the same.

NAPTIP worked to change the mindset of migrant women—to persuade them to accept intervention, turn against their sponsors, and decide not to try leaving again. Although intertwined with the detention, rehabilitation was imagined not as a punitive measure but as a benevolent one. The following chapters examine how this effort took form around several issues that were central to the counseling process—migration, sex, fate, and livelihood. Across each of them, we can see counselors' efforts to *convince* women that this intervention, however challenging and unwelcome, was still ultimately "for the best."

RISK ASSESSMENT

"You *wan go, eh?* You will be forced into prostitution, if you are going like that," the counselor Kenny warned casually as she walked by. Florence was reclining dejectedly on the sofa, groaning *I wan go, I wan go,* while staff and residents slowly assembled plastic chairs in a circle around her, readying the common room for a group counseling session. "You, you don't even know. Do you even know this trafficking thing?" Kenny asked.

One irony of NAPTIP's preemptive intervention scheme is that counselors were constantly having to explain the harms of human trafficking to its supposed victims. Most of the shelter residents had not experienced violence or abuse in their journeys, many still trusted the brokers they had hired, and they continued to believe in the purpose of their choices. Women accepted trafficking as a synonym for migrant sex work but still did not see themselves as victims. The first step in rehabilitation was therefore to convince women of the danger of their original travel plans—that they were being trafficked, would likely have suffered great harm, and should not attempt the journey again.

Others had settled quietly into their seats, waiting for Kenny to finish so they could begin the day's lesson on contentment. They watched expectantly as Kenny began listing the many dangers of trafficking: forced prostitution, dangerous deserts, men who will shoot you. Counselors often borrowed the grisliest details from United Nations information campaigns and popular Nollywood movies about trafficking and prostitution, blending together macabre scenes in grisly detail. Florence scoffed back, saying that those stories did not apply to her because she trusted her sponsor. Kenny replied sharply, "Of course the traffickers would not tell you the truth, because then you would not make the journey. So, they deceive you."

"My own brother *DECEIVE* me?!" Florence exclaimed, annoyed.

"Your blood brother?" the counselor Ben jumped in.

"He's my cousin," Florence conceded.

"Well, they deceive," another counselor, Foluke, affirmed, straightening two chairs and taking a seat in one to lean in. Foluke did not know the details of Florence's case and, as evidenced in her retort, she did not feel she needed to. When arguing with women about the circumstances of their travel, counselors rarely based their assessment on details of the given case but instead on generalizations about trafficking writ large, affirming that all traffickers deceive, coerce, and abuse. Although Florence's case was still under investigation, the counselors presumed that all the accusations would prove justified.

"You are even lucky that Gambia is so close," Kenny continued, referencing Florence's original flight ticket. "If you go to Egypt, you know they go by desert. And then, most of them, they drink their own piss!"

Florence had been intercepted before boarding a flight to the Gambia, and from there everyone expected that she would have traveled on to Italy. She told me later that she was planning to reach Italy by plane, but it is also possible that she would have faced a journey by boat through the Canary Islands.[1] Either way, it was unlikely that she would have attempted the desert crossing after flying to this westernmost part of the continent, and if so, she certainly would not have crossed back to Egypt in the opposite direction. In this context, Foluke's warning alerted Florence not to the dangers of her own choices but to those of illicit migration in general—of the type of activity she has associated herself with, whether or not she personally faced those risks. Other horror stories that counselors often repeated in the shelter included similarly graphic accounts: women forced to have sex with dogs, travelers abandoned in the desert, and capsized boats in the Mediterranean.

Migrants do face incredible danger in crossing oceans and deserts by clandestine routes, and many migrant women are subjected to exploitive working and living conditions once they arrive. As sex workers, they are doubly illicit: undocumented workers in a criminalized industry. While the counselors' stories are not all fabricated, their recurrence in the shelter betrays a deeper project not only to inform migrant women but also to denounce all forms of undocumented migration. Even where those risks are real, accounts that focus exclusively on the dark and dangerous elements of migration depict anyone who pursues these journeys as ignorant of the truth about these hazards, too lazy to learn more about the destination's abusive labor practices, or too stupid to make better decisions with that information.[2] These stories are used not only to educate women in the shelter but also to demarcate categories of migrants, distinguishing between the good and bad, the rational and irrational, the responsible and irresponsible.

This chapter shows how ostensibly neutral education campaigns, both in and out of the shelter, aim to revise the social and moral framework that gives meaning to migration aspirations and choices. I show how migration deterrence messages reframe the common desire to leave Nigeria into a personal, moral flaw. I argue that this is a gendered and classed distinction, validating the mobility of Nigerian elites while demonizing migrants without access to visas as naive and undeserving. This claim is supported by evidence from public awareness materials targeting aspiring migrants around Nigeria and from ethnographic accounts of debates about migration from the shelter, including repeated conversations about why residents originally tried to leave and whether they would try to migrate again. I recount here the ways staff and residents sparred over the appeals of traveling abroad, the kind of work they hoped to find there, and the risks they were willing to take on to do so.

By situating counselors' and residents' arguments within other strategies of migrant education, protection, and prevention, this chapter challenges the presumption that anti-trafficking campaigns deliver information that is different from other kinds of migration management. It instead explores the changing methods to police illicit migration—techniques that are not only imposed by faraway, rich nations but are also championed by public officials of migrant-sending states, specifically through the moral policing of women's ambitions to move. Ultimately, what makes anti-trafficking campaigns unique is not the kind of discipline they impose but the wide license they are granted to impose it. This practice is gendered through both the implied irrationality of migrant women as well as the concurrent legitimization of paternalistic state efforts to "protect" them.

Information Campaigns

Counselors' messages about the dangers of migration were consistent with the larger NAPTIP campaign to inform women generally about the risks of travel and life abroad. Separate from the Department of Counseling and Rehabilitation, NAPTIP's Department of Public Enlightenment has organized widespread public information campaigns since the agency's founding in 2003. These campaigns discourage all forms of clandestine migration in the name of preventing trafficking. In collaboration with local NGOs, politicians, media outlets, and celebrities, the information campaigns serve as the public face of NAPTIP, targeting not just migrants in the act of travel but also anyone who might be at risk of trafficking or those who might be bystanders to it. The NAPTIP website lists public enlightenment strategies that include the following:

Conferences, seminars, and workshops
Strategic alliances and cooperation
Production and distribution of sensitization materials such as caps, t-shirts, stickers and posters
Courtesy calls or visits
Awareness campaign rallies
Organized excursions
Pre-sensitization tours to endemic areas of human trafficking
Research projects
Newspaper sensitization and awareness publications
Electronic media messages
Outdoor publicity vans
Jingles
Local media
Newsletter publications
Traditional methods of communication, such as the Town Crier[3]

This diversity of methods presents the agency as achieving communication coverage that is both comprehensive and adaptable, adjusting the means of delivery to suit different communities and their needs. Still, the message delivered is consistent: trafficking entails a horrific journey full of hazardous environmental and human threats. Corrupt, deceitful, and violent men target vulnerable or naive women, who need to be warned about these dangerous schemes. Once trafficked women reach their destination, they will be forced into prostitution without compensation and exposed to disease, violence, and incarceration or death.

Like Foluke's warnings to Florence, these messages were often presented in salacious form. One billboard outside Benin City uses a collage of images to present a young woman turned to the sea but smiling coyly over her shoulder as a whale leaps before her (see figure 6). The ocean fades into a tomb with skeletons lying in open graves, the visual counterpart and narrative end to the smiling woman's journey. Though sponsored by NAPTIP to fight trafficking, the billboard discourages all clandestine migration, alerting passersby: "Many Nigerians using irregular routes die in hot deserts or drown in seas. Be wise! Safe your life and your future." The billboard's prominence within its particular site is also revealing. The colorful graphic design had been printed and pasted atop a sturdy raised billboard in a field of shorter government signboards, most hand-stenciled,

FIGURE 6.   "Be Wise." NAPTIP billboard posted among rusted stencil signs for state services. Uromi, Edo State (photo by author).

tilted, and long rusted over, including warnings about promiscuity and HIV and signs with directions to local police and immigration offices. Amongst this array, NAPTIP distinguishes itself in a bureaucratic landscape of underfunded and long-neglected state-sponsored programs.

Similar campaigns inform would-be migrants about the kind of work that awaits them abroad. In a poster hung in Lagos airports, a headless man and woman in business suits walk toward a departing plane and urban cityscape (see figure 7). Together, they illustrate the quoted promise—"I'll get you a job in Italy"—but their visual decapitation emphasizes that such a respectable version of this journey is impossible. "Beware of strangers with attractive offers. . . . Human traffickers have many tricks" the text continues.

These signs are directed not to potential traffickers—recruiters, brokers, or sponsors—or to the families and communities that supposedly pressure women into accepting these arrangements: like the rest of these awareness campaigns, they are directed to would-be migrant women themselves. "Save your life and future," the first one warns. "Just say no!" urges the second. By identifying individual migrants as the audience for these messages, they assert that women are responsible, in part, for their own trafficking. Whether that trafficking is due to

FIGURE 7. "I'll get you a JOB in ITALY." Banner displayed at the First National Anti Human Trafficking Awareness Week / Presidential Launch of the Red Card to Human Trafficking. Abuja, FCT (photo by author).

their culpability or vulnerability, these messages position migrant women themselves as the object of intervention, whose minds must be changed to prevent trafficking from happening.

But despite these attributions of blame and responsibility, these campaigns do not openly acknowledge the moral framework for their messaging. Instead, they pose as neutral sources of information that can help people assess opportunities to travel by arming them with data that might puncture the false hopes and promises offered by human traffickers and smugglers. The International Organization for Migration, which pioneered these tactics, describes them as follows:

> Information campaigns aim at helping potential migrants make well-informed decisions regarding migration. Experience has shown that the most credible information is a balanced and neutral one that offers facts on the possibilities and advantages of regular migration, as well as on the disadvantages of irregular departure. . . . In the anti-trafficking campaigns, information is given about the risks and dangers involved.[4]

The IOM distinguishes here between information campaigns that target potential migrants and those that target potential victims of human trafficking, implying that there is a meaningful difference between those two groups of people before travel even begins. Instead, the anti-trafficking paradigm justifies the provision of exclusively negative information, even when a more "balanced" perspective is shown to be more effective in encouraging regular migration. Even then, this "balanced" information merely recognizes the possibilities that documented migration offers, rather than the possibilities that other kinds of illicit modes of movement may provide, such as access to employment and educational opportunities, access to health care, the possibility of having a baby in a country with birthright citizenship, access to flows of capital and markets of goods unavailable in one's home country, and the possibility of new romantic and social connections in cosmopolitan locales, among many other motivations to move. In this IOM framework, "the key feature of 'objective' information is darkness," and the "realities" of migration are almost exclusively described as negative.[5]

These strategies reveal how information presented, even when technically accurate (migrants *do* die in irregular routes), is not neutral. These campaigns assume that seeking clandestine migration opportunities can never be a rational, informed choice, regardless of the circumstances people leave behind or of what they want for their future. By prioritizing certain information and imposing foregone conclusions, these campaigns deploy the danger of those routes not as information, but as a deterrent.

FIGURE 8. "Abroad Good-o!" A woman scolds her friend for envying the wealth others earned abroad. Illustration by Okanlawon Oladele, published in NAPTIP News, August 2010.

By the same logic, anyone who ignores these campaigns and chooses to migrate despite these warnings is implied to be irresponsible and even deserving of any violent outcomes of that decision. One comic strip published in NAPTIP's promotional magazine illustrates this belief by showing a poor village woman who is charmed by the lure of foreign money (see figure 8). It ostensibly promotes better information, encouraging the woman to "be sure" and "look beneath the surface." But the comic strip itself does not demonstrate why the source is not credible; it just urges the woman to do more research herself, assuming that she must be wrong while shaming her with a wagging finger for not being more skeptical in the first place. By addressing the woman's attitude, it imposes a moral correction.

The audiences for such images extend beyond potential victims of trafficking to instruct a wider pool of community members and stakeholders. This comic strip was distributed to foreign donors, local partners, and NAPTIP's own staff, teaching them how to understand and approach victims. The naive woman appears as a bureaucratic fantasy, as the kind of would-be victim that enlightenment campaigns are equipped to inform and therefore the kind of victim they must imagine.[6] In this way, disciplinary projects not only act on the given population but also structure how "experts" understand the problem at hand. To implement any intervention, they must first establish consensus about what deviance looks like, in the process often transforming the ordinary into something pathological. In this case, a Nigerian woman's interest in life abroad is framed as pathological because it renders her willfully oblivious to the costs of accessing that world.

Risk and Reward

Popular understandings of migration and sex work challenge such ready dismissals of migrant aspirations. Around the time of NAPTIP's founding in 2003, a team of researchers conducted a random household survey of 1,456 women in Benin City, aged fifteen to twenty-five. The results demonstrate how prevalent the discourse of trafficking and direct connections to migrant sex workers already were:

> 97.4 percent of the women had heard of international sex trafficking.
> 70 percent had female relatives who lived in the receiving countries of Italy, Spain, and the Netherlands.
> 44 percent knew of someone who was currently engaged in sex work abroad.
> 32 percent of the women reported that they had been approached by someone offering to assist them to travel abroad.[7]

In short, most women in the region already had direct contacts abroad, and many of them knew that those women were engaged in sex work. Women often migrate to work in sex industries rather than work in local sex industries because it allows them to maintain some discretion about the nature of their labor in their home communities: as long as they continue to send remittances, their families will not ask where the money is coming from. The number of women who "knew of someone currently engaged in sex work abroad" reflects *known* sex workers, likely a lower estimate than total contacts in the industry. With this network, women considering migration were not naive about the kind of work that awaited their friends, their relatives, and likely themselves. Since the time of this survey, NAPTIP information campaigns have only affirmed the notion all women who migrate illicitly are trafficked into sex work, making discretion impossible and promoting the stigmatization of all migrant women.

Women are also not naive about the risks of travelling without papers, as indicated by the number of women who willingly make multiple attempts at the journey—the founding fear of "retrafficking" that motivates "preventive rehabilitation" at the shelter. The documentary short *Becky's Journey* features one woman's failed efforts to migrate to Europe to sell sex, told in her own words.[8] An immigration officer at the Lagos airport blocks her first attempt to leave the country after discovering that her papers are false. Next, she turns to much more dangerous routes and joins a group to cross the Sahara. She describes the lack of water, the dangerous road conditions, and the heat that ultimately take the life of another woman traveling with her, who dies in childbirth. Becky decides to turn around to return the infant to her family in Benin, but still, she considers trying again, saying simply, "I want to change my life." This determination revolves not around a strict calculus of risk and reward but from a larger sensibility about what meaningful change looks like. As she told the Danish filmmaker after she had brought her chocolate bars as a gift, "Yes—I ate it all. I love your chocolate. It's real. Everything in Nigeria is fake. I love the shoes my aunt in Italy sent me too. They are real. That's why I love Europe. Europe is real."[9]

Despite my skepticism about NAPTIP's anti-migration message, I sometimes found myself sympathetic to the agency's concerns. For example, when some residents of the shelter spoke casually of traveling without documents or with hired agents at exorbitantly high prices, I felt obligated to interject about the extraordinary risks these choices implied. Like the counselors I worked with, I too was dismayed by the blank stares and shrugs I would receive in reply, privately fearing for women who spoke candidly with me on so many matters, and yet refused to acknowledge the dangers I described. However, I would later learn that those stares did not necessarily indicate their ignorance or irresponsibility.

One day, we were discussing the pros and cons of leaving Nigeria, a conversation that we had engaged in dozens of times. Each of the women there had been intercepted trying to travel to Europe without papers, and they kept asking me, half-jokingly, if they could follow me to the United States when I went home. Perhaps spoiling the fun of the fantasy, I admitted in seriousness that I could not arrange anyone's visas, and then we began debating the importance of having one's papers in order before traveling. I described some of the vulnerabilities associated with undocumented migration in the United States, offering what I hoped was a more nuanced and sympathetic portrayal of migrant vulnerability. I said, for example, that life can be hard because if you are not paid your wages, or if your contract is otherwise not honored, you may not want to go to the police to seek help. Your travel sponsor can increase your debt, and there is little you can do to fight it. If you do not have papers, I explained, sometimes the police will not listen to your complaints and could end up putting you in detention, without the legal recourses available to citizens and those with documents. They all listened to me politely but were not nearly as shocked as I had expected. I expressed indignance at these injustices, but they remained entirely unfazed. Then you could be *deported*, I added, and finally they agreed this would be disgraceful. Still, they were undeterred in their plans to travel abroad, regardless of their access to proper paperwork. How did these regular abuses of migrant labor not burst their hopeful impressions of life abroad? I thought. Why were they not outraged by this maltreatment? At first, I worried that they did not believe that the United States or Europe could be that bad, but over time, I have come to see it differently.

It was not that they failed to understand the realities of life abroad; I simply had not yet come to understand life in Nigeria. The threats I earnestly listed as risks of undocumented migration—unreliable police support, labor exploitation, unstable housing, and a constant sense of precarity in daily life—were ordinary and unremarkable features of life for them already. In Nigeria, no one turns to the police for help; state security forces are more known for extracting bribes at roadside checkpoints and assaulting those who refuse to pay than for fighting crime. Employers—not only those in petty trade markets but across the entire civil service and other large-scale operations—regularly delay wages for months at a time. Even NAPTIP regularly falls months behind in paying salaries to its staff, despite its reputation as a more responsibly managed government agency.

Anthropologists of migration have described how illegality and deportability are experienced in day-to-day life as a constant sense of insecurity.[10] The Nigerians with whom I lived and worked also complained often about this perpetual sense of uncertainty. It was a lesson that women from the shelter and other friends outside of it labored to teach me whenever we moved through the city—avoiding area boys in sprawling bus lots known as motorparks, avoiding stampedes in the market, avoiding confrontations at police and military checkpoints, avoiding armed robbers on public transport. Don't trust anyone. "This is Lagos," they always cautioned, invoking the famously foreboding sign outside the international airport that greets newcomers into the city not with a welcome but with a warning.

After months of these repeated warnings from women at the shelter, I changed how I navigated the city of Lagos. I learned to face traffic police, government officials, and dodgy market vendors with a practiced and steady blank stare, just as I observed women doing at the shelter that day. I sought to communicate my suspicion and my refusal to be exploited, as well as to masquerade my own everyday fears and uncertainty, all through my posture, the pitch of my voice, making sly jokes with raised eyebrows and harmless insults, and sometimes through boldfaced eruptions of anger—often mimicking the encounters I observed between the staff and residents of the shelter.

I came to recognize my initial reaction to these women's unfazed responses as being a reflection of my own privilege. I had taken basic protections for granted. Even when I knew about the ubiquitous presence of corrupt officials and petty criminals around the city, I had not carried that vigilance in my body the way others needed to. My status as a white, relatively wealthy, and legally documented foreigner in Nigeria still protected me from the worst of these threats.

Just because these threats were so commonplace in Nigeria did not numb anyone to their injustice; each woman I talked to might express great outrage over these issues in other contexts. However, in conversations about migrating, this outrage did little to make the question of living abroad without papers seem any less desirable by comparison. At least traveling abroad would trade these risks for a chance at something else, whereas Nigeria felt bleak and stagnate. After decades of devastating colonial occupation, subsequent eras of independence, structural adjustment, and democratic reform each promised a bright new future for Nigeria, to no avail.[11] Across Africa and the global south, foreign aid has likewise had little impact other than to create entire industries of professional projects for international experts and well-connected, entrepreneurial local elites.[12] Local benefits from foreign investment have proven even more scarce and uneven.[13] State-sponsored anti-trafficking and migration deterrence programs aim to convince people that life in Nigeria has improved, although everyday life remains objectively more difficult there—due to poverty, political insecurity, the crumbling urban infrastructure, overburdened health systems, unfunded schools, and an absent social welfare system. The question Nigerians face is only whether they should tolerate it. This is a moral question, rather than a factual one.

Culture of Exile

Understanding how would-be migrants make sense of these disparities between life in the global north and south is essential to understanding how high-risk migration can seem not just desirable but also necessary. While anthropologists and other scholars have grown uneasy with the teleology and hierarchy of labels like "developing nation" and "third world," Africans are acutely aware of their exclusion from the comforts and opportunities of the neoliberal world order.[14] For example, many Nigerians I met were more familiar with the resources and pensions available in the United Kingdom than British citizens may be. Against the broken promises of modernization, Africans understand their position as one of abjection—"not a matter of being merely *excluded* from a status to which one had never had a claim but of being *expelled*, cast out-and-down from that status by the formation of a new (or newly impermeable) boundary."[15] It is not only that Nigerians lack access to a similar safety net of services provided in North American and European countries but also that those nations actively exclude Africans from these privileges—through terms of foreign assistance, uneven trade policies, and rigid migration policies.

Inside the shelter and out of it, I was surprised at the many ways this interpretation would be expressed. "It must be different," Florence told me once, "because Nigeria's own celebrities will go to US, but American celebrities will not want to come to Nigeria. Even when Rihanna came to Nigeria, she had her own hotel basically; they just bought the whole thing, so she wouldn't go anywhere. . . . But most people won't come here, and it's because the US has more."[16] To migrate, then, is not to steal someone else's piece of the pie but to make a "claim for equal rights of membership in a spectacularly unequal global society."[17] Like Becky explained in the documentary, "Everything in Nigeria is fake . . . Europe is real." She wanted to live in the "real" world.

This widespread sensibility has fostered an sizable field of aspirant migrants worldwide. The 2013–2016 Gallup World Poll estimated that 700 million people around the world—14 percent of the population worldwide—share this desire to migrate, including almost one-third of adult Africans (31 percent). Of the 156 countries surveyed, Nigeria recorded the twelfth highest desire to migrate, with 43 percent of the total adult population reporting an interest in leaving the country.[18] That figure of 43 percent means that four out of every ten adults in Nigeria would rather be living elsewhere. Anthropologist Charles Piot describes this sentiment as a "culture of exile," a way of living life in the constant shadow of the foreign. He recounts the phone booths, Western Union stations, and internet cafes that increasingly populate the streets of Togo, fostering both physical and imaginary landscapes permeated with signs of wealth and opportunity abroad.[19] Women in Benin City live surrounded by similar reminders, from advertisements for foreign-language classes to conspicuous new construction projects, funded by money sent from abroad. A "culture of exile," then, is not just the desire to go elsewhere but also the feeling of being already exiled in one's own homeland.[20] It makes staying in Nigeria feel not settled but stuck.

This collective sensibility does help fortify people's desires to migrate, as NAPTIP's information campaigns depict through images of excited and hopeful women. However, the feeling of exile is not factually inaccurate or mistaken; it is not an empirical claim to begin with. Rather, the feeling of belonging elsewhere provides a moral framework to assert one's place in the "first-class" world, to seek those opportunities, and to accept the costs incurred along the way. Nigerian understandings of "abroad" *are* mythological, but they are not myths in the sense that they are false. Rather, they are myths insofar as they help structure people's understanding of the world and provide meaning to the choices they make. Florence viewed the United States as a place where celebrities like Rihanna could move freely and not be confined to hotels when they travel. Similarly confined to this Nigerian shelter, Florence sought that same freedom and access to a country with "more."

The obstinate desire to gain access to that world confounded counselors, who shared the belief that the only rational decision was to stay in Nigeria. Counselors saw rehabilitation, then, as the opportunity to fix that broken way of thinking or, more specifically, to reframe the moral frameworks that, in their view, so erroneously supported it.

Ambition and Greed

Counselors understood women's determination to leave Nigeria as founded in the misplaced desires for a better life, so they made ambition a key object of intervention for the rehabilitation process. The group counseling session that followed Foluke's warnings was typical. After borrowing and arranging chairs from around the building, the half-dozen counselors working that day shuffled through the building to find all the residents and call them to the common room. There were seven new women who had been intercepted at international borders, including Florence and her travel mate Blessing, as well as four children, both boys and girls, who were brought in from working as domestic house help. We began the session by introducing ourselves in the usual way: I introduced myself and my project, and then the residents shared their names and their home states, while insisting they *wan go*.

Kenny, the lead counselor for the day, rolled her eyes a little at their complaints and began. "Ok, the topic for today is contentment. Do you know what this is—contentment? Is this grammar too high?" Ben, the other counselor, nodded, indicating that he did not think everyone understood the question.

"Ok, what of satisfaction? Do you know what it means to be satisfied?" Kenny continued. "What does it mean when you eat food and feel satisfied? That is satisfaction. Has anyone ever felt good about something they have done? Something that made them feel, *ahehn*, that was nice. . . . No one?" She looked around the room. "What about you, Florence?"

"When my uncle asked me to come to Gambia. I felt happy to travel. Happy to go abroad," Florence replied brusquely, glaring back at her.

Kenny just nodded and moved along. "And you, Blessing?" she asked, turning to the woman Florence had been traveling with.

"For me it is the same. We were to travel together, and I was so happy to go," Blessing added softly, looking down into her lap.

"Well," Kenny continued, "some people can be satisfied with one naira. They take it home, and think to themselves, *ahehn*, I have this naira. But others, they go out, they want more. They are not satisfied with 100 naira, or 500, or 1,000."

Some of the women in the room scoffed audibly at that thought. It was true that more than half the people in Nigeria lived on less than a few hundred naira a day.[21] Still, suggesting that anyone would be content with these conditions seemed both insincere and condescending. A single naira was worth less than an American penny. Yet the lesson was clear: these women should be satisfied with less and, implicitly, not desire the wealth that lured people into making bad decisions.

"So, some people even have something, but they still aren't satisfied. *No be happy-o*," Kenny continued. "I have my own food, but I see someone else and want his. I have this my own shirt, but I see Uncle Ben's and want his. Some of us, our families are not too rich and not too poor, but no *dey* satisfied with what you get." These examples illustrate that the problem is not only wanting more but also wanting what is not yours and what you have no right to have. Greed, according to these counselors, makes a person blind to her own advantages and to covet anything new or different.

Suddenly one of the younger residents interrupted Kenny to complain fervently about a rat living in his bedroom, who had bitten into a bag of instant noodles and a new bar of soap given to him by a recent group of visitors. Florence snidely quipped that the rat was not contented—"Not *satisfied*," she enunciated sarcastically. The room broke into laughter, including myself, the counselors, and the residents alike. I was impressed with the metaphor: the rat's insatiable desire for unfamiliar goods led him to eat that which he does not need and risked poisoning himself in the process.

"See! This is therapy," Kenny announced as our chuckles quieted down. "Before you were tense and upset and now you are laughing. This is group therapy." She tried to carry the good energy back toward her discussion. "So, when you were not satisfied, what happened? How did you feel? When you got to travel, you were satisfied, but what about a time when you weren't?"

"Right now," Florence replied, only slightly more willing to engage after sharing in the joke. "Right now, I'm not *satisfied* here," she explained, begrudging the language, "because I want to go to Gambia. I have family there now. I have a plane ticket. *I wan go*," she declared firmly.

Florence did not have family in Gambia, and everybody tacitly understood that. Yet counselors did not challenge the veracity of her claim, because that was not what mattered here. Her desire to leave to go anywhere was the problem, and it was rooted in a materialist greed for nicer things, for feeling entitled to what others have, and refusing to accept anything less.

Naivete and Optimism

Kenny continued to press for details about Florence's expectations for life abroad, shifting the conversation to what opportunities she was seeking. As Florence's assigned counselor, Kenny had recently completed an intake interview with Florence and knew the story she had given for traveling, but by modeling her skepticism in a live debate, other residents in the room could learn from it as well. So, she nodded and played along as Florence talked, not disputing the truth of the story, but letting Gambia stand in for any foreign destination.

"Okay, okay, so, I've never been to Gambia, so let me ask you," Kenny countered, in a tentative but friendly tone. "How do you know what it is like there? How do you know this salon, where you would work, is as big as he says? How do you know there is room for you?" Counselors often used this tactic with residents at the shelter, cultivating doubt in unnamed travel brokers. But by framing this as a question of conviction ("how do you know?"), these inquiries again place responsibility on the women themselves, for being so naive in their trust, lazy in their research, or shallow in their planning.

Florence and Blessing both replied that, yes, they had seen a photo of the place and it was very nice. "It's my uncle's, so I know," Florence reminded them.

"Ah, but you can find this here," Kenny insisted, shifting gears from the facts regarding the destination to its comparative advantage over Nigerian counterparts. Even if the broker's promises were true, she asserts, any eagerness to travel was still misguided.

When Florence and Blessing insisted that the prices paid by salon clients in Benin could not support them, Kenny proceeded to analyze the costs. "What is the price then?" Kenny pressed. "300 naira? With that, you *no dey* satisfied?" The two women shook their heads. "What of 500 naira? 1,000? 2,500 naira?" They then started to laugh, still shaking their heads no, suggesting that they would never find a price in Nigeria that would be worthwhile. Kenny started listing the other women around the room and naming the hairstyles they might choose. "Ok, so say Hope comes into the salon for plaits. And then I come in for Ghana weaving. And Titi too. So, it's 1.5, 2, 2.5 [thousand naira—about $10 to $15 a piece], and together you can make 5,000 or 10,000 in a day! It is good now." That was the equivalent of $30 to $60, but the rest of the women in the room all still looked skeptical. Maybe if they could really make this much money, it would be a different story. Florence explained later how hard it is to make any profit at all as a hairdresser, especially working under others like she did, while waiting to accumulate the capital she needed to open her own salon.

"Or is their money just better than our money? You just like Gambian money better?" Kenny asked, teasing them and again trying to undermine their reasoning. I heard this phrase often, and it was always meant sarcastically. Of course all money is interchangeable, but the value of the naira shifted so dramatically just between my own annual visits to Nigeria that this accusation never seemed so preposterous to me. Indeed, in the lifetime of anyone in that room, the naira had fluctuated from being worth more than a dollar during the oil boom of the 1980s to ranging between a penny and a halfpenny during the decade of my research. Both in terms of value and stability, other currencies really were better.

"What is even the money there?" Kenny pressed, now again calling into doubt their knowledge of their destination.

"Dalasi," they responded in unison.

"No, no, it's shillings now!" two counselors corrected them—wrongly.

Florence frowned at all of this, tired of defending her case. Finally, she just said, "I'm willing to suffer to go."

"Better to suffer there and make it than to just suffer here," Blessing agreed.

Foluke interceded. "But how do you know you will not suffer there? Even after two weeks, or a month, your uncle will not be smiling at you any longer."

The women shrugged.

"How much was your ticket?" Ben asked.

Florence said that her ticket cost ₦70,000 or nearly $500. "I will have to work for it for one year," she added.

"But why go there? You like their money more than our money?" Kenny repeated. "You have a house now, you can start there, in the street, in your own place." The girls replied that there is no space in their area. "Even if there is no space there," she answered, "you are telling me there is no space on the next street? You start there. You start anywhere."

"It's a village," they said, suggesting that too few people would pay for higher cost services.

"Well, even in a village now people are going to salon. You are just not thinking of all of your options," Kenny insisted.

In conversations like these, the counselors alternated tactics to discredit the women's desires and plans to leave Nigeria. After questioning the reliability of their knowledge, they asserted repeatedly that Florence and Blessing had failed to make rational, informed decisions about leaving. The counselors implied that they did not know enough about the debts they would incur or the employment conditions they would face elsewhere and that they underestimated alternative opportunities for work within Nigeria. With their logic and their sources deemed to be unfounded, counselors then insisted the women must have been charmed only by a blind faith in what is foreign: "you like their money better than ours."

Later that week, Ben elaborated on their assumed lack of knowledge as he pursued these questions again with Blessing. She was tall, angular, and a lot quieter than Florence ever was. He began asking her more questions about their destination: "Did you see photos of the shop where you were to work? How can you know what it is like there? You have never been there, and I have never been there. How can we know?" But before giving her a chance to answer, he leaned toward me to explain his take.

"I have seen that there is an excitement that comes with leaving and getting ready to leave, where people feel like it is all going to happen, and they have complete faith in the plan, and don't want to believe any other facts. There is opti-mism that comes with it, and I know how people don't want to consider the rest. *Abi?*" Ben asked. Isn't that so? He looked to Blessing, and she nodded respect-fully, almost repentantly, before he continued. "And with that excitement about leaving is this anger about Nigeria, too. The grass is always greener, they say. People think other places have jobs and everything that they can't find here. So they lose faith in their country."

Ben shook his head in pity. He at least seemed to sympathize with the deter-mination and optimism that motivated women to travel, even if he eventually dismissed the decision to go as misguided. His assessment of their despair re-garding Nigeria also seemed accurate, explaining Blessing's own frustrations that she expressed earlier in the conversation when she complained about having "nothing going," no money, no opportunity to use her skills.[22] Yet, to dismiss it all as "the grass is greener" also seemed unfair. At the core of Ben's argument, like that of the other counselors, is the belief that that women are fundamen-tally unable to see clearly enough to make rational decisions—that any enthusi-asm for their choice is discrediting, and any confidence only proves their gullibility. Ben not only encourages healthy skepticism but also discounts every conclusion that does not match his own.

I waited to hear if Blessing would challenge him on this point about losing faith in her country and not looking for solutions at home, but she just looked down and shifted in her seat uneasily. Eventually, she nodded in agreement, but exactly which point she was affirming, I was not sure.

Desperation and Documents

Unlike other counselors at the shelter, Ben often would concede that migration itself was not the problem. Given the time to parse out details of his philosophy of intervention, he worried more specifically about how women became depen-dent on and indebted to brokers both while traveling and once abroad, leaving them without recourse if anything went wrong. "I want you to go," Ben would sometimes tell residents, "but then you should save your money, so then when you travel, you can do it independently."

By traveling independently, Uncle Ben meant doing without a "sponsor," who would finance and organize the initial part of travel as a loan, in amounts some-times as high as $60,000. These arrangements are often the grounds for exploi-tation that becomes known as human trafficking, though the point at which that line is crossed from debt to indentured servitude or trafficking is often difficult to identify.[23] Of course, anyone would agree with Ben that it is preferable to travel independently, including the women at the shelter, but it simply was not a reasonable option. Women wanted to travel to make money precisely because they did not have access to savings of that size and they would not be eligible for papers through regular visa systems. With a sponsor women only had to assemble a small down payment to cover initial costs, which brokers used to arrange counterfeit passports and visas as well as travel expenses.[24] Dependence on brokers not only for loans but also for travel documents renders migrants more vulnerable at their destination, where they might live in fear of deportation and without access to their own passports.[25]

A few days after the "contentment" discussion, I found Ben lecturing Blessing again about the conditions of traveling out. "Do you think that you are the only one in this condition, here? Go to the airport," he suggested hypothetically. "Most flights to the US and the UK are long and they leave at night, so you can arrive there in the morning." His insight on flight times established some authority on the matter before he continued. "So, go there around the evening time and you can see everyone—checking out, checking out." She nodded, sympathizing with their plight. "But," Ben interjected, "if you then go to arrivals, you will see people being thrown back, thrown back, because they didn't have the proper business."

Human trafficking victims were sometimes repatriated back to Nigeria alongside deportees in groups coordinated by the IOM, which collaborated closely with NAPTIP. Ben had been on these trips and had worked with deportees who were later designated as human trafficking victims. He began to paint this scenario in more detail: "Okay, say you are going, but what is your business there? Like my friend, from Michigan, in the US, he called me to say they were deporting 34 Nigerians—34!—who were involved with fraud. And you are a second-class citizen there, so people do these things." I appreciated his emphasis on structural causes of illicit activity, but in this scenario, it was used only to render Blessing's own intentions irrelevant.

"This place has a bad reputation," he asserted, "like when people hear you lived in [notorious Lagos neighborhood] Oshodi and they say *ehehn*." He was right about this reputation; Nigerian migrants were notorious across Europe for drug trafficking, advance-fee email scams, and, of course, prostitution. "They can do any fraud. If you want an American passport, they will make one, and it will look genuine. They can do it, but then they come back." Ben here emphasized the practical dangers of deportability—that the cycle of return shows how failure is inevitable—as well as the moral ones. "You, you don't want to have that mindset, that anything I can find I will do. You want to have this standard, and then don't settle for anything less than that." Even as he appealed to her sense of self-worth, he dismissed her ambition and determination as a bad mindset, suggesting that to willingly do "anything" reflected poorly on her: "You don't want to do just *any* business. So, ok, you are going to Gambia, but what are you going to do?"

Blessing paused, hesitant as usual, and then tried to tell him as much. "But there is money to be made there," she insisted. "You can make lots of money there."

"Yes, yes, okay, I want you to go," he repeated, "But I want you to be independent. I don't want you to go running—"

"But I *am* running," she interrupted. "I am running . . . to Gambia. There is no food to chop. I am *running*."

"Well, that is exactly the mindset I want to change," Ben announced, pleased to have isolated it. "You to not be running, just—*going*." Ben's point throughout this conversation seemed to be that desperation breeds bad decision making, enticing people to take on risks that are not worth the reward. But to go casually, leisurely, is a luxury Blessing said she cannot afford. Blessing saw traveling as a chance for her to do something, to take control, to make something from nothing, or to at least try, even if the odds were against her. His only answer was for her to wait longer.

She paused for a moment, thinking about what he had said. "We were not going for business," she insisted finally, "just to visit."

"Okay, so you are going to visit, but then you need a proper travel allowance," he explained. "If you go with 150,000 naira, you can travel there, no problem. You can even call Mr. Tunde, Director of Operations at Ikeja, if you get stuck then." Blessing complained about the costs. "No, no, NAPTIP won't ask for bribe," he insisted, laughing. "We are well fed here. And we are here to help."

Passport Control

Even though few counselors other than Ben supported women's choices to migrate, they all insisted that the agency would support their travel if it proved to be legitimate. These promises were not entirely erroneous, as one of the first women I met at the shelter, to my surprise, was waiting for exactly that support. Ben explained Helen's case to me like this:

> What happened was she went to travel, and then the man at the airport, he asked her for a €100 bribe. She refused, but she fit the profile—a certain age, a look. So they had to investigate. And then she had to

improve her passport, because she had the old one, so we had to help her get the new e-passport.[26] But when she was finished I took her myself to the airport, and she showed me the man. She had filed a complaint with his superior even. But she had genuine papers and she left.

Although Helen would certainly prove to be the exception, I heard her story repeated often over the next year. Once, while a group of us were taking out braids from one of the younger residents in the makeshift salon room, Florence complained about the ₦87,000 (about $600) she had lost on her ticket after she was kept from boarding the flight. The vocational trainer was a part-time member of the shelter staff, who usually avoided the work of direct counseling, but she jumped in to assure Florence that not all was lost. "Aunty . . . Eh, what was her name?" the trainer asked the room, knowing we had all heard the stories before. "Aunty Helen! Aunty Helen was here at the shelter but they replaced everything. All her papers were genuine, so if everything you have is genuine then they will replace it too. They can buy you a new ticket and even replace your visa if your visa expired. They will go to embassy, no problem. They won't charge you a fee or anything, if everything you had was genuine."

This attitude toward legitimate travel papers troubled me for a few reasons. On the one hand, it assumed that people with authentic travel papers could not be human trafficking victims. On the other hand, it suggested that those who did not have proper documents were legitimately detained as human trafficking victims. Or, perhaps more accurately, lacking proper travel documents made them either victims or criminals, so in any event they had to be stopped. Even the way in which shelter staff continued to refer to Helen as "Aunty" conferred greater respect, because she was a migrant with the proper papers, than was common in referencing any of the other residents of the shelter.

As the trainer's enthusiasm suggests, Helen's story always seemed to be offered as providing a modicum of hope, and I imagine many women did hope that their papers, however obtained, might pass NAPTIP's inspection. Regardless, the result of so often referring to Helen's situation was to consecrate the distinction between legitimate and illegitimate travel. Indeed, although Helen had her papers returned and then updated, other residents had trouble recouping their own passports at all. Florence believed her Nigerian passport to be genuine, and she demanded for months that NAPTIP return it to her, to no avail. It may have just been lost within the agency, or NAPTIP may have also kept her documents because they were altered or falsified. Either way, such dispossession further restricted Florence's and the other women's mobility; it was especially distressing for those who believed their passports to be valid.

Returning Florence's passport (or at least explaining why they disposed of it) would likely have facilitated opportunities for her to obtain valid papers, enabling her to leave in the future—ostensibly an important role of the agency in reducing her vulnerability to traffickers. But the agency's resistance affirms its preference that she not travel at all, as Florence's frequent requests only prompted greater suspicion that her sole desire was to migrate. "Your passport?!" they exclaimed. "Why do you need your passport if you say you don't need to travel?" Both in their messaging and in their handling of her passport, the agency effectively made it harder for Florence to travel with papers, not easier.

Fear and Response

Although a state's commitment to support only documented migration may seem to be a matter of commonsense, it is far from the only option available to serve those countries that take on high-risk migration projects. While Nigeria expanded border interception and deterrence campaigns over the past three decades, the Mexican government has tried a different approach.

During the 1990s, Mexico's emigration control police force, known as "Grupo Beta," targeted illicit smuggling activities, but the government ultimately decided that migrants could not be constitutionally prevented from leaving the country. In 2001, they shifted to new intervention tactics, providing information and support for safer crossings instead of focusing on deterrence and control.[27] Some people argue that the Mexican federal government's argument for a constitutional right of exit is a convenient way of legitimating their minimal efforts to restrict unauthorized emigration and evading their responsibility to enforce the border and protect their citizens. However, those critiques conflate border enforcement with migrant protection, much like border security efforts that have been supported under the banner of human trafficking prevention. If migrant aspirations and attempts are recognized as a permanent part of the current world order, more substantive information campaigns like Grupo Beta's can better serve and protect vulnerable migrants.

Nigeria, in contrast, offers little in the way of mitigating the risks of migration or reducing the harm they cause. In an analogy to sex education, the Nigerian government promotes abstinence-only intervention, warning women at the shelter to abstain from migrating entirely while failing to give them any tools to address the real dangers that undocumented migrants face. NAPTIP does warn women about false promises of employment, both at the shelter and through countrywide public education campaigns. But they do not offer concrete resources for assessing brokers' services or for researching the reliability of information agents offer about different destinations. Like abstinence-only sex education, any determination to migrate despite these warnings is deemed a private moral liability.[28]

The risks of clandestine crossings are very real, and abuse of indebted and undocumented migrants occurs frequently, especially in criminalized sex industries. However, this reality is sustained and normalized by systems that continue to validate regular migration and renounce anything else. In places like Nigeria, documented migration is only available to elites and to the lucky few, often those who make services of brokers operating in gray areas of the law. For Nigeria's remaining aspirant migrants, clandestine, undocumented migration is the only option, as are the dangers that come with it. Rather than challenge the sociolegal systems that perpetuate these risks and support migrants to navigate them more safely, warnings about the dangers of migrating illegally only reify those structures—to naturalize class-based barriers and even legitimize them in the process.

"Information campaigns" do not make overt moral claims. In declaring the rational position ("Just say no!" "Safe your life and future") they disavow those who would pursue the behavior anyway, suggesting they are irrational at best or immoral at worst. Tracing how simple signposted warnings of danger and deceit elide into more extended arguments in the shelter helps us understand that slippage, suggesting that high-risk migration can never be rational or reasonable. Ambition, however, is a moral claim to one's place in the world; no "neutral" information will revise that assertion. Instead, these campaigns help people *assess* the information they have already acquired, suggesting their desires were fundamentally unsound and immoral. Migrant women believed they were behaving morally, and they defended both the logic of their choices and the urgency of their ambition. Together, these competing frames reveal the social context for migration aspirations. The shelter rehabilitation program worked to shift women's thinking on these questions, not just by providing new information but also by reframing the moral landscape in which those risks are deemed worthwhile.

These competing claims are summarized in this list:[29]

Risk	versus	Opportunity
Many people die on that route.		*Those who made it overcame these hurdles.*
Exile Abroad	versus	Exile at Home
You belong in Nigeria.		*I belong in the world.*

Greed	versus	Ambition
You want too much.		*I want more.*
Naivete	versus	Hope
The project could fail		*I must at least try.*
Ignorance	versus	Irrelevance
You should consider the risks.		*There is nothing to do except face them.*

These debates reveal the moral questions inherent to all migration projects. In many ways, they reflect broader arguments against all undocumented migration, including men's migration, which is rarely classified as trafficking. These arguments are compelling within the context of the anti-trafficking program because sexist gender norms naturalize the paternalistic urge to question women's rationality, accuse them of emotional decision making, and protect them from danger, whether they want it or not. Modeled as rational agents, male migrants are culturally recognized as taking such risks for themselves (and sometimes demonized for it). Women migrants, in contrast, are presumed, prima facia, to be hysterical, materialistic, or just mistaken.

These distinctions took on new valences of immorality and greed when counselors talked about migrating into sex work.

SEXUAL AMBITION

"Today we are going to talk about patience," Kenny began another group counseling session. "The shelter is one example of patience because we have told you
that you will go but you are still complaining. God will ordain the day you will
go. Last week, everyone was just shouting, *I wan go, I wan go*. We know. The reason that you are in the shelter is that you are not patient."

Kenny recognized here that no one wants to be in the shelter but uses their
protests only as evidence that they need exactly the kind of counseling that rehabilitation promises—to learn to be patient. "You want everything, but you are
not willing to wait for your time," she continued. "You are looking at fine cloth
and you want it, but you are not willing to suffer. Because you are not patient is
one of the reasons you are in the shelter today. You want everything. Just want
to get it, get it, and it will lead you to the shelter. Determination can change to
desperation. But to be patient is not to be lazy. Fine, we have to struggle, but only
desperation will make someone . . . misbehave."

These comments echo other group counseling discussions of "satisfaction"
and "contentment" that encouraged women not to migrate. But while those discussions suggested women were misled or mistaken, Kenny here directly accuses
women of wrongdoing. Specifically, she uses the euphemism "misbehave" to talk
about sexual propriety. She elaborated,

> God says in the Bible that your body is your temple and the more men
> who come, you are destroying your temple. Some of you know what
> I am saying but others I know will just say, ah, I don't care. But those

people who are coming, they are killing you. *Abeg* [please], just use this place as an avenue to find a new road. I am trying to talk to you, but I am not trying to disgrace you or embarrass you. Don't let your present determine your future.

In Nigeria, conversations often move swiftly from talking about greed to talking about sex because many young women use sexual exchange relationships to support themselves. Although it is culturally appropriate for men to provide for their sexual partners, women are also accused of exploiting and manipulating these ties. Conflating sexual exchange and prostitution as immoral "shortcuts" to wealth, as Kenny does, is common in public discourse. Being willing to "suffer" means working hard to achieve slow gains through other forms of commerce, but to use sex to acquire resources is to be too impatient, too determined, and too desperate. When Kenny accuses the women of greed—"you want everything"—she holds them morally culpable for whatever they might do to pursue it. Importantly, these censures apply as much to women's ordinary lives in Nigeria as they do to foreign sex industries they might encounter in migrating.

"So if you leave this place, plan for your future. I want you to think, please, why am I here in this shelter? The mistake you have done—are you going to go back to that place?" Kenny asked.

"No, no," the women mumbled, penitently. All of the residents present had all been intercepted preemptively and, to my knowledge, had never practiced commercial sex work in Nigeria. Kenny was not referencing any actual physical place; instead she meant "that place" figuratively, as a mindset. She continued,

> Maybe the way you talk to your parents, the way you move around. Think about it. Don't just say, *Me I wan go, Me I wan go*. Think about what led you to this place and think about the steps you will take after it. This is an opportunity to plan your life. If you are just thinking how to get that *bobo* [boyfriend], how to get anything, you will not be planning your life. If you are complaining that the soup is not sweet, there is no meat, you will not be planning your life. But you were eating fine food before? Some of you, you want jollof rice, but garri [dried cassava] doesn't kill. I have seen so many people hawking pure water, and they are going to school. That is how life is, rotating.

Kenny paused for them to take in her comments. She wanted them to think not only about how ambition had led them to consider migrant sex work but also how it had affected all parts of their lives—"the way you talk to your parents, the way you move around." Prostitution was not the only temptation; all boyfriends were.

After Kenny sat back in her chair, having finished the main lecture for the day, the other counselor present in the discussion, Sandra, jumped in with more explicit advice: "Have patience because just taking shortcuts, like doing prostitution for material things, means that your new things will be gone in three months." Again, she locates the failure in their impatience, but frames her advice in prudential, economic terms. "It will soon be in your record if you are not patient. Go apply for a post and it will destroy your career. Do prostitution and no one will want to marry you if you are a prostitute." Although Nigeria's official criminal record system is rudimentary, Sandra suggests that the social records or reputations of women too will be forever marked by their sexual decisions. Their marital careers will be ruined as readily as their professional ones:

> No one will respect you, as a lady. If you look at your achievements, those clothes will be gone but if you make a good name for yourself, it will not deteriorate. Those [material] things, though, will not last long. Some of you want to have nice hair weaving but what about your dignity? What have you really achieved? What you are losing is not worth what you are gaining. All clothes, that is all. If you have a shop, though, people will greet you—"Good morning, madam"—but these customers you have are not treating you with respect. What are you going to tell your child when he asks Mommy, who is my Daddy, or, Mommy, what do you do for a living? If you are working in a salon, people will respect you more.

Counselors often invoked the Yoruba saying, *Oruko rere san ju wura ati fadaka lo*, meaning "a good name is better than gold," to emphasize the importance of maintaining one's reputation. Though presented in a pragmatic tone, their advice still sounded like more than mere strategy. In describing the stigma that comes with these practices, counselors also appeared to endorse it as a deserved consequence of that behavior. As the women sunk in their chairs around me that day, they too seemed to understand the shame put on them. Just as with counseling on the risks of migration, counseling on the risks of sex and sex work expanded well beyond simple information to invoke deeper moral questions of personal character and desire.

In this group counseling session and throughout the rehabilitation process, counselors spoke directly about sex and sexual promiscuity but indirectly about sex work itself. Assuming that all forms of sexual relationships are intertwined with material desire—"how to get that *bobo*, how to get anything"—they addressed the topic of sexual exchange very broadly, not only focusing on the kinds practiced in commercial sex work abroad. This approach locates the root cause of women's sexual immorality not in desire for sexual pleasure but in greed for material things, especially comfort and luxury items like fine cloth or fine food. It frames their willingness to trade sex for resources—whether in romantic relationships or otherwise—as a condemnation of their work ethic. Paradoxically, alongside near constant lectures about how migrants suffer, counselors accuse residents of being unwilling to suffer or struggle to obtain what they want.

This chapter examines how Nigeria's anti-trafficking campaigns disciplined women's sexuality by discouraging not only prostitution (as it was called) but also the broader range of sexual exchange practices understood to be rampant among Nigerian youth. If counselors understood the decision to migrate as a single choice that should be made rationally and informatively, they discussed the closely related decision to enter foreign sex work much differently. Perhaps they understood that women wanted to migrate and would tolerate sex work only as a means to that end. As a result, they addressed women's openness to migrant sex work as part of a much larger continuum of wrongdoing, shaming women not only for sexual immorality but also for the outsized ambition that drove their choices.

This thinking may result in part from the specific circumstances of women's interception. Because most women at the shelter were intercepted preemptively and had not yet entered commercial sex work, they could still deny their intentions or plans for work abroad. However, they could not deny their aspirations to improve their lives and the compromised sexual morality that, according to counselors, would lead them to consider migrating into foreign sex industries. Since they had not yet entered that work, women were treated both as morally culpable for their choices and as still salvageable from the dire future they had chosen. Counselors regularly affirmed residents' innocence in conversation, convincing them that they still had the opportunity to reform their ways. They then used the stories of the few women at the shelter who had already engaged in sex work to model both good and bad reactions to it, encouraging others to take note and "plan their lives" accordingly.

None of these exchanges between counselors and residents addressed the very real threats that migrant sex workers face. They were instead geared to influence women's choices to take on those risks. By encouraging women to denounce all their sexual relationships that involved money, these messages conflate women's sexual appetites and material appetites and again discredit the kind of ambition that would lead them to ever want more for themselves.

Ambition and Ambivalence

To understand how counselors articulated these issues at the shelter, it is important to first understand how women talked about sex work themselves or, more accurately, how they avoided talking about it in these spaces. The women I met at the shelter rarely shared with me their thoughts about entering foreign sex industries.[1] When they did, they usually hinted at that possibility with a knowing look or buried it deep in euphemisms. Most also expressed ambivalence about their choices. In discussing these choices even obliquely, they shared little with the unabashedly self-described sex workers who have spoken out against anti-prostitution and anti-trafficking campaigns around the world.[2] None of the women intercepted preemptively while traveling openly acknowledged an intention to do sex work abroad, none of them reported doing sex work within Nigeria, and none of them identified herself as a sex worker or by using any related terms during their time at the shelter or in our conversations afterward.

Of course, the social stigma around sex work discourages this kind of disclosure, in Nigeria and elsewhere. NAPTIP's ongoing criminal investigations into the alleged trafficking of shelter residents made it even harder for them to speak freely. They understood that such admissions might delay their release from the shelter and affect their eligibility for "empowerment" materials down the road. There were many incentives for women to deny or obscure their true intentions in traveling abroad. But more than that, I came to understand that their intentions, willingness, and consent surrounding sex work were, for them, much more complicated than the legal binary of voluntary versus involuntary behavior.

Human trafficking is characterized by a lack of consent, so identifying what women really knew about their travel and work arrangements is critical to discerning who should be counted as a trafficking victim. However, these legal frameworks do not map easily onto how the women I knew talked about sex and sexual exchange in their lives, especially when sex work was still considered in hypothetical terms—a challenge to be confronted rather than an experience to be appraised. Indeed, I asked some women directly about what they knew and did not know before they traveled. But such questions inevitably invoked the replies in the tones of either guilt or innocence that obscured other ways of understanding their choices. Ultimately, I found it useful to resist the desire to pin down whether any given woman "actually" agreed to become a sex worker or whether she "really" knew what kind of conditions that would entail, especially because sex work still existed as a future possibility that she had not yet encountered.

Because they were intercepted preemptively, women at the shelter mostly seemed to think about sex work as something that might happen or probably would happen and therefore was something to be confronted. But it was not something they were seeking out in its own right. Sine Plambech has studied migrant women from Nigeria who were able to make it to Italy, those who were deported back home, and those who evaded state programming like that delivered by NAPTIP.[3] Sex work, she writes, "appears both as a problem, which the women hope will be temporary, and as a solution, since it is the fastest way to get out of debt and remit as much money as possible to Nigeria."[4] For these women, sex work is understood as one of many forms of suffering they might encounter in high-risk migration, and a kind of suffering they may have to endure to be successful.

Mixed Judgment

These sensibilities were evident in the way women at the shelter talked about sex and sex work. Florence often professed refusals to enter sex work, but she entertained opportunities for sexual exchange, balancing the virtues of independence and respectability differently in conversations with me while living in the shelter and in the months and years that followed. The first time the topic came up, we were sitting together in the common room, peering out the barred windows and watching the line of cars enter the compound. Suddenly, a helicopter flew past the horizon, and Florence shook her head. "Seven days by car to get to Gambia," she said, "and how many days have we been here? Ten?"

"Ah," Blessing sighed from the couch behind us, "when I leave here, I no go Gambia, I go straight to US." She smiled at me, joking again about how I should bring her with me back to my country. I laughed some with her and then, in a tone I soon realized was patronizing, mentioned something about how hard life is for people in the United States without visas.

"You know," Florence said, turning to me, "in Benin they do prostitution just to survive. You can go to this road and see them, one thousand of them, doing prostitution there. There is no food and no work." She looked back out the window.

"But me, I can't do it," she clarified. "I will see them at clubs, when I go with my fiancé. In fact, I won't go to those places alone, without my fiancé, because of them. They are in their shorts, dancing, and they are not ashamed."

"Should they be ashamed?" I asked.

"Yes!" she replied, as if the answer was obvious. "I could not do it. I only go there with my boyfriend, my fiancé." Months later I would go to one of these clubs in Benin City with Florence, her fiancé, and a few of his friends. While walking in, she muttered insults as we passed these women, grew angry at her boyfriend when he left us near them to buy snacks across the street, and chastised me directly for greeting one who had passed through the NAPTIP shelter after police raided a Lagos hotel that had been operating as a brothel. She disparagingly called them all "dirty prostitutes" as we left.

"It's true," Blessing agreed, "life is harder in Benin." She told us about the time someone gave her a phone number that led to another number and another about doing prostitution in Port Harcourt, about two hundred miles southwest of Benin

City. "They said they had a nice room, nice furniture, everything was okay, but I never called back."

In recalling this offer, Blessing's tone did not suggest outrage or offense but a sort of mild intrigue about an opportunity that she just never pursued, perhaps still wondering whether it would have worked out. Sex work is often practiced as migrant work within Africa, historically and currently, both to gain access to more lucrative markets and to maintain discretion by working outside one's community.[5] Going to Port Harcourt, the largest city in the region and a hub for Nigeria's lucrative oil industry, would achieve both these things.

Florence replied that she too had been invited to go to Port Harcourt, though she declined immediately. "I said no to that but if you have a salon then I'll come," she explained. "But I know this girl there. She met a white man and married him, and now she drives a jeep and has a baby. This baby—*so white!*" She marveled, pausing. "But she is happily married now. I think I could do that."

Even as she affirmed her own refusal of this offer, Florence here understands it as an opportunity to meet a different pool of men, and she recognizes its appeal. Whiteness comes with financial assurances and elite status: "now she drives a jeep." Many women enter sex work with the goal of converting brief transactional encounters into more formal and long-lasting relationships, including marriage and childrearing, and indeed many succeed in doing so.[6]

Still, Blessing laughed at Florence's declaration: "But just yesterday Mr. Ben just asked you about getting married! He said you should be ready, and you said no, no, no, you were not interested, not for another ten years, no, no, no."

Florence laughed too, blushing. "My fiancé—he doesn't have the money now. Someday we will marry. But only when he has the money. Not yet."

Florence's position was not uncommon. She had met the man she would like to marry, but he was unable to fully provide for her. Even though Florence was committed to her fiancé, she had to pursue financial support elsewhere, whether that was in fixing hair, in migrating abroad, or in exchange relationships with other men.

Sex and Mobility

Even though Florence had reportedly declined these opportunities to pursue commercial sex work within Nigeria, she still depended on other relationships for money. Even before she decided to migrate, sex, money, and mobility were already closely related in her life, as they are for many women in Nigeria.

Although she always gave special recognition to her fiancé, Florence had several men in her life that she called boyfriends. They were mostly older men who were married, and they provided most of the income she lived on. One was a family friend she saw only occasionally, when he visited Benin every couple of months; "he will give me in one visit more than I can make in a month fixing hair," she told me. There was a former city council member whom she saw more regularly, up to several times a week. She referred to him fondly as "my politician" and knew his friends, went out with him around town, and felt she could rely on him. He lavished her with gifts, dinner in Chinese restaurants, and generous tokens of his appreciation, often in cash.

Keeping multiple boyfriends is a common practice in Nigeria, understood as a pragmatic strategy for women to maintain financial independence. In one popular YouTube video, two dozen female university students respond to the question, "How many boyfriends can a Nigerian girl have?" Their responses vary and a couple of the women answer only one, but the majority said at least two or three. "Three is responsible," one puts it, implying any fewer would be reckless.[7] Managing these relationships is understood as part of being a self-respecting, autonomous woman. In contexts like these, it is not only that women can extract benefits from men in their lives but also that they should.

In Nigeria, as in many parts of Africa, all kinds of relationships are made real through exchange—whether with romantic partners, extended kin networks, or visiting anthropologists.[8] Making sure that men maintain their financial responsibilities to their sexual partners is part of how women lead responsible, autonomous, and moral lives. Women at the shelter shared and acted upon these expectations as much as anyone else in Nigeria. Indeed, while at the shelter, several collected the phone numbers of the NAPTIP security guards and drivers, building relationships with the government-salaried young men available to them. When counselors urged them to use their time productively, they meant that the women should reflect on their choices and perhaps develop interest in a new vocational skill. Instead, women were using their time productively in ways that seemed most reasonable to them: building potential romantic connections that might provide access to institutional knowhow and resources.

This expectation that men should provide resources to their sexual partners is in no way tantamount to sex work; Florence's disparaging remarks remind us of important distinctions she sees between her own romantic relationships and "dirty prostitution" practiced publicly in nightclubs. However, the exchange of resources in both scenarios means that sex work is distinguished by a more nuanced understanding of the role money plays within sexual relationships. While she insisted repeatedly in different contexts that she would never—could never—join the women outside the dance hall that her own boyfriend frequented, she herself did keep "boyfriends" for similar ends. Like many other women her age, she spent most of her weekends in social excursions called "going on runs." Compared to more spontaneous and brief encounters that Florence would recognize as prostitution, runs operate like informal escort services, often to out-of-town parties and events. Women exchange invitations among themselves, creating social networks known as "runs girls." Indeed, the female friendships affirmed in these connections can be as important as their romantic and economic aspects.[9] Not all outings end in sex, but all women expect "thanks for coming" gifts and "transportation allowances" in exchange for their attendance.

In all these encounters, women use sex to move physically and socially between worlds. Although not direct avenues to migration, going on runs offers a similar appeal, including access to wealth, luxury, novelty, and comfort, as well as the discretion afforded by geographic mobility—whether to clubs that friends would never visit within Benin City or in air travel to Abuja or Dubai. Sex with wealthier men offers women access to both income and mobility, and migrant sex work provides one avenue to potentially lucrative contacts. Like most women their age in Nigeria, women at the shelter relied on sexual relationships for their income, but they had not yet engaged in commercial sex work. It existed only as a hypothetical, a problem to be confronted. Intercepted preemptively, they were not certain how they would navigate this world, and that uncertainty is where counselors aimed to intervene.

Innocence and Ignorance

"You are innocent girls and do not know," Kenny said as she concluded another group counseling session. "You refuse to go to school because you want fine cloth like that girl, but you don't know how she gets her own money. It will lead you to that. Following men—men are human beings and they can deceive you and even if anything happens to you he can deny you."

The half-dozen women in the shelter that week had all been intercepted preemptively, so Kenny spoke again of sexual exchange in broad terms. Calling the women innocent and unknowing effectively set aside the question of their true intentions around sex work, while still holding them culpable for the desire that would "lead to that." Rather than provide practical advice on how to organize or defend themselves from abusive men, the counselors instead shamed women for pursuing too much, implying that such abuses are an inevitable consequence of their own "determination."

Insisting upon their innocence seems intended as an act of generosity on the part of the counselors: it is a refusal to accuse them outright of bigger moral violations, and it holds on to the hope that they would change their course before committing to that life. But by pardoning them so eagerly, Kenny also obscures the way they might defend these interactions, urging women instead to comply with her narrative, denounce sexual exchange, and reclaim their own virtue. Although Florence said that she would not be able to practice sex work like the women she saw at clubs in Benin, she still sometimes seemed to resent the supposed wholesomeness that shelter staff tried to project onto her. Most of these exchanges were implicit, as suggested in Kenny's comment about "following men." But a few weeks into her stay at the shelter, Aunty Ola, the shelter's part-time teacher, tried a different route.

It had been a particularly difficult day for Ola, as residents kept disrupting her lesson on the concept of human rights. She was reviewing vocabulary definitions from a United Nations handbook written for young children, but no one seemed to be interested. Ola eventually gave up and walked around the room, chatting with the residents—mostly children around the age of ten—before eventually turning to Florence. Florence returned her stare directly, seeming determined not to give in to such a patronizing show of friendliness. But the teacher ignored the hostility and pulled up a chair next to us "just to talk," she said.

"So, you want to travel out, *abi*? That is why you are here?" Ola asked softly. Her question was a common one among counselors, but it was unusual for her to broach the subject. As a teacher she was not trained in counseling, and she was not expected to engage residents directly on the issues that brought them to the shelter.

"Yes," Florence sighed, tired of defending her plans yet again.

"To do what? What business?"

"Any business. Any business I can do to make money," she mumbled, looking away.

Ola leaned in. "Ah . . . any business? Even . . . if it is to use this??" she whispered, motioning both hands below her waist. I was surprised. Other NAPTIP staff speculated about women's relative willingness and naivety in traveling abroad, but never had I seen one of them ask outright about sex.

Florence paused for a moment and then turned directly to face her again. "I will use it!" she stated defiantly.

Ola turned from Florence to look at me, eyes wide, shocked either by her willingness to do sex work or her candor in admitting it, I was not sure. She looked a little embarrassed, maybe for them both, and began to quietly discourage her. I could not make out all her words, but I could tell by the tone that she was pleading. "*Na wa o*," she repeated, as she warned her about AIDS and God's judgment.

I do not take Florence's declaration at face value; it felt more like a provocation than a confession. She seemed sick of the feigned concern and dismay habitually displayed by the shelter staff, and her open defiance made a mockery of the inquiry. Florence also may have been parsing her own thoughts about sex work, considering that this could have been her fate, and trying out the idea that she could in fact do it so willfully.

Still, I was surprised by Ola's bluntness as much as I was by Florence's: it would be the only time I heard NAPTIP staff interrogate residents' intentions around sex work directly. If the counselors had overheard, I think that they would have criticized Ola's efforts as soliciting an opinion about something that Florence simply could not understand. Rather than prompting preemptively intercepted women to defend hypothetical choices and fortify their resolve, counselors preferred to set the terms of these conversations by sharing the experiences of select women at the shelter who had entered sex work.

A/Typical Victim

Although most residents had been stopped at international border checkpoints in or near Nigeria, the shelter also occasionally hosted women intercepted directly from commercial sex work venues, both in Nigeria and abroad. Most of those repatriated from foreign sex industries were just as frustrated with their return as those who had been intercepted en route, but one nineteen-year-old shelter resident named Juliet was different, always expressing her gratitude for NAPTIP's support. Naturally, the counselors encouraged Juliet to share her story.

One Friday, a team of volunteers from the National Youth Service Corps, known as corpers, visited the shelter to meet a group of residents. They were participating in public awareness campaigns about the harms of trafficking, so they came to the shelter to learn more about the problem and to be inspired to pursue their work more diligently. The two dozen residents sat in rows of chairs in the dining room foyer while the visitors assembled against the walls of the room, circling them. Ben invited all the residents to share their experiences, but they remained silent. He reiterated that the stories would not go beyond the shelter's walls but would just serve to "push the corpers further" in what they are doing.

"OK, just one or two of you," he said, eyeing Juliet, urging her to speak up. Unlike the women at the shelter who had been intercepted early in their journeys to Europe, Juliet had made it all the way to Libya, and she readily described her experience as trafficking. In the rehabilitative model described by the NAPTIP counseling director, she was already "sober" to the harmful intentions of traffickers and the undesirability of life abroad. Because she already accepted and affirmed the NAPTIP narrative against migration, the counseling staff spent less time with her day to day, but often highlighted her case for residents and for guests of the shelter.

Eventually, she yielded to Ben's prompting and stepped forward from her seat in the front row. "My name is Juliet, and I am supposed to be in SS3"—finishing secondary school. At nineteen, she was one of the youngest women currently at the shelter, and she looked it.

"After I finished SS2, I wanted to make some money, and I planned to go to Osun State," she recalled. "My mother's pastor, though, convinced me that I should give one year and go outside." Osun was less than one hundred miles from her home, so the reference frames her original intentions as modest. That she needed convincing to go abroad affirms her own innocence and places the blame on trusted authority figures.[10]

"So, he talked to my mother, and she talked to me, and I went. We traveled through Niger, and from there to Libya. I saw many things, many bad things. I saw many things on the way . . ." she trailed off and took a deep breath. "We even saw dead bodies," she divulged hastily. "But when we got to Libya, I am too stubborn, and I said I wanted to go back to Nigeria. So eventually I came back by plane." She did not detail these negotiations but instead emphasized everything she had seen along the way.

"Many lives are being wasted over there, I can tell you that. Pretty, pretty girls," she said, pointedly. "There are still many beautiful ladies there; some of them were even office workers before they traveled." She never suggested these women were deceived or distraught, only that they were "wasting" their beauty and their potential, as indicated by their prior experience in the respectable middle-class profession of office work.

"But now I am happy," she concluded, looking back at Ben as her usual smile returned. "And that is why I say I am the happiest girl in the whole world." The corpers clapped as she returned to her seat.

Like the naive migrant dupes described in anti-trafficking propaganda, Juliet presents herself as an inexperienced and innocent girl who trusted others to make plans for her. On arrival in Libya, her refusal to engage in commercial sex (being "too stubborn") confirms the purity of her intentions and strength of character. In welcoming the return to Nigeria, she shows how thoroughly she had changed her mind, unlike most migrants, who resist repatriation even from the direst conditions. Finally, she assures her audience of a happy ending in the shelter, an affirmation of her own growth and an implicit affirmation of NAPTIP's rehabilitation programs.

Selecting these elements to share was not an arbitrary process but was the product of the regular practice Juliet had in sharing her story. Indeed, most people who experience trauma like the kind Juliet describes struggle to assemble such a coherent narrative about their experiences.[11] However, repeat interviews by intervention teams along the way help women like Juliet develop a more legible story, often in exchange for access to services and legal protection.[12] During the six weeks Juliet spent at the shelter, in addition to speaking to these youth corpers and answering questions from NAPTIP counselors and investigators, I also saw her provide interviews to a foreign documentary film crew and an international fact-finding mission representing several European governments—two groups who never interacted with the other residents. Others at the shelter did not want to share their own stories, but they still found the snub insulting, reporting it back to me: "They did not even come to greet us! Can you imagine!" A few months after she left the shelter, I saw Juliet on a national television news program thanking the agency for sponsoring her schooling; more recently I noticed on social media that she had attended the wedding of a NAPTIP administrator's son. She was a darling of the agency for many years, not only because her case affirmed the NAPTIP mission but also because it was so exceptional in doing so.

Importantly, audiences for this narrative were not only outsiders like the corpers but also the other women at the shelter. Most had never reached their final destinations, so, as counselors often reminded them, they could not know for certain what kind of work and living conditions awaited them. Testimony from women like Juliet suggested that, had they been allowed to continue on their journeys, their own lives would be "wasted," regardless of whether they consented to the work. For women who had yet to fully confront that prospect themselves, Juliet also modeled the appropriate reaction to it—sexual innocence, revised ambitions, and moral purity. With the evident approval of the counselors and administrators, her story was a lesson to other migrant women still wrestling with their own feelings about sex work.

Such simple morality tales, however, elide other details. In my own time with Juliet, I came to see how this version of her story, although not untrue, left out insights that did not fit conventional narrative expectations of what trafficking, rescue, and recovery should look like. When I first asked her how she came to be in the shelter, she did not say she was rescued or in need of protection, but that she came to report what she saw going on in Libya. "When I returned to Nigeria, I wanted to tell these people about what is going on, about what everyone was doing over there," she told me. By framing her contributions proactively, as a cause taken up by a concerned citizen, she took ownership of her own story and disrupted raid-and-rescue accounts that conjure images of passive women in the throes of evildoers.

As in the testimony she provided to others, she described her own resolute refusal to engage in sex work as the reason she left Libya. When I asked her to explain how she left, she told me that she did so on her own. "I was just so stubborn that they let me go," she said, simply. A few weeks after Juliet left the shelter, I visited her at the long-term group housing facility where she was living under NAPTIP's sponsorship. "Some other people are calling me here too," she mentioned. "The leaders from that place, in Libya, are returned, and they've been calling. They have been telling me that it's good to just move on from the past, to do new things and move forward. They heard about the court case and everything."

"So they don't want you to continue in court?" I asked. Based on the testimonies she had provided in the shelter, I worried that she might face retribution both for leaving and for reporting what happened. I was wrong.

"No, no, they encouraged me to report everything originally, and they said I was a good girl for doing it. They were the ones who helped me come back," she explained. "Those men, they were the leaders there, and they were not happy with how I came. They did not want girls like me. Before, they would go to hotel and get girls there, but me, I was a virgin when I went. It was only inside that place that I was disvirgined . . ." she trailed off. I assured her that she did not have to tell me that part of the story if she did not want to. She resumed, "So, they were not happy with how they were bringing people over like me. They knew it was not good, so they came together and helped me return and told me to report everything to take those ones to court." In this version, it was the bosses of the network—those who could be held as traffickers themselves—who helped her get out of Libya and prosecute those who brought her there dishonestly.

"They got my travel certificates and plane ticket and paid for everything. It was only after I returned that I took some rest and then went to NAPTIP. My mother had contacted the lawyer even before I had arrived, and he was the one to take us there." She emphasized that she was not afraid of the men in Libya but was in fact deeply thankful for their help.

In the context of ongoing NAPTIP investigations around Juliet's case and the NAPTIP financial support she depended on for housing, I did not try to verify the details Juliet described. But whichever version is more accurate, the differences between the two versions of her story are still revealing. The first narrative I heard—that practiced for guests and media audiences—denounces an entire network of migrant sex work as trafficking, including both those who organized it and those who participated in it. The second version suggests that leaders of this network also rejected coercion, deceit, and exploitation within its ranks, or tried to. Juliet's suffering is evident in both scenarios, but only one serves the broad political mandate of anti-trafficking campaigns. That is the version she learned to tell audiences within the shelter and outside it, reinforcing the ideal type of true trafficking victims and discouraging all versions of migrant sex work.

Acknowledged "Ashawo"

Women brought into the shelter from Lagos-area hotels and brothels provided an important contrast to stories like Juliet's. Whereas Juliet fulfilled a vision of pure innocence, women like Mary, a twenty-four-year-old brought to NAPTIP from a nearby hotel, were denounced outright.

One morning Mary got into a shouting match with Bisi, a preteen who had been working as household help for a distant relative. The counselors interrupted the argument and corralled all the two dozen residents into the common room to address the situation. Bisi was invited to talk first. "So she said she was *ashawo*," she explained, in pleading tones, still crying.

Ashawo is a derogatory Yoruba and pidgin term for a sex worker. In the shelter and outside it, women often slung it as an insult against each other, but here Mary had evidently identified herself that way.

"Then I told her to read First Corinthians 6:12," Bisi reported, calming down and speaking more assertively.

Sandra and Kenny nodded, praising her choice of the passage. "When you cannot fight your fight, God will fight for you," Sandra said, pulling a Bible e-reader out of her handbag. Bisi tried to continue, but Sandra interrupted her to read aloud the cited passage from the New Testament:

> "I have the right to do anything," you say—but not everything is beneficial. "I have the right to do anything"—but I will not be mastered by anything. You say, "Food for the stomach and the stomach for food, and God will destroy them both." The body, however, is not meant for sexual immorality but for the Lord, and the Lord for the body. By his power God raised the Lord from the dead, and he will raise us also. Do you not know that your bodies are members of Christ himself? Shall I then take the members of Christ and unite them with a prostitute? Never! Do you not know that he who unites himself with a prostitute is one with her in body? For it is said, "The two will become one flesh." But whoever is united with the Lord is one with him in spirit. Flee from sexual immorality. All other sins a person commits are outside the body, but whoever sins sexually, sins against their own body. Do you not know that your bodies are temples of the Holy Spirit, who is in you, whom you have received from God? You are not your own; you were bought at a price. Therefore honor God with your bodies.[13]

The passage is a popular reference on sexual immorality, disparaging both formal prostitution and other kinds of sexual promiscuity. Kenny nodded throughout the reading, affirming each line. Sandra thanked Bisi again and scolded Mary for being corrected by someone so junior to her.

"What do you have to say?" Sandra finally asked her.

Mary replied, "I know my work is not good, but she accused me of having one-one cloth and I even gave her cloth because I had many—"

Kenny interrupted. "But why would you call yourself names, Mary? She did not call you that name, you did. And what will you say about it? What will you tell your daughter you do to earn these cloths? Even, we are all women here, and you will want to marry someday! This attitude is not good."

Kenny seemed sincere in her pleas, urging Mary to rethink her work and especially her attitude for the sake of her own future. But in the process, Kenny also dismisses Mary's own explanation for her choices and chastises her "attitude" for so boldly claiming her work. By using the term *ashawo*, Mary acknowledges the great shame and stigmatization this identity brings. And unsurprisingly, Kenny's reprimand does little to help change the conditions for her choices. As Mary had said, she knew already that her work was "not good," but it was providing for her daughter, leaving enough even to share. Although counselors often blamed women for greedily pursuing the satisfaction of every desire, here Mary positioned herself as someone who worked selflessly for both her family and for others.

After lunch, I passed Mary in the hallway and asked how she was doing. She shook her head. "*I wan go*," she said, with a quivering lip and distant gaze that suggested tears barely held back. "My mates, we were eight altogether, and they have all left, and now I am the only one here. I want to go." We talked about the bureaucratic hurdles still keeping her there even after the seven other women from the same hotel had already been returned to their home states. I could see why she felt hopeless.

"So, you have a daughter?" I asked next, shifting the conversation. Mary smiled softly. "Yes. Her name is Rosemary, and she is three, staying with my grand[mother]. I came here to find work, so I can provide for her. It is only for my daughter that I want to get money, and that is why I hope they will help me, for my daughter. I used to be a tailor." She lifted a limp and bent left hand that had been crushed in a car accident. "But now that is not possible. Government cannot give help so I will become a trader, a small shop, so I can care for my daughter. That is why I came to Lagos, to work in a hotel, not forever but to save, enough to start another business. But then they came to the hotel and arrested me, and now all of my things are gone—stolen."

I asked her how long she had been in Lagos and she says she had not even spent one Christmas here, though she was in Ibadan before that. "Do you remember

Joyce?" she asked me, referring to one of the other women who had already left. "We were in Ibadan together, in a hotel there, before we came to Lagos."

I asked if someone helped her move from Ibadan to Lagos.

"No, not really. There was one woman who helped me set up," she explained, "but she didn't take any money, or anything like that, because of my baby."

"So no one deceived you?" I asked, to be clear.

"No, no," she said, shaking her head. "I was just there to make some money, but then we got caught." She looked down with the thought of such lost progress.

Many counselors expressed frustration that women like Mary were brought from hotels to the shelter, blaming poor referral systems and other state agencies' misuse of NAPTIP services. The counselors did not think of these women as trafficking victims, and they did not seem to know what to do with them. Whereas those intercepted preemptively could be claimed as too "innocent" to know better, these women had already entered commercial sex work, had seen the truth of it, and evidently had decided to keep doing it. Mary's experiences could provide a meaningful rejoinder to the images counselors projected of prostitutes and prostitution. She was by no means proud of the work, but she took on the challenges it presented, in the hopes of securing enough money to raise her daughter. Perhaps because of that, there was no room for her story in the shelter program. She was publicly reprimanded for even mentioning it. The cases of such women were processed more quickly than the rest, and they stayed at the shelter only until NAPTIP could arrange transport to their home states.[14]

Coercion and Conditions of Labor

Instead of acknowledging the possibility that women could willingly engage in sex work and that it could be profitable, counselors circulated the stories of those who fit the trafficking narrative, presenting the exploitation of sex workers as inevitable. The counselor Ben was particularly likely to emphasize the risks of sex work through these narratives. In some ways, this was generous: just as he was more willing to acknowledge the appeals of migrating abroad but emphasize the risks of illicit routes, he was also more likely to acknowledge women's good intentions but emphasize the poor treatment of sex workers abroad. This tactic was especially effective in conversations with migrant women who considered the moral questions of sex work less pressing than the practical returns it might bring.[15]

One afternoon at the shelter, Ben, Florence, and I were chatting about a few famous Nollywood films when his phone rang in his pocket. He apologized and took the call a few steps away, confirming an upcoming court date and promising to save the phone number. After he hung up, he returned and described the situation in a soft tone:

> This girl, she was going to come to Lagos, but was deceived. Instead they stopped in Ogun State and forced her into prostitution. And, you know, there are lots of places like this in Lagos. Lots of hotels that seem normal in the front, with a regular bar and restaurant, but then you go to the back, and they have girls, young girls. There is no law against prostitution, but I think the two laws are, if I can summarize, that, one, you shouldn't bring anyone with you and, two, you shouldn't deceive or trick anyone. And these girls, they just eat what they are given, stay where they are told, and work all night, whenever they are told to work.

I had my notebook out to record his comments, as usual. "You're writing all this down?" he confirmed, and I nodded. "Good, he replied. "These are the stories we need to share"—stories not only of prostitution but of coercion and poor working conditions.

As Ben left the room to take notes on the call, Florence said, "I am surprised. This isn't happening in Benin. You have prostitution there, but no one is giving money to another person—a madam, no. You just go when you want to go, and you are free. You can go whenever you like, and, yes, it is flexible." She repeated an estimate she had offered before, herself impressed by the ubiquity of sex work in Benin or perhaps just wanting to impress the number on me. "They have 500, maybe 1,000 girls."

Ben explained to me when he returned,

> This is the one I told you about the other day, the one whose brother is a police officer, who could just pay anyone to take care of her, if he wanted only to prevent his sister from going to jail. But instead they are doing full prosecution. She is the prosecuting witness, and if there is no witness the case will be dismissed. So now this girl is being harassed, she keeps changing her phone number to avoid certain people. Even her mom is not staying in her own place. She came to the shelter last week to be safe.

It surprised me at first that Ben would relay this story to Florence, because it seemed likely to discourage her from cooperating as a witness in the prosecution of her own purported trafficker. However, the continued harassment in the story validates the woman and her family as righteous in their decision to proceed with prosecutions, and it also affirms that the supposed traffickers were malevolent in their intentions. As with warnings about clandestine migration, the counselors used other women's cases to emphasize risk by association—that this kind of exploitation exists, and therefore they would have likely encountered it, no matter how different the circumstances or the networks. Like Ben said, "These are the stories we need to share."

Conclusion

Because most of the women at the shelter were intercepted preemptively, the shelter rehabilitation scheme does not treat prior trauma but instead aims to convince women to reject migrant sex work and thereby reduce their vulnerability to being trafficked again after they are released. As described in the previous chapter, to convince them not to migrate, counselors question their reasoning, their understanding, and their incentives. Although there are moral underpinnings to those questions about migrating, this chapter has shown how counselors extend that moral interrogation to discourage sex work. This was not a simple denunciation of immoral sex. No one at the shelter entertained the idea that women possessed sexual appetites or desires of her own. Rather, sex was only imagined as a tool women would use to get something else. In lectures at the shelter, women were deemed immoral not simply for pursuing immoral sexual activity but for pursuing their desires for material goods and comforts.

These accusations were far removed from the particular landscapes of foreign sex industries because counselors understood the root of the problem to lie within each woman herself. Counselors admonished women at the shelter for pursuing fine cloth and fine food—everyday luxuries that are common gifts from good and generous boyfriends within Nigeria. Women were warned about being lazy, in search of shortcuts, and unwilling to suffer and struggle to do hard work. By choosing to pursue opportunities abroad, they jeopardized their futures not in the physical abuse many sex workers face but in the damage to their reputation, their careers, and their dignity before daughters they had yet to bear.

In stressing these harms, counselors echoed a much wider moral panic around young women's sexuality that gripped much of the country. Newspaper editorials and Nollywood films popularize sensational tales of devious university-age women, fresh out of the family home, who string along well-meaning sugar daddies, unwitting professors, and earnest bachelors to steal their wealth. Unaccompanied women are regularly prohibited from patronizing restaurants and bars in Nigeria, for fear they will bother the (male) clientele. In the capital city of Abuja, women moving through the city alone at night are regularly arrested as prostitutes.[16]

Counselors feared that mundane participation in sexual exchange in ordinary relationships made women underestimate the social and moral harms of commercial sex work in other contexts. They used the rehabilitation process to impress on women the specific shame of prostitution, valorizing the stories of women who resisted its lures and urging other residents to "correct" women who openly acknowledged participation in the sex industry, even as they expressed remorse about it.

As best as I could tell, most women at the shelter who had been intercepted preemptively did feel ambivalent about the prospect of selling sex to be able to make it abroad. They agreed that it was not an honorable or desirable path, but it appeared to be the one only available if they wanted to make the journey. This was a big decision, and to imagine that women had not already given due credence to its moral or reputational implications perpetuates sexist assumptions about how young women manage their lives. Indeed, the fact that women like Florence themselves expressed different views on it over time—resisting any simple narrative of their own choices or willingness—suggested to me that they still wrestled with these choices.

The counseling they received, in contrast, offered moral absolutes about the virtues of sexual purity and the degradation of all promiscuous sex and sexual exchange. Targeting not only the morality of sex work but also the morality of sex in general pitched women's individual ambition against broadly shared cultural sensibilities that took for granted how mobility, sex, and desire are so often intertwined for women in Nigeria. The staff deployed discourses of shame and fear to intimidate women to change, reinforcing social stigmas that made many women in sex industries—and in ordinary life—so vulnerable to abuse in the first place.

Like alternatives to the "orderly" principles of migration management, there are other well-established forms of intervention and support for people entering the sex work industry. Protection and prevention programs could help equip women to address the real violence that sex workers can face, and they could provide safe sex and reproductive health resources to avoid pregnancy where, as Kenny warned, "man can deny" them. However, these programs would not serve the underlying disciplinary project of the shelter, which urges women to avoid migrating into sex work altogether. Instead, the rehabilitation program left aspiring migrant women who were already well aware of these conditions to confront these hazards on their own.

Aware of the shame and danger associated with migrant sex work, women managed these choices as they had before: through private prayer and contemplation. They were, of course, familiar with the biblical references that counselors and even other residents dogmatically deployed in arguments against sex work, but they still believed God had guided their decisions to leave Nigeria. Ultimately, rather than imposing strict rules of church teaching about sex or greed, talk of God's plan would prove to be a much more effective way to engage women's sense of right and wrong.

GOD'S PLAN

The conversation was so familiar that everyone seemed to carry on almost out of habit.[1]

"*I wan go*," Florence repeated.

"So open up," counselors Sandra and Kenny replied together, matter-of-factly, back and forth, once again.

Eventually, accepting the impasse they had reached, Florence gave up and tried to change the subject. She insisted that it did not matter anyway; she just wanted to go home now, to start her business back in her hometown. I thought she was partly acquiescing, saying what she assumed they wanted to hear, by stating intentions to find work at home instead of traveling out. But then she added that she just needed her international passport back from the NAPTIP staff first, and then she would go.

"Your passport?!" Sandra exclaimed.

"Why do you need your passport if you don't need to travel?" Kenny demanded.

"It's not only for travel. For bank," Florence replied, "and school."

"No, you can't use it there," Sandra countered, narrowing her eyes suspiciously, as Kenny shook her head.

"OK, I want to go to Libya. Not Gambia, now it's Libya," she teased them, smiling, testing their reaction. Libya was a hub for sub-Saharan migrants trying to reach Europe, and many Nigerian women sold sex there while waiting to cross the Mediterranean Sea. Sandra and Kenny were not amused.

"Look, if travel is what is in your mind," Kenny finally conceded, "then it doesn't matter what you say, that you don't want to travel. God will let you go because he has already rescued you once."

"God wants me to go," Florence insisted, her brow lowering as the humor dropped from her voice. "I prayed for direction before traveling. God *wants* me to go."

"Everyone who tells you not to travel, you hate," Kenny replied, "so that is why God let you go so far. But when you got to the airport, he rescued you . . . but he may not do it again."

Florence glanced back at them as if she were about to speak, but then paused, stood, and walked to the window in silence. She was still looking out at the parking lot below with her back to the rest of the room as Kenny and Sandra eventually made their way back to their offices, shrugging their shoulders at me as they left.

In confrontations like these, the back and forth of the usual debates could quickly prove fruitless. Residents demanded to know why they are being held, counselors demanded to know why they were traveling, and no one was satisfied with the answers offered in reply. Even when Florence tried to change the subject, the counselors returned again to her plans to travel. But then Kenny mentioned God. Southern Nigeria is a primarily Christian region, with Muslim and animist minorities. In encounters like this, counselors took for granted that Florence already believed in God, but that she might not be prioritizing faith in her life and so might need help identifying God's true plan for her future.

Importantly, this assertion of religious authority did not silence disagreement or immediately unify residents and counselors around religious doctrine. Instead, faith in God provided a common ground for arguing about everything else. It was a usefully different register from the truth-telling matches over what any given resident *really* wanted in migrating abroad. The suggestion that it was God's plan to rescue Florence moved their conversation beyond whether she was *actually* being trafficked, or what risks she had entertained, or what her travel agent had planned to do with her. Instead, more important than her own intentions, or her sponsor's, or even NAPTIP's was what God wanted for her. Kenny contended that God was guiding the whole process, both when he "let" her go in the beginning and when he later intervened to keep her from completing the trip—sending her to NAPTIP instead. Florence, too, believed God had guided her, but out of Nigeria and not toward the shelter. Who was correct, which path God had ordained for her, and, most importantly, what this meant for her future ultimately proved a more engaging debate than arguments based in accusations of greed, naivety, and poor judgment.

The terms for debating God's plan were familiar to Florence and the staff alike, reflecting the ordinary hermeneutics of Christian religious practice in Nigeria. Pentecostal churches dominate the religious landscape in Lagos and Benin City, and Pentecostal theology has influenced popular religious thinking and popular culture even across other Christian denominations.[2] Formally, Pentecostalism is characterized by a belief in direct experiences with the Holy Spirit, in baptism and in daily life. In this tradition and in others influenced by it, the continued discernment of and submission to God's plan constitute the primary practice of an ethical life. This version of introspection and interpretation is common to people's faith lives throughout Christian Nigeria and shapes how they make important decisions, including the decision to travel abroad.

Florence and many other women I met at the shelter reported fasting for days in sustained prayer and contemplation at their church before deciding to leave Nigeria. They repeated the process again to secure God's blessing before they left, and when that journey was interrupted, many turned again to pray for direction within the shelter. However, these habits took on new significance as the shelter staff actively participated in this process of introspection, redirecting its conclusions. They asserted that not only did NAPTIP want them to reform, but God also endorsed this purpose by leading them there. As Florence and Kenny argue over God's real plan for her—did God want Florence to travel or did God intervene to bring her to NAPTIP?—counselors co-opt this common religious practice in the political project to reform migrant women.

This chapter discusses how shelter staff and residents alike invoked God's plan in trying to understand the experiences that brought them to the shelter. In formal weekly worship sessions, in passing comments, and in ongoing debates like those between Kenny and Florence, counselors regularly claimed that God must have wanted everyone to come to the shelter. "Why else would you be here?" they would ask rhetorically. These assertions retroactively legitimized the actions of state actors responsible for stopping women in their journeys and delegitimized women's determination to leave. They prompted intense self-reflection that residents took more seriously than other conversations with staff about the risk and morality of migration, which were often met with sarcasm, irreverence, and plain indifference. Heated arguments over different possible fates—what would have happened had they not been intercepted, which of these paths God had destined for them, and what they should do about it now—consistently made women at the shelter contemplate, articulate, and defend their prior life choices.

Trusting God in Government

If we understand NAPTIP's rehabilitation project as a moral one, then it makes sense that counselors needed to establish their own moral footing to engage residents effectively in conversations about their choices. This was especially important because so many of the women understood their detention at the shelter as an unfair abuse of power, and they saw counselors as complicit in this abuse. One strategy that counselors used was to separate their authority as individuals from their authority as bureaucratic agents of the state. These practices raise important questions about affective dynamics of governance in the shelter rehabilitation effort.

For example, after a particularly adamant morning of protestation and demands to be released, a resident named Mary repeated, once again, that she *wan go*. Kenny looked exasperated. "By the grace of God, you will go!" she cried. "Even you, Mary, your papers are ready; it is just *money* that is keeping you here." The distinction seemed insignificant to Mary, but to Kenny, it spoke to the commitment and hard work of the staff, who had to do this work with limited resources. "Do you think the counselor who took those other eight girls on Saturday did not actually pay for the fuel? Do you know how long it will be for her to be reimbursed?" She urged the group to have sympathy for the staff who were doing their best:

> Me, if I could just buy a plane ticket to get you home, I would. We are all just trying to make you happy, so we will do things even government would not be doing. Like those three days I spent to return those girls to Enugu. It could be June before I see that ₦30,000 [$200] reimbursement, or even December next year. We all will make that sacrifice, just to see you happy, but you don't appreciate it. You just say, "*Me I wan go, me I wan go.*"

Kenny finally acknowledged the arbitrary nature of return procedures, conceding that much of the NAPTIP bureaucracy was impenetrable, even to her. But just as quickly, she insisted that the residents should not be so unappreciative of her own personal goodwill. In recognition of the agency's shortcomings and of unrealized expectations for state authorities in general, these personal declarations asserted that staff were advocates for the women's return, even as they were simultaneously tasked with enforcing their confinement at the shelter. Such stories often endeared women to individual counselors at the shelter, even as they protested their detention generally.

Relationships between shelter staff and residents continued to develop over the six weeks women typically stayed in the shelter, and, for some, they continued months and years after they were released. In my own follow-up interviews with women after they left the shelter, many recalled particular counselors fondly. Although they protested wholeheartedly the initial basis and conditions of their detention, most women slowly came to respect individual staff members. Many kept counselors' contact information and occasionally called them after returning home to say hello and even to ask for advice. In short, the extent to which each woman listened to counseling, "opened up" to other aspects of rehabilitation, or in any way accepted the governing message of the agency was largely due to the affective and charismatic authority of creative state agents—in many ways despite their state affiliation, not due to it.[3]

Given the importance of religion in Nigeria, these interpersonal affective bonds were often founded in shared religious practice. For example, in one afternoon group worship session, Ben offered a sermon inspired by *The Purpose Driven Life,* a book by the popular American pastor Rick Warren.[4]

"Do you know what it means—a purpose-driven life?" he asked. I had seen this book sold everywhere in Nigeria, from street vendors hawking them in traffic jams to kiosks in university plazas, and I expected that everyone was familiar with the reference. "It means knowing the reason you are here and then living for that reason," he continued. A few women nodded in agreement.

"So, if you tried to travel, and you were stopped by immigration, and you were made to come to NAPTIP, are you asking why did this happen, why am I here?"

"*Ahehn!*" Florence affirmed, determined to have her frustrations recognized, however briefly. Ben forged ahead.

"Well, the answer is in Romans 8:28: 'And we know that all things work together for good to them that love God, to them who are the called according to his purpose.'" A few women recited the passage with him, recognizing it immediately.

"It means *all* that happens will come together in God," Ben proceeded. "It's *good* for you that you were stopped when you tried to travel. . . . All things are for good. You must see any problems as challenges, not as barriers."

The room was silent now as Florence and the others stared back at him skeptically.

"Don't see us as wicked," he pleaded in reply. "Government is trying to help you, trying to help you out of this problem. You may not see it as problem, but by the time you do, it may be too late." Ben was acknowledging the most fundamental contradiction of their rescue mission: that the women at the shelter may have deliberately chosen their previous travel plans and saw their detention at the shelter as the problem in their lives. But just as quickly as he had acknowledged this contradiction, he dismissed it as naive and disingenuous—an imposed story from elsewhere that women should not accept. "Don't let people deceive you," he warned, "because I am not God, but he will judge you."

Finally, he turned back to *The Purpose Driven Life*. "Remember that you are here because it was destined by God. Nothing happens that is not under God's plan." He paused. "And God wants you to learn something from being here."

In saying that the government was trying to help, Ben directly challenged the women's ingrained and often justified distrust of Nigerian government—"Don't see us as wicked," he had implored. Interestingly, to do so, he moved beyond the virtues of individuals within NAPTIP.[5] Instead, he asked for faith in the whole system, by implication, even the corrupt or arbitrary acts that brought them to NAPTIP. In the end, he suggested, no one had to trust government directly to find reason to accept their time in the shelter; it was not government alone who brought them there. Actually, they had been brought by God's hand—to fulfill each woman's own destiny—and the state agents working there were only doing God's work. By this reasoning, residents could no more be angry with the government than they could be angry with God himself.

This rationale was also evident in debates about Nigeria that collapsed any difference between the nation and the government. Florence happened to spend the fiftieth anniversary of Nigeria's independence inside the shelter. In honor of the occasion, the staff led a group counseling session to encourage patriotism and love for Nigeria. That most of the residents of the shelter had been trying to leave the country and now considered themselves captives of the government was not lost on the counselors—instead, it lent weight to the exercise. Each counselor took turns describing what they liked about Nigeria, listing things like a survivor's spirit, increased accountability in politics, and the mobile phone revolution. Then they turned the floor over to the residents and asked them to do the same. Florence refused. She shook her head with a sort of indignant dismay and insisted that Nigeria did nothing for her. In warm spirits, the counselors together egged her on, saying Nigeria must have done something good.

"But Nigeria rescued you-*o*!" Benjamin suggested, smiling, almost joking, knowing she did not see things this way.

A pause. "God rescued me," Florence murmured carefully.

"Through NAPTIP, he did," Prudence rejoined. The other counselors nodded in agreement.

Florence rolled her eyes and slumped back in the couch. Even if she had accepted God's change of plans for her, it was difficult to reconcile submission to that new path with the more immediate sense of injustice she still expressed at being detained in the shelter. When she refused to recognize the state's role in God's work, the counselors specifically interjected that NAPTIP deserved credit.

To recognize God's plan, therefore, was also to recognize the government's beneficent contributions to their lives.

In Nigeria, religious institutions—rather than political or secular institutions—provide structure, meaning, and accountability to daily life.[6] Like most Nigerians, the shelter staff also subscribed to these ways of thinking. Although counseling was not designed to be religious in nature, these shared systems of belief naturally informed their work. In so doing, shelter staff appropriated religious discourses of suffering and God's plan, working as agents of the state in the ad hoc, day-to-day, face-to-face tasks of governing—including their efforts to convince women not to migrate.

Discerning God's Plan

Invocations of God's plan can strike secular audiences as easy dismissals of protest and discontent, but that interpretation misses what is important to these women in those moments. Some religious traditions *do* emphasize a tolerance of present suffering, including several earlier sects of Pentecostal Christianity that were popular in Nigeria. These sects encouraged an ascetic, minimalist lifestyle and promised true reward in the afterlife. Critiquing these conventions, Afrobeat superstar Fela Kuti admonished Nigerians who "suffer suffer for world, enjoy heaven." By contrast, most contemporary churches in Nigeria promise decidedly worldly rewards. Part of a global theological interpretation known as the "prosperity gospel," believers are promised great material success while on earth, in addition to the riches of heaven. Indeed, this faith-based sense of entitlement arguably makes religious Nigerians expect *more* out of their lives, not less.

In the context of Nigerian religious culture, especially in the contemporary Pentecostal faith, references to God's plan do not simply condemn people to endure suffering but rather engage them in an interpretive debate about how best to pursue wealth. Pentecostal teachings emphasize that it requires constant effort to achieve the promise of God's riches, both spiritually *and* materially. Merely believing in God is not enough to secure his miracles, nor will following a simple set of rules guarantee any person's virtue. The spiritual work is considered just as important as the worldly labor. Recognizing God's plan requires a perpetual interrogation of the present, so one can avoid the devil's temptations and follow instead the true signs from God that will mark the path to success.

These practices of making good and ethical choices are distinctive in important ways. Whereas Enlightenment traditions favor logic and impartial reason as the foundations of responsible decision making, Pentecostal traditions establish responsibility through prayer and reflection.[7] Rather than weighing options, choosing to travel, and accepting the risks, women like Florence instead defend their decisions by talking about their work of fasting and worship; "God wants me to go," she insisted. Through this lens, the meanings of events leading to their detention are not evaluated in terms of the motives and choices of the individuals involved. The state officials who demanded bribes at the airport and detained women without cause very well may have been corrupt. However, those actors may still serve God's will, working to bring everyone to this moment. This is how Florence saw the world before she reached the shelter, as she contemplated leaving and fashioned plans for a prosperous future. At the shelter, the counselors offered a different interpretation, challenging the righteousness of her decision and urging a reconsideration of her plans.

Another worship session was typical of these efforts. Everyone stood to sing the series of popular gospel tunes that opened the hour. Each song ran into the next, from the slow, mournful call for God to "Do Something New in My Life," to the joyfully triumphant "Everything Na Double Double," which prophesies how everyone's wealth will multiply in thanks to God. They were popular tunes that everyone knew well. The residents sang emphatically, swaying to the tunes and occasionally raising their hands and closing their eyes in praise. About ten minutes in, the counselors near me started nudging each other and whispering about who would lead the sermon portion next. The homily was always extemporaneous, loosely inspired by a specific biblical passage and filled with messages that resembled the lectures and lessons of the group counseling sessions. Eventually, Kenny gave in, rolling her eyes at the many others who refused to contribute each week. She stepped forward to take over for the last song and then, with a deep breath, she began the oration.

"I was not supposed to lead today. But the person [who was supposed to] is not around, so I will lead. I was just looking through my bible, and the spirit led me to read Psalms 23. Does anyone know Psalms 23? No?"

Florence grumbled from her seat, "We know it . . . we know it." Kenny then looked at her expectantly, waiting for the recitation. "I can't remember it," Florence trailed off.

Kenny turned to the room again and asked, "Ah, do you know, 'The Lord is my shepherd, I shall not want . . .'"

"Yes, yes," several residents affirmed.

Kenny nodded and resumed. "So, many of us, we are . . . moody, shall we say. 'I wan go,' abi [right]? So let us read."

She read the entirety of Psalms 23 aloud. Several residents spoke softly along with her, reciting key phrases as they recognized them.

Kenny looked up. "Let us take it piece by piece now. 'The Lord is my shepherd.' Most of you left your homes for Nigeria or for Lagos or for another place. Someone must have brought you. But now we are talking about God. It was God who brought you here to NAPTIP Lagos Zonal Shelter. And God will not lead you astray."

The residents nodded along as she spoke. "There are people who passed through here and received items. You can even see their shops if you go down the road. They are thanking God that they came to the shelter. I pray that your stay too will not be in vain. You know the Fulani saying—is it sheep leading the man or the man leading the sheep? It is the same with God. He will always be leading you."[8]

Everyone seemed to be listening intently. A few counselors and even Florence echoed, "*Eh-heh*," before Kenny continued.

"The next part: '*he makes me lie down in green pastures, he leads me beside quiet waters.*' You will sometimes be tempted by things, but with God you can resist temptation. No one ever plans to find trouble, but by the end of the day they will, so you have to have God to guide you. I pray you will make the right decisions with God's direction."

"Amen, *eh-heh*," a few more replied.

Kenny resumed reading. "'*Even though I walk through the valley of the shadow of death.*' What this is saying is that when *wahalla dey happen* [trouble happens], you have nothing to fear. '*All the days of my life.*' You *no go* worry. God *no go* forget you."

"Amen," the room repeated in unison.

"So I want us to rise up and thank God, for the day, for our food, for we are living. There are people who cannot eat, who are in hospital, but today we woke up and ate, so let us thank God. I pray for the families of everyone here. . . . I pray for our president and leaders that they may not be corrupt and work for the good of our country. . . . I pray for Nigeria and our future. . . . I pray for our visitors and those traveling, that they may have safe journeys . . . and I pray that Mary's dream of going home may come true . . ."

Kenny began by acknowledging God's hand in even ordinary actions, such as her role in leading that day and the page of the Bible that God brought before her. She delicately framed traveling as something guided by someone else, whereas "it was God who brought you to shelter." She implied that his warnings to resist temptation and avoid trouble, for example, are omens about the dangers of migrating abroad in search of material wealth. Ultimately, in referencing one resident's dream, she acknowledged the residents' desire to leave the shelter but implored them to have patience whatever their frustrations ("*wahala dey happen*") and to trust in God that his plan for them was good, including the time they must spend there.

"In Jesus name we pray," Kenny concluded, bowing her head.

"Amen," everyone replied.

Planning for Submission

Accepting that God's plan was to stop women from migrating and to bring them to the shelter required women to reorient their expectations for traveling abroad. Not only should they externally accept NAPTIP's intervention but also internally surrender their desire to leave Nigeria in the first place. As Kenny suggested to Florence in the opening vignette, it was only when she disregarded God's true plans that he intervened to stop her at the airport. This approach directs the residents' frustrations toward their own stubbornness, prompting further contemplation to truly submit to God. Because intervention was intended to reduce women's vulnerability to retrafficking, the most direct application of this reflection was to the plans each woman had made before and the plans she might make again.

Another group worship session articulated this message. As was typical, counselors feigned reluctance to step forward when it came time to lead the sermon. Eventually Ben agreed and announced that he would just let God speak through him.

"If you fail to plan, you plan to fail," he began. "Our stories may be different, but surely each one of you had a plan when you traveled. Was it you who made that plan, or did you let someone else do the thinking for you? And if you let someone else do your thinking for you, what are the outcomes? If you can survive the mosquitos here and the food here you will live and leave and you will need a plan. And I promise this is not the end of your life here. You will leave, and you will need a plan. So let us turn to Proverbs 16:1–9."

A resident named Rose read the passage aloud from the Bible she had carried on her journey: "To humans belong the plans of the heart, but from the Lord comes the proper answer of the tongue. All a person's ways seem pure to them, but motives are weighed by the Lord. Commit to the Lord whatever you do, and he will establish your plans." The passage urged women not to confuse their own confidence with God's blessing and to surrender to his plans by relinquishing their own desires.

Ben began to elaborate. "So what are the plans that brought you here to NAPTIP shelter and what are the plans that will lead you out?" He paused to let them think about their answers. "Everyone makes mistakes," he assured them, "but the question now is what you learn from those mistakes. You had an opportunity and you took it. Opportunities will definitely come, but you need to be ready for them." The problem here was not that they had seized an opportunity but that they were underprepared and therefore exercised poor judgement. "That's one thing about adolescence, those years between childhood and teenage years. In adolescence you crave freedom and think you can do anything to upgrade your social status, to run with the big boys or big girls in town. So you will make bad decisions to try to upgrade your social status." Of the ten residents who had assembled that day, the eight women intercepted while traveling were in their late teens and early twenties, and the two house-help children were younger than ten. Nobody was an adolescent, so the story served to suggest that the grown women had acted like impulsive children.

"And if God asks you on the day of blame, and you say, 'It was my friend!' it will not be enough," he warned. "It is like Adam and Eve in the Bible. Adam said it was Eve who made him eat the fruit from the tree of good and evil, and it was God who gave him Eve, but it was not God's fault. Adam had to take responsibility." He paused again for emphasis. "If you are wondering 'why me?' then who would you rather experience what you experienced? They say experience is the best teacher." Here Ben insists that all the residents should take responsibility for what brought them to the shelter—emphasizing their moral responsibility for these events, even as victims. In asking "who would you rather experience" this, he does not commend them for confronting hardship, but urges them to resist self-pity and instead welcome the lesson in discerning God's true intentions.

"Life is like a movie, and we each have roles to play," he continued, "but God has the master plan. Whose plan do you think is better—yours or God's? For our own plan, we don't ever have all the information, and that makes us weak and vulnerable, when people don't know the right thing to do." He caught himself, wanting to get things exactly right. "I'm not saying you shouldn't plan, but that, you should say it will get better and not suffer so much while you let God's plan reach you. That is why we are here today, to ask God to let us fall into his plan."

The women seated around me nodded and affirmed Ben's message, saying "yes, yes" to each of his claims. They shared this worldview and had only ever disagreed on its application to their choices. Ben continued to address that interpretation specifically, encouraging them to think differently about migration than they had before.

"When you go home people might be expecting you to return bigger, since you traveled." Indeed, these expectations discouraged many of the women from sharing their plans to travel in the first place, feeling that the stigma of failure would be worse than not going at all. "They won't be expecting that you will return worse," Ben recognized. "They might even call you a loser. But we are not losers. Are there any losers here? No." The women agreed but twinged awkwardly with the suggestion.

"Once you accept God's plan, you are on the expressway," Ben quickly interjected. "You are on the expressway but you don't know where you are going. You have to ask God for directions. You say you need a plan. Say it out loud: I need a plan."

A few women repeated that phrase with him in call-and-response, "I need a plan, I need a plan."

Finally Ben concluded, "If you don't have a plan there is nothing God can do for you. You need a plan but let it fit in with God's plan." Here, Ben unambiguously affirms that God's plan for each of them is not to migrate, no matter what social pressure and disappointment they might feel. They should find solace in knowing this is truly the path God ordained for them—that their own plans have finally aligned with God's.

Ultimately these sermons claim that God not only wanted to stop women from the immediate dangers they faced on a single journey but also intervened to stop them from wanting to migrate altogether. By contrasting God's plan with each woman's intentions, Ben denounces not only the wrongdoing of traffickers who, like the biblical Eve, presented the opportunity to stray. He also denounces the desires of women who so welcome those paths, confusing their own ambition for God's blessing. In drawing the comparison to Adam and Eve, however, Ben's admonishment turns from a problem of misrecognition—of seeking God's plan but "mistaking" it due to a lack of "information"—to a sin of greed and desire. This sin is not irredeemable, as Christianity teaches that because of Adam and Eve's original sin, all people are sinful by nature. However, it does prompt different models of reform than merely adjusting one's plans.

Confession

Women at the shelter were urged regularly to talk about the arrangements they had made to migrate. This disclosure invoked many different paradigms of intervention. It was essential to advancing the legal investigation and the potential prosecution of traffickers, and it was key to the psychosocial support presented within the therapeutic aims of rehabilitation. However, women at the shelter largely resisted counselors' urges to "open up" and disclose their true intentions for travel and work abroad, because they resented NAPTIP's intervention, did not want to entangle themselves in legal proceedings, and often did not support the prosecution of their accused trafficker or travel broker. Disclosing personal experiences in the idiom of confession was different. It offered the space for women to reflect on their motives and possibly to acknowledge any remorse without directly conceding the legal or trauma narratives of trafficking.

Although counselors hosted weekly group worship services addressing themes similar to the group counseling topics, they did not invite confession per se. Every Sunday a Catholic priest came to give mass at shelter, and about once a month, women from a local ministry group came to visit the residents and offer them prayer services. On one such day, three women arrived in bright, closely tailored ankara dresses with large *gele* head ties. The guests introduced themselves by name and shared doughnuts and yogurt drinks with everyone gathered, about twenty residents in total. Most residents at the time were adult women intercepted while traveling. "We are here to bring love," one of the visiting women declared. "We are here to tell you that you are loved by God, and you are also loved by us, every one of you. You are loved by God and he will come for each one of you on his time."

After leading the residents in song and discussing a reading on Lazarus— "God has his own timing, and we must be patient for him to help us"—the counselors invited anyone who wished to come forward to say her own prayers aloud to the group. Mary spoke up first, asking that her mother forgive her for her sinful past and accept her once again as her daughter when she returned home. Blessing asked next that God help and protect all those outside Nigeria. Another woman asked that she turn from bad to good. After a long pause, Florence asked simply for the grace of God. "Yes, it is a good prayer," one of the visitors said, "We all need it."

When no one else spoke up, the visitors invited everyone to come forward with private prayers if they wished. Several of the residents lined up beside the table where the women were sitting to take turns hunching down, whispering requests into their ears as the women nodded and made notes on legal pads. After several minutes, when they were all finished, the three visitors conferred quietly with each other. Then one stood to lead the final prayer session.

"All of you have the same story, from the same sweet tongue," she announced. "From what you are telling us, from what you are asking for, it is the same. Someone convinced you and your family that you will earn dollars." I do not know what each of the residents shared in their private prayers, so what version of "the same story" they prayed for is unclear: for release from the shelter, for safe passage to Europe, or for grace on their return home. The woman from a local ministry group concluded only that all the residents have been promised money abroad. However, she then shifted her comments from what she had been told to what she makes of it.

"But you will do prostitution and you will not see the money," she cautioned. "You will see twenty to thirty men a day, and they will even make you sleep with dogs, with animals, if you can believe that. But you must believe it. Some of you have even seen it." This was a reprimand, rather than a recitation of their requests or a prayer in response to them. Each whispered exchange had lasted no more than a few seconds, so these warnings about what they would find in the journey—men, animals, misery—were necessarily an extrapolation, perhaps learned from the counselors on previous visits or from news and popular media accounts.

"Some have prayers of going back," she continued, "but God sent for people to stop you from that. Pray for little money, enough to eat. Pray for money for vocational training, in fashion design or in hairdressing. Even in petty trading or selling phone cards, you will eat." She corrects their prayers, offering more humble aspirations and alternative paths.

"You all pray for forgiveness for a sinful past, and we pray also that your families will forgive you." Like the counselors and other NAPTIP staff, the visitors seemed sincere in their wishes that the women at the shelter would find full and happy lives. Still, encouraging forgiveness for these desires ultimately affirms their sinful nature and the culpability of each woman for following them. Christian prayer often acknowledges one's sinful past and asks for forgiveness. By correcting their prayers, emphasizing the risks of migrating, and directing them toward a different life, the session appropriates these practices to discourage women's migration.

Testimony and Salvation

Women at the shelter both contested and conceded these moral claims throughout the rehabilitation process; for instance, Florence argued with various counselors about what path God had truly ordained for her. As with the proclamations offered by shelter staff, I have no reason to believe that these shifting understandings were insincere or offered as mere performance. However, it is useful to explore the function of these statements, independent of their intention. By tracking how these kinds of statements were deployed and the visions of redemption they contained, we can observe the interpretive landscape that structured these conversations and the choices that followed. Ultimately, accepting God's plan for one's future required one to take action in achieving it.[9] Just as shelter staff represented the righteousness of the state through religious idioms, women at the shelter used religious language to make claims on the state as well, actively seeking material support for their new goals on the same terms.

Counselors pointed out to me early on that Florence would likely never receive additional support after leaving the shelter, having consistently failed to impress the shelter staff because she remained outspokenly skeptical of NAP-TIP and still talked about trying to travel again.[10] Other women, however, were more compliant, even emphatically so. These residents performed their own worthiness for support in a manner akin to religious testimony, as was the case with Rose.

Rose celebrated her twentieth birthday inside the shelter just a few days before she was released. Like Florence, she had been stopped while traveling. However, except for a couple of turbulent days after arrival, which counselors always said were to be expected, she rarely complained the way Florence did. Slowly, Rose earned a reputation as an arbitrator of resident disputes; she also ran small errands for the counselors, fetching water for their bathroom and cold beverages from the provisions stand across the lot. As she gained their favor, her assigned counselor, Prudence, invited her to compose a special letter to high-ranking NAPTIP officials to help "advance her case." Rose showed me the final copy and allowed me to photograph it before turning it in. Handwritten on sheets torn from a donated composition notebook, it read,

> WITH ALL DUE RESPECT TO THE HEAD OF MANAGEMENT AND STAFFS OF NAPTIP ORGANISATION
>
> U all have been so nice to me and U all have been treating me so kind. Just the way U all have done to me the Most High God will do the same to you all, the blessings of the Lord in your life shall be so much that you all will have to cry for stop. God bless you all for your hospitality toward me, remain bless.
>
> My coming to the NAPTIP was not a mistake and I know it's all planned by God. During my stay at the shelter I discover that very step a man takes is ordered by the Lord so I wasn't surprise when I found myself here in the shelter. From the day I step into the shelter I kept on praying and reading Bibles, Novels and there is this portion of the Bible I read that says "IN ANY SITUATION YOU FIND YOURSELF GIVE THANKS." So I keep thanking God from that very moment and till the day I will leave.
>
> I want to use this Opportunity to beg all staff and the Head Management of NAPTIP that I want to go back to school, I want to see myself as a great person, and I want to say that I am very sorry for my sinful past and I want to look forward to a brighter future.
>
> After my Secondary School here in Lagos state, I went to my State, Bayelsa hoping there will be somebody to assist me farther my education but there wasn't anybody. I kept on praying and believing

because there is a saying which they use to say "*IF THE LORD IS FOR YOU NOBODY CAN BE AGAINST YOU.*" In this world I have nobody but God and finally God has ordered my step to the NAPTIP.

To the NAPTIP I see my helpers, my Fathers, Mothers, Brothers, Sisters and my Everything. I have come to notice that I adour [*sic*] most staffs and I learn from them and they also change my life: You people are my saviour. Please assist me and make my dead mother proud, don't disappoint my dead mother dream. It means a lot to me.

I love all staffs of NAPTIP Organisation. Please God and help me.

Miss Rose

This letter articulates a sentiment that many women at the shelter expressed. Although they at first resisted the messages that the staff presented, with time they often took them seriously. They described feeling God's hand dramatically intervening to stop them from an earlier path they had chosen, and many ultimately told me that they found the advice of the counselors to be valuable. Indeed, in a nonrandom survey of 148 women rehabilitated in NAPTIP shelters, the vast majority reported improved emotional well-being, and more than two-thirds indicated relative satisfaction with the program.[11] I suspect that survey results may have been influenced by the respondents' ongoing pursuit of agency support, which was premised on their cooperation, broadly understood. To that end, Rose's own letter can be read as a performance of submission, both to God and to NAPTIP, more than it might indicate the sincerity of her contrition or reform. It reveals her understanding of the agency's vision of rehabilitation success and her best attempt to meet their expectations for how victims should behave to qualify for further support.

Narrating an experience of victimhood is a common path to obtaining resources, as has been especially well documented in anthropological studies of aid, governance, and citizenship. For example, ready expression of an HIV-positive identity shaped access to rare antiretrovirals in the early days of West Africa's AIDS epidemic.[12] In Europe, legible accounts of certain kinds of suffering provide access to immigration rights for both refugees and human trafficking victims.[13] However, in this very purposeful display of gratitude within the NAPTIP system, Rose articulates a different kind of story. She describes feeling saved and even praises the NAPTIP staff explicitly as her saviors, but she does so in a religious idiom, not the raid-and-rescue narrative common to trafficking stories.[14] In terms of her alleged trafficking, she concedes only that her "coming to NAPTIP was not a mistake;" she says nothing of any dangers from which the agency may have protected her. If anything, she shows contrition for her own sins, apologizing for her past rather than lamenting her suffering.[15] In this sense, the letter suggests Rose sees herself as saved—not necessarily from human traffickers but from a journey God did not intend for her to pursue.

Next, Rose turns these claims on the state itself. Just as counselors at the shelter based their own authority on God's plan, she legitimizes her own requests for state support through religious means, expressing submission and gratitude to God and NAPTIP alike. She admits to a "sinful past" and states plans to pursue "a brighter future." She gives thanks and insists she is on a new path to righteousness. This conversion is the ultimate purpose of rehabilitation: counselors aim to convince women to adopt a new narrative of their past and future. Rose expressly insists they "change my life."

Rose thereby makes claims on the state, but bases those claims outside the language of the state. This choice makes sense in Nigeria, where there is little symbolic or material purchase to ideals of citizenship and governance. Like most ordinary Nigerians, she "lacks the modalities and social instrumentalities [to demand] egalitarian intervention from the state."[16] Indeed, she notes explicitly that the government failed to help her advance her education, so she instead prayed to God. Opening the letter by showering God's praise and well wishes on the NAPTIP staff, she frames their kindness as generous exceeding her expectations. Even her reference to their "hospitality" at the shelter implies a more personal rather than institutional relationship with the staff, while also displaying her own obsequiousness. Mentioning her deceased mother's wishes, and insisting they would "mean a lot to me," emphasizes again a more affective connection to the staff and organization. Then, as she makes explicit claims on the NAPTIP organization, she also uses the language of religion. After weeks of being told that she was being detained as part of God's plan and that she would be permitted to go when it was God's plan to do so, she now turns the tables—asking the NAPTIP staff and organization to honor God and his new plan for her by materially supporting her revised ambitions. She compels them to "please God and help [her]." Just as counselors at the shelter invoked a vision of divine providence to legitimize their own actions of intervention, so Rose employs this this frame to make moral claims on the state in return.

Ad Hoc Claims

In her account of Nigerian Pentecostalism, Ruth Marshall describes how popular theology promotes constant introspection and self-evaluation as means to submit to the will of God. Rather than teaching an ethics based on a universal moral code, as is common in other Christian churches, born-again spirituality advances an ethic of individualism by emphasizing interiority, discipline, and techniques of self-fashioning, especially self-examination and what Marshall describes as "giving an account of oneself."[17] In this sense, submission is not a passive process but rather one that requires the active interrogation of events and signs in one's daily life. Although these analytical skills are individualist in that each person is responsible for her own interpretation of God's work, they are still learned and practiced in community and affirmed through testimony shared with others.

The counselors' secular conversations with women at the shelter also asserted universal moral codes, shaming women for their sexual choices, ambition, and risk-taking. By contrast, conversations that foregrounded God's plan reflected the kind of moral reasoning that women had used to arrive at these decisions in the first place. Counselors still urged women to cooperate with NAPTIP and discouraging them from pursuing migrant sex work, but the religious framework offered a more effective opportunity for women to reflect on their own motives.

In the context of widespread state failure and corruption, NAPTIP's programs have been widely regarded as a successful case of "good governance." To make that work possible, however, shelter staff and residents must supplant expectations of the state that have otherwise been corrupted. When Florence, Rose, and the counselors alike invoke the common language of God's plan instead of discourses of citizenship and politics, they construct ad hoc relationships between the state and its citizens. Because the Nigerian government is largely perceived to be absent from the daily lives of its residents, these links must be forged anew in places such as the rehabilitation shelter. State ambivalence and neglect of community needs may be the norm in Nigeria, but trafficked women are the exception. Unlike other poor, vulnerable, or exploited groups, they are targeted by state intervention programs and invited to make claims on the state for further resources. Together with the shelter staff, migrant women crafted narratives that justified both the need for state intervention and their worthiness to receive its support. What makes these claims remarkable is that they were made in distinctly religious terms.

Shared references to God and religious purpose are commonplace outside the shelter, but they take on new significance within it. Where vulnerability reduction requires the work of persuasion, counselors are ultimately effective insofar as they can relate to women beyond the immediate authority of the state itself.[18] They reveal alternative ways that citizens and the state interact in day-to-day practices of discipline, resistance, and claims making. These relationships fracture and fail in a number of ways, but ultimately strengthen state power by co-opting a means of discipline that otherwise might supplant it. That is, the state succeeds where it finds the moral framework to convince women to discipline themselves.

CONCLUSION

Throughout the rehabilitation process, counselors spoke encouragingly about the possibility that NAPTIP might offer women additional support after their release from the shelter. Such goods were awarded to select groups of women in public events called "empowerment ceremonies," before an audience of local news media, politicians, NGO leaders, and foreign stakeholders. NAPTIP public relations materials featured uplifting narratives of lives turned around in an instant:

7 SURVIVORS GET NEW LEASE OF LIFE
ANOTHER ROUND OF VICTIMS EMPOWERED WITH SKILLS AND TRADE
  EQUIPMENT
JOYOUS ATMOSPHERE AS VICTIMS GET EMPOWERMENT

As headlines like these suggest, empowerment at NAPTIP is neither an abstract concept nor an internal form of personal growth. It is not something that emerges over the course of time, in weeks of rehabilitation or in the months of reintegration and vocational training that might follow. In these headlines, and in other contexts across the agency, empowerment is something material. It can be handed over, literally. Typically, it is distributed on a weekday afternoon, in an air-conditioned hotel banquet hall, to women wearing matching NAPTIP-branded baseball caps: "Seven victims empowered with hairdressing and fashion designing equipment, including generator sets" (see figure 9).

In global development and public health lexicon, *empowerment* usually describes transformation that goes beyond access to material goods, indicating

FIGURE 9. "Empowerment Ceremony." Journalists photograph a woman receiving a sewing machine in a NAPTIP empowerment ceremony. Benin City, Edo State (photo by author).

deeper, internal shifts, especially in self-understanding.[1] NAPTIP staff broadly think of their work in this way, but in practice, they use the term to mean something much more specific: the transfer of equipment to start a new business. A victim receives empowerment in its material form, through which she is declared empowered in the existential sense. "With the empowerment she is now an owner of a shop, hairdressing equipment and ready for a new life," one report states. "A girl rescued from Oyo state also chose to be a hairdresser; she was also empowered and as at the time of this report, she is married with a child and a legitimate source of livelihood. The other two girls, from Lagos and Ogun states both choose to go into the fashion industry and were trained as fashion designers and empowered." In one newspaper interview, the Lagos Zonal Commander, Joseph Famakin, describes empowerment as the "provision of all needed equipment with which the victim will start life all over." Empowerment therefore might come in the form of a sewing machine, a hair dryer, or an oven. Famakin also clarified that the agency did not distribute cash to victims "to prevent their retrafficking themselves."[2]

In this parlance, a given woman is either empowered, or she is not, or she may be scheduled to be empowered next week. NAPTIP reports that it costs between ₦400,000 and ₦500,000 to empower a victim, and they regrettably had to deny many women empowerment due to lack of funds. One write-up celebrating the dispersal of goods to seven women emphasizes their "visible elation" at being chosen from among five hundred victims reportedly rescued and rehabilitated by the agency, while promising other women that "efforts were being made to empower them in the same manner."

Because resources are so limited, empowerment is not a typical postscript to the rehabilitation process; it is reserved for the deserving few. Shelter staff must evaluate each woman's case to determine their suitability for empowerment, and they remind residents constantly of these stakes. "You know when they are staying here, we are not only rehabilitating them," Kenny once explained. "We are also watching them, talking with them, to see how they are." Although the terms of this evaluation were not made transparent, neither to me nor to the women under its lens, exploring its contours further reveals NAPTIP's vision for success and how shelter residents understood and navigated those expectations.

This chapter describes how shelter counselors and residents attempted to convert stories of personal transformation into support for release, reintegration, and empowerment. Through an examination of stern staff lectures and dubious detention rumors, it explores how women at the shelter tried to figure out when and under what circumstances they would be allowed to leave the shelter and to receive financial support afterward. These understandings circulated through the shelter in stories of success and failure shared by both counselors and residents. By paying attention to how women navigate these choices, we can also better understand how they weigh high-risk migration projects against other unlikely opportunities to get "something going."

Reform and Redemption

Demand for empowerment programs among current and former shelter residents far exceeded the supply of dedicated NAPTIP funding. Even after establishing the Victims Trust Fund from the forfeited assets of convicted traffickers, more victims passed through NAPTIP's care than could be supported by full empowerment packages. This funding gap necessitated a sorting process, one that prioritized certain women for access to resources based on the attitudes they demonstrated inside the shelter. When Kenny explained, "We are not only rehabilitating them. . . . We are also watching them, talking with them, to see how they are," she meant that staff not only encouraged women at the shelter to change but also monitored this progress to inform later decisions. "There are some, who if you give them money or school fees, or apprenticeship fees, it won't matter," she continued. "Even after some months, you will just see them go. Like that girl Florence, all the time she is here she is saying she will still travel, so you will not be surprised that when you return to [her home for follow-up], she will be gone to travel out." Kenny here affirms the fundamental goal of rehabilitation—ceasing migration projects—and describes prioritizing different types of attitudes to support that goal. "So, we don't want to waste money by giving it to people like that, who are only going to leave without even completing the program. Instead we must give it to those who are really serious, who will want the help and will stay."

If NAPTIP cast a wide net in its initial interception and rehabilitation efforts, Kenny's explanation and others like it illuminate how they narrowed that agenda to serve a select victim population: those who sufficiently demonstrated that they would not attempt to emigrate again. There are different logics available to counselors in explaining these choices. Talk of "wasting" resources suggests a selection process like medical triage, which frames treatment priorities as regrettable but necessary, based not only on the severity or urgency of their case but also on the likelihood of their recovery.[3] Preference for "serious" candidates evokes meritocratic scholarship systems in education, awarded to students based on their abilities and potential contributions to society, rather on their need or experience of harm.[4] But neither of these comparisons evokes the full moral weight implied in the shelter's projects of personal reform.

Kenny dismisses Florence as a candidate for empowerment not for her complicity in the original act of migrating but for the dispositions she demonstrated afterward.[5] She makes no mention of Florence's individual talent, experience, or professional aptitude and instead tracks her evolving attitudes toward traveling out, contrasting her with someone who "is really serious, who will want the help and will stay." Ben lamented something similar in another conversation: "You invest and you spend all this time and money and eventually they go and just get retrafficked. Like this one victim—you remember Thelma?" He gestured over to Prudence who knowingly shook her head with regret, as Ben continued to explain the case. "She was here a while back in 2007, and she was really bright. She had seven [secondary school] credits already, and five of them were A's, including maths and English." He seemed dismayed that Thelma had tried to migrate despite her academic promise. "After her rehabilitation," he continued, "we bought a computer to empower her, so she could continue school. But by the time we brought it to her, she had already left again, retrafficked. Just one month later."

Such complaints do not blame aggressive recruiters or greedy traffickers for incidents of retrafficking. To the counselors, these cases did not suggest a failure to protect and support women like Thelma, but proved the futility of any efforts to do just that. By their account, she was trafficked again because she wanted to be, or was even determined to be, and any empowerment support would have been misdirected. She did not want their help to begin with, they assessed, and that was why it was a waste. Theirs was both a moral and a practical evaluation.

Good Behavior

Although counselors were vague about the standards for these evaluations, they were vocal about their importance. Whenever they visited the zonal headquarters where release and reintegration decisions were made, the counselors reminded the women that "everyone should be on best behavior—remember I told you I was going to Ikeja?" The shelter manager would visit once a week or so, offering lofty, extemporaneous speeches about what everyone needed to do to impress her. In one lecture she declared to the two dozen residents that she had just been in conversation with the zonal director and that they should all improve their attitudes accordingly.

"Well," she began, "I talked to the *oga* [boss] when I was there, and we discussed everyone's cases, and as a result of that some of you will be going home soon, but there are some conditions." She looked around to see who was paying attention. "And I will be calling some of you up to my office later to discuss those conditions. We are watching everyone," she warned. "And we are noticing who is having a good attitude and who is not. We are watching during group counseling, all the time, to see who is refusing to cook or refusing to do this or refusing to do that. We will see some leave by tomorrow if all goes well." With these remarks, the shelter manager incentivizes a range of behaviors—some simple compliance with orders, such as cooking and cleaning, but also participation in projects of personal reform, such as group counseling. She holds release as leverage to get women to cooperate with whatever "conditions" she is prepared to set. Days later, no one had left the shelter, but counselors were still repeating the shelter manager's warnings about keeping good attitudes.

Residents took this information and in response developed strategies on their own and with one another, angling for advantages with counseling staff and administrators. They pursued a range of tactics to perform the "good attitude" demanded of them, alternating between earnest attempts at submission to the process and exasperated frustration when that ultimately failed to produce any evidence that they would be released. Indeed, the latter may be overrepresented in my notes and retellings, if only because quiet patience and compliance seem less noteworthy to document than dramatic outbursts and confrontation.

Residents articulated these strategies explicitly in conferrals among themselves, especially as new women arrived. When a woman named Obas first came to the shelter, she sat in a bedroom alone and hollered "*I wan go!!*" intermittently for over an hour. Her shouts echoed down the long cement dormitory hallways as we sat just one room over, lounging in creaky bunk beds for some mid-afternoon rest. Rose rolled her eyes at each outburst and told me that Obas had been annoying them like that all morning and the night before too. Finally

Rose and the other women present called her to come over. Obas came to the doorway, her eyes red, breathing heavily, and visibly upset. The other residents encouraged her softly to keep a better attitude if she really wanted to go. "Listen, you shouldn't just yell like that," Rose advised. "If you really want to go, go talk to shelter manager upstairs. Don't just yell at us. It depends on *how* you talk to them—you should be nice and not a problem, not angry and screaming, if you want them to work on your case."

Rose's emphasis on tact reflects common bureaucratic practices in Nigeria, where people do not expect bureaucrats to work for just anyone. Citizen–state encounters often rely on a play of affect and identity in Africa, and good favor is especially needed from those with the discretion to dispense social services.[6] Charm and personal connection are ordinary strategies for Nigerians dealing with bureaucratic barriers from police checkpoints to school enrollment.[7] Where the state is understood to be ultimately arbitrary and oppressive by nature, it is manageable in Nigeria at the indulgence (often via bribery) of a well-placed bureaucrat.

In the context of the rehabilitation program, the stakes of this affective performance are especially high. The calm and careful interactions that Rose advises—"nice and not a problem, not angry and screaming"—not only curry personal favor and goodwill but also perform the attitudinal shifts that are imagined to index each woman's successful reform.

Earning Empowerment

In accordance with NAPTIP policy, most preemptively intercepted women were detained at the shelter for six weeks. Although everyone would eventually be released, not all the women who passed through the shelter would eventually be empowered. Counselors and administrators often welcomed new residents with broad assurances that NAPTIP would help them pursue the new life paths that they so ardently encouraged them to consider. But over the time of their stay, that message evolved not only to acknowledge the scarcity of funds available to support women after their release, but to stress this scarcity as a form of motivation. Instead of implying that everyone would be eligible to receive funds, counselors ultimately promised that only serious women would be considered. The sorting process thereby served as a tool to reward certain kinds of attitudes.

NAPTIP staff modeled these stakes through two narrative archetypes of shelter residents—one representing the path of submission and sponsorship, and another representing that of resistance and retrafficking. The successful women in counselors' stories first passed through the shelter without complaint and then went on to see great success under NAPTIP's reintegration programs after leaving. They undertook yearlong training courses and ran profitable small businesses that supported their families with modest but comfortable lifestyles. These stories provided incentives for women to take their stay at the shelter more seriously, seeing it as a small opportunity for help after dashed hopes of securing much greater wealth abroad.

One young woman's story of success was passed around most of all, perhaps because she still sometimes spent time at the shelter. By the time of my fieldwork, Hope had been living under NAPTIP support for nearly four years, including full government sponsorship for her accommodations, secondary education, and job training. During my research year, she revisited the shelter whenever she got into arguments with staff or roommates at the long-term women's shelter where she lived, which was also sponsored by NAPTIP. One day, in yet another group therapy session about being patient and appreciative, the counselor Kenny asked Hope if she would like to share her experiences. Hope said that she did not mind, but then sat quietly, so Kenny went on to narrate them.

"Okay," Kenny began cautiously, "just tell me if there is anything I am saying that is not accurate." Hope nodded.

"Hope here first came to shelter four years ago, just like all of you are here now. And when they came they were many. They said, *"Me I wan go, me I wan go."* Kenny looked around at those who had made similar protestations that morning, establishing some common ground in their experiences. "But *then*," she emphasized, "when it came time for them to leave, Hope and the other girl decided that they did *not* want to go, that they wanted to do something else."

Kenny smiled and checked in with Hope before continuing the story. "So, NAPTIP helped them find another place where they could continue education. The other girl was in secondary school, but then she decided that she wanted to leave the school and go back to her mother's place." Kenny shook her head in disappointment. "We all came and talked to her—I did, and the *oga* [boss] did. But she was determined to go back, so we let her." Support of this decision recognized some of the woman's autonomy but was still presented with censure. "Only months later," Kenny continued, "her mother passed, and then she moved into her father's place, but he kicked her out. Can you imagine?" She paused for suspense, looking around the room with her eyes wide.

"Then you can guess what she did—she called us begging to come back to us. But we had already signed those papers, closed her file, and we could not help her." Kenny's tone expressed some pity for the woman's situation but also some acknowledgment that this was the choice she had made. But then she gestured again at Hope, sitting before her. "So now Hope has graduated with a certificate in fashion design, but we do not even know what came of the other girl. Hope had patience to do the program, and that is what made the difference."

By beginning this story with Hope's demands to leave—*I wan go*—Kenny confirms that counselors understand this resistance to detention as resistance to rehabilitation. Still, she invites everyone to change their course, noting that in contrast to the other disgruntled residents, Hope and her friend decided specifically that they "did not want to go." If *I wan go* is a protest, then wanting to stay indicates compliance with the NAPTIP program. Counselors saw in them a sincere change of attitude, fulfilling the goals of rehabilitation. When they did finally leave the shelter, it was under the auspices of NAPTIP support.

Here, cooperation meant more than doing regular chores around the building and displaying patience with staff. It was also more than the simple divulging of information about travel plans or known travel agents, or "opening up." It meant exhibiting those *internal* signs of change that were the hallmarks of rehabilitation. As described in a NAPTIP magazine, "The beneficiaries of the scheme [are] carefully selected based on their various voluntary desire[s] to forge ahead in life after their aborted foreign trip"—they are rewarded for changing their minds, for being *convinced*. The headline formatting of the same article reinforces this image, "TURNING Around the Captivity of 28 GIRLS," such that at a glance it could be read simply as "turning girls." The intervention celebrated here is not just their rescue but also their internal reform. Recall Rose's letter: "I want to use this Opportunity to beg all staff and the Head Management of NAPTIP that I want to go back to school, I want to see myself as a great person, and I want to say that I am very sorry for my sinful past and I want to look forward to a brighter future. . . . I adour [*sic*] most staffs and I learn from them and they also change my life: You people are my saviour." She frames her story as one of transformation and choice. These strategies deployed the performance of compliance and goodwill specifically to assure NAPTIP staff of the residents' successful rehabilitation.

Vocational Training

Vocational training programs inside the shelter offered another opportunity for women to demonstrate their personal reform and their commitment not to migrate after release. In addition to basic educational classes in math and reading, "master trainers" visited the shelter twice a week to supervise women in hairdressing, tailoring, and sometimes beading. Most counselors were quick to admit that few students would really learn enough skills from these programs alone; they would need much more than six weeks of training to run a proper business after their release. In the end, however, the vocational training classes seemed intended to do something else altogether.

"You know there is this girl who was here a few years ago," Ben once recalled in a conversation with Florence's traveling partner Blessing. "I went to her graduation on Thursday, because after she was here, she chose to go back to school. She came to Lagos because she was orphaned, and the family members that took her in, they abused her, and left her. So, she decided to come to Lagos . . . to hustle . . . if you know what I mean—"

Patience interrupted him. "That's not her fault!" she said, defending her.

"Of course, it's not," Ben agreed, "but then she had to *choose* to return to school, to do something new."

"It's been two years since I was in school," Blessing admitted. "But there are no jobs, and I can't work, so I had to take this opportunity. If I leave now I will return to my mommy's house . . . but I will leave again. I will travel to Gambia."

Blessing here connects her decision to travel the lack of other opportunities in her community, while Ben counters with the choice the previous resident had made to resume schooling. While classes at the shelter were unlikely to teach Blessing new skills, they were well positioned to address the kind of resignation that she reports. No one was going to learn to be a hairdresser in six weeks at the shelter. But vocational training could teach residents that they simply had the capacity to start again—that they could sit in a classroom, even if they had dropped out years before, or that they could enter new training programs and take on new professions. By seeing that this path was possible, Blessing could then choose it for her own future, one to plan for from within the shelter and then pursue in earnest after returning home.

Consistent with those goals, women's plans for the future functioned as a sort of litmus test for the effectiveness of rehabilitation. Another day, I was sitting in the common room with two dozen residents. Shelter staff always encouraged residents to attend available classes but rarely enforced their attendance. On this day the counselors Ben and Sandra had walked through the shelter reminding everyone to assemble for informal education, but the residents were indignant about this request: they felt attending class was an imposition. They gathered in the room but kept interrupting the class to ask to watch television instead. The teacher, Aunty Ola, eventually gave up on her lesson plan. She pulled a chair to the board where she had been teaching, took a seat in it, and just stared across the room, arms folded across her chest.

Florence pointed out from a seat in the corner that since she was not teaching anyway, and since the electricity was on for the first time in days, she should just permit them to watch a television program. When Ola shook her head in refusal, Florence insisted, "Here, let me teach then." She retrieved a marker and marched to the dry-erase board and wrote in large letters, *I want to go home.*

"To do what?" Ola asked.

Please let me go, Florence wrote next.

"To do what?" she asked again.

When Florence did not respond, Ola said, "No, write it," meaning write down what she would like to do, but instead Florence wrote the question, *To do what?*

Ben joined in urging Florence to respond. *I want to do hairdressing work,* she finally wrote.

"You want to learn or own your own shop?" they asked her.

"I've already learned!" Florence exclaimed, once again exasperated by the idea that she needed training. Counselors in every encounter seemed to forget her qualifications in the field.

Embarrassed by his forgetfulness, Ben made vague promises about possibly being able to help with that but retreated from the conversation in the face of her frustration. His solutions for Florence were facile in the face of her history. She had already trained for two years as a hairdresser but could not make real money working in someone else's shop, and she could not afford to open her own. That frustration had motivated her to leave. But the counter-trafficking campaign hinged on the idea of rehabilitation through vocational training and reorientation, primarily in catering, tailoring, and hairdressing. I heard mention at anti-trafficking workshops that there were more than 140 counter-trafficking NGOs now offering this kind of training in Florence's hometown alone. This was reported as a point of pride, but even if the number was exaggerated, everyone seemed to agree that such training programs were ubiquitous. The chances of women like Florence securing a stable income as a hairdresser were arguably worse now that so many counter-trafficking NGOs were training women with the same skills and overwhelming this market. When her stunt at the white board turned into an opportunity to convince the counselors that she really would not travel again if they would just let her go, she acquiesced and declared that she would work as a hairdresser, but it still felt half-hearted. As she had told me before, she could make more in one night with a generous boyfriend than in a month working at someone else's salon.

Release and Reintegration

Eventually, all the women did leave the shelter. Counselors reported these decisions as reflecting the spontaneous conclusion of investigation and reintegration research, but they almost always lined up with the six-week benchmark established in

NAPTIP policy. Release announcements prompted squeals of delight and running up and down the halls, collecting things and saying goodbye, often with only a few hours' notice. Residents would pack their belongings in large nylon bags and knot them closed at the top, tucking in donated items like rolls of toilet paper and bars of soap they had used during their stay. When possible, NAPTIP would arrange for several victims to leave together, therefore saving on transport fees. Big group departures always seemed to compound the emotions of the day, provoking an increased sense of despondency among those left behind. After processing paperwork at the zonal headquarters offices, case managers or counselors accompanied all residents on the journey home, taking them on either agency vans or public buses on daylong drives across the country. If they were being returned to a different NAPTIP zone, officers would first introduce the women to the local office, perhaps staying there overnight, before finally escorting them to the family home. I never observed these family reunions, but I was told they were generally conducted without fanfare. The women themselves preferred to be discreet in their return—embarrassed more for squandering their chance at leaving than by the stigma of leaving itself.

After reintegration, NAPTIP staff would offer the same vague assurances about follow-up tracking, vocational training, and empowerment support that they offered during rehabilitation, but their actual help varied. "They told me they would give investment for materials, so I can be working," Florence told me, "but I never saw any of it." Other counselors had told me how unlikely her empowerment would be, but I imagine she technically sat on the waiting list for years, her name far toward the bottom. I asked if they called to check on her, and she shook her head. "I am the one calling them," she explained, still holding out some hope that her turn might come up. Every few months, she would call one of the local staff from the Benin office, one or two of the administrators from the Lagos Zonal Headquarters, and Ben, her favorite counselor, "just to greet him," and to follow up on her status, just in case. She called me often too, in Nigeria and in the United States, mostly to offer greetings, often to ask when I would return to Benin, and occasionally to ask for money or for the phone numbers of NAPTIP staff members.

In the meantime, she tried to keep up her good humor at home. I visited Benin every couple of months in the year immediately after her release from the shelter. Whenever I would call to ask about visiting, she would insist, "Of course, I'm around," laughing dolefully at the thought that she would have something else to do. Tellingly, on more than one visit she did prove to be busy, as I found myself waiting at her family house while she returned from "going on runs" with different men who continued to provide support and entertainment in this otherwise idle time of her life.

When I first visited Florence in Benin, about two months after she was released from the shelter, she was spending most days at home. She had resumed helping her mother run the provisions stall out of the front of their house, selling Coca-Cola, small sachets of spices, and basic produce like tomatoes, onion, and yam. When I asked about her other plans, she sneered at the idea of working in hairdressing. "Working in someone else's shop, they earn 10,000 a month ($65)," she explains. "The politician will give me that sometimes. I even visited my mommy's friend the other day, and he gave me 20,000! He's a married man, so he pays well." Instead, she wanted to set up a fashion boutique. Her boyfriend's mother had spent time in Italy, and she used the contacts she made there to import women's clothing and accessories. Florence hoped she might help her establish her own shop sometime soon.

A few months later, she had indeed set up a small shop with money from an older boyfriend. He had covered her rent in advance, and she planned to sell lotion, perfumes, small handbags, and accessories. She could not afford a full inventory, however, and had a hard time turning a profit. When I visited her, she was still spending most of her time at home, so I requested we visit the shop. We walked through a busy market to a quiet side street, where she unlocked a heavy metal gate. The narrow room was only sparsely filled: it was like a deep cement closet, with barren glass shelves lining the walls and a display box that sat mostly empty. She had stopped even going to the store every day, knowing she could still make better money elsewhere, through other relationships. She told me that the rent money would run out anyway in a few months, suggesting that without another large capital investment, her fate was already sealed. "At least it's something," she said, "something going, for now."

Spectacles of Success

The few women I knew who received NAPTIP reintegration support were only marginally better off than Florence, but they were at least occupied with training after returning from the shelter. Whereas Florence had often complained to me that she had "nothing going," they were busy with training every day and were provided a small stipend to supplement tuition costs. However, transportation to the classes by public bus cost up to 200 naira ($1.33) each way, and NAPTIP provided only 2,000 naira per month. Training was a full-time commitment, but many of the participants were only able to attend intermittently, given their conflicting care and work responsibilities.

Others I knew sat idly in different apprenticeships, restless but at least trying. One woman learned to sew and sell coral beading for traditional Benin weddings.

Several more were in catering courses at a large youth-focused organization in the town center. Four trainees I knew from the shelter eagerly escorted me around the space, ducking out of the instruction on meat pies to show me their white hairnets and NGO-branded powder-blue aprons. Many of the other woman in the program were from NAPTIP too, they told me, over a spicy jollof rice they prepared for our lunch. One apologized for not having any meat to add. They smiled politely when I insisted I that did not mind, until another sighed that she still doubted whether they could make money with this rice anyway. Everyone else agreed.

Florence had always been skeptical of the empowerment schemes, insisting that if she were selected, she would only pursue hairdressing if NAPTIP required her to repeat her previous training. Indeed, many NAPTIP-sponsored women were starting the same style of provisions shop that Florence helped run from the family home. Florence knew what narrow margins those shops offered, and others seems to suspect as much. The catering trainees were not the only ones doubtful of their prospects for running effective businesses after completing the program.

Eventually, the women who finished training and apprenticeships would become eligible for official empowerment: the provisioning of materials to start their own businesses. I observed several events where this aid was disbursed, including one two-day combined empowerment workshop and ceremony, hosted at a recently refurbished hotel in Benin City. Invited guests, staff photographers, and journalists far outnumbered the two dozen women invited to participate. To open the affair, NAPTIP zonal directors gave speeches recounting the women's suffering and the horrors of human trafficking in broad terms before turning to their great promise as renewed citizens and businesswomen. Basic skills training followed, as local NGO staff lectured on bookkeeping, marketing, and sexual health. On the second day, NAPTIP administrators took turns to ceremoniously transfer supplies to each woman, pausing for photos beside tables stacked high with sewing machines, hair dryers, kerosene cookers, small fridges, and diesel generators.

The optics of these occasions fulfill the NAPTIP vision of itself as an exceptional agency in the Nigerian state bureaucracy. With no cameras and limited media access to the shelter rehabilitation process, NAPTIP widely broadcasts empowerment stories to demonstrate its successes. Empowerment ceremonies were featured regularly in news programs on the state-owned television channel, where twice I caught glimpses of women I had known from the shelter, grimacing modestly under the same bright-orange caps, standing in rows behind men in suits and women in formal *gele* head ties. In these stories, the triumph of empowerment is claimed not only for individuals receiving equipment but also for the agency, and for the government at large. One NAPTIP magazine feature makes this narrative even more explicit as it paints the scene of another ceremony:

> Even though the items to be given to the beneficiaries of the Empowerment Scheme were conspicuously displayed at the premises of the Agency, it could be seen from the body language and mixed reaction on the faces of some of the beneficiaries that they were still in doubt about the reality of the event. They had thought it was impossible for any Government Agency to pick somebody on the street of foreign land, transport the person to Nigeria and even his home town at no cost to the victim, shelter them in a facility of International standard, train the person on vocation of his or her choice with stipends that covered feeding and transportation during the training and eventually empower the person with items that were of international value in addition to some seed money. While some put on their best attires, a handful of them who were doubting Thomases simply appeared in their normal outing dress and turned up for the event.
>
> However, few hours later, it dawned on them that the event was real. This is real! This is real!! This is real!!!, one of them who could not hold back her joy shouted as she rushed out of the premises to call her mother on the phone to hurry to the Agency's office to witness what had happened and to help her convey some of the items home.

Here, NAPTIP again proudly fights the expectations of a corrupt state and proclaims renewed faith in the government—for these women, their families, and now anyone else who might witness their success in media outlets.

Ironically, the question of how "real" their empowerment might be was not resolved so easily. I would learn later that many of these items distributed at the ceremony I attended were essentially props because about half of the money expected from the national headquarters had failed to arrive in time to distribute all the recipients' actual equipment. Nevertheless, the officials took turns holding the microphone and giving speeches to each woman as photographers documented the transfer. The recipients wore baseball caps printed with NAPTIP insignia, and they mostly looked to the ground, out of modesty or discomfort I was not sure. They were then formally assigned to two local NGO leaders who would be responsible for supervising their progress for the next six months. Both directors gave speeches on the importance of hard work and strong character and passed around business cards to their delegated groups. Everyone parted with promises to follow up within the coming weeks, especially for those still awaiting their supplies. That process would ultimately take several more months to complete.[8]

Sex and the Unserious

I passed by Kenny and Sandra one day while they worked on empowerment requests, handwriting reports to pass along to the zonal headquarters, when Sandra called me over through the doorway to explain what she regarded to be a particularly troubling case. She was reviewing the files of someone who had already been empowered, but follow-up checks had revealed the business to be stalled. "The girl is just not serious, so we are going to go reclaim the materials and give them to someone who will make better use of them," Sandra said. While NAPTIP staff spoke often of materials that had been wasted, I had never heard of someone losing equipment, that had already been distributed, so I asked her to explain the offense.

"We organized for this girl to have rehabilitation materials, so she could open up a shop," Sandra began, "and the girl even collected the materials. But then when we called to learn about her progress, her mother explained that she was learning about the business from another shop owner before she ventured out on her own."

"That was fine," Kenny interjected, making sure to acknowledge the importance of training and apprenticeship.

"Yes, of course," Sandra continued, "so we just asked would she please give us the number of the master trainer, so we could inquire about her status there. The mother claimed not to have the number, which, isn't that suspicious? You'd give your daughter to train with someone whose number you do not even know!?" She clapped the back of her hand into her palm for emphasis. "The woman eventually called us back later to explain that her daughter had since become impregnated and wouldn't be able to open the shop for even longer!" Outraged, her voice then dropped to lower tones. "If she was serious she wouldn't be opening her legs like that," she pronounced soberly. "I just don't see how she could let someone get her pregnant when we had just invested all of that. The girl is just not serious," she repeated.

Sandra was therefore writing to request permission from the zonal office to conduct what is called a "social inquiry," a process usually used to investigate the family environment before release from the shelter. "I need to confirm the story and reacquisition the materials to pass along to someone else who is more serious," she declared.

I do not know if Sandra's efforts were successful, but they reflect the naive presumption that women receiving empowerment would somehow be instantly disentangled from the other relationships that sustain them, both socially and materially. NAPTIP presented itself as offering a universal form of economic empowerment that was necessarily chaste and sexless. It assumed that entrepreneurship should lend women financial independence from relationships of sexual exchange and help them resist the lure of migrant sex work for foreign money. NAPTIP's own promotional coverage of another empowerment ceremony summarizes a zonal head's inspirational speech urging women to "contribute to the community by being employers of legitimate labour" and by rejecting "the get-rich-quick syndrome that has infected most youths in the Nigerian society today." Although offered in gender-free terms, the underlying message is clear, discouraging women from engaging in transactional sex generally and migrant sex work specifically. These implied values explain why lessons on sexual health accompany those on bookkeeping. But sexuality, ambition, and opportunity of course remain entangled for women both within and outside those empowerment schemes.

In her own recounting of professional and personal goals, Florence sought support from NAPTIP, as well as from her fiancé, his kin, and her other boyfriends. Sexual relationships were not alternatives or backups to her business goals but potentially provided direct support for them, especially when NAPTIP, her own family, and other would-be patrons did not deliver. Likewise, women in vocational programs had to subsidize their own expenses while working and training without pay. Even those who would go on to open proper businesses still had little confidence in their success, and they knew that any income they might make would compare poorly to what they expected to make abroad.

Even setting material needs aside, NAPTIP-sponsored business skills classes always acknowledge the importance of expanding networks to market goods and services for new businesses. In all these cases, sexual relationships remain a resource to help women bridge the gap between their incomes, needs, and ambitions. While ostensibly helping women build alternative sources of income, empowerment programs like these still compel women to return to their known resources for growth. Ironically, those relationships of sexual exchange subsidize not only women's own needs but also implicitly the exact empowerment schemes that NAPTIP so eagerly broadcasts in its visions of successful rehabilitation—while dismissing those who expose these contradictions as somehow "unserious."

Resourcefulness Reconfigured

Empowerment is the culmination of NAPTIP's rehabilitation program. It represents the happy conclusion to a rescue story, even if it is reserved for only a portion of the women who pass through the NAPTIP shelter. These ceremonies manifest NAPTIP's own achievement in saving certain migrant women, while those women in return affirm their commitment and gratitude to NAPTIP and the life it has ordained for them. They do this work photogenically, with plain evidence of support, easily relayed in newspaper headlines, state television reels, and agency promotional materials.

These women are accustomed to pursuing multiple opportunities and maintaining multiple potential income sources, as do so many people living in precarious economic landscapes. It is little surprise that women remain entangled in their previous networks and routines, even as they remain grateful to have "something going" with NAPTIP's empowerment support. However, counselors' skepticism of other opportunities confirms that the goals of the agency are not merely to see the women become economically independent. They show how ambition, focus, and responsibility are evaluated in the rehabilitation process and incentivized with empowerment. Across intervention schemes, migrant sex work is consistently presented as a moral problem of ambition rather than a practical problem of economic desperation. Empowerment therefore must be leveraged not only to provide alternative income streams but to reward the reform of women's desires.

Epilogue

Before my first steps on Nigerian soil, colleagues at my university advised me that unadvertised expediting fees might be necessary to secure my visa, so I tucked an extra money order in the slim Express Mail envelope to mail to the Nigerian consulate in New York. The envelope also included an invitation to visit Lagos from a friend of a friend I had never met. Unlike my hosts for the summer, this contact had access to institutional letterhead and the proper government-issued identification required to endorse my visa application. Next, I was coached on how to talk my way into being given a ninety-day permit when I approached the immigration podium in the Lagos International Airport arrivals hall. My multi-entry visa would be valid for a year, but visitors obtain limited clearance to stay with each entry. A less careful traveler might just be allowed thirty days at a time, ensuring more frequent trips to immigration offices to extend their pass.

Throughout my research in Nigeria, I have variously been afforded thirty-, sixty-, and ninety-day permits, and every time I needed an extension, I found myself genuinely confused about how to proceed through Nigeria's formal visa system. I rifled through half-built websites and wandered half-vacant office complexes of the Nigeria Immigration Service (NIS), where only touts seemed available to help me. Eventually I would sit down with someone in a fresher-looking uniform, not sure of their formal ties to the office, but also not sure what other options I had. The processing fees were never consistent or transparent, and my paperwork was never considered sufficient on the first attempt. I was sent away once for not using boldface formatting on the subject line of my request letter, and everyone always initially insisted that I must personally travel to Abuja (a short flight or overnight bus ride) if I wanted to see real progress on my case. After some persistence, someone would eventually agree to pass along my materials for review, sliding my passport, money, and letters in a manila folder or tucking them in the ruffled pages of a composition notebook. Then, they would write a mobile phone number down on a scrap of paper, inviting me to call them personally to check on the status of my visa. If I was so determined to stay, this was how the system worked—daunting and impenetrable, in constant tension between trust and trickery, with no clear alternative but to accede to it all. I left many exchanges not knowing if I had interacted with an NIS official or an informal broker, and even less confident whether I had paid the appropriate fees, been manipulated to pay more, unwittingly bribed someone, or all three. Still, I was relieved to have at least thirty days before I had to do it again.

Moving through the world with my fair skin and an American passport is fundamentally a different experience than anything Florence has ever known, and these minor visa sagas suggest plenty more about my naive privilege as a white foreigner in Nigeria than they might reflect about her experience of migrating. To waltz into government offices and demand a fair and formal solution to a problem takes entirely for granted that I might make a system work in my favor by sheer force of my will—without connections, without bribes, without acknowledging the people involved in each step.[1] Where I was successful (and I always eventually was), the system yielded not because I was honest or deserving, but because my whiteness ensured that people would accommodate me. Despite my stubbornness, I still needed to manage these systems through interpersonal contacts as anyone else would, and those relationships, however fleeting, were always structured across race and class difference. In the end, whatever unease I was made to feel in these exchanges, my "fees" were always accepted and my papers always extended.

This contrast was made clearest to me in the one trip I took to Nigeria's land border, which also happened to also be a common interception site for women eventually referred to the shelter. Exhausted by the bureaucratic labyrinths of extension requests at the NIS offices, I decided to try renewing my visitor's stamp by passing through the Seme border checkpoint into the Benin Republic. It was just seventy-five miles west of Lagos, but the freeway was notorious for traffic and armed robberies, so I did not want to travel alone. I hired someone to drive my car, and then I invited two friends, Joy and Chichi, along for company as well. They both owned international passports—Chichi had traveled once with a boyfriend to Dubai, and Joy had lived in Cotonou as a teen. Still, it took some explaining to get them to understand I did not want to cross by bush as they said they usually did—convenience aside, the whole purpose of this trip was to stamp my visa. Chichi had misplaced her own international passport some weeks earlier, and she was not about to get a new one for this minor journey. No problem, they both assured me, they had crossed that way without papers many, many times before.

The checkpoints began miles before the border, and although many cars passed freely, we were directed aside each time. Perhaps we had bad luck, or perhaps they purposefully targeted a white woman unaccompanied by the security escorts usually afforded to expatriates in the area. Joy and Chichi deflected the officers' inquiries from the backseat of the sedan, insisting they did not need passports since they were just traveling with me up to the border, not through it. Lacking a valid passport, Chichi eventually gave up and returned to Lagos by bus. Joy pretended to join her but then returned on a motorcycle taxi, wearing a teal jeweled scarf over her head to avoid being spotted by the officers who had initially questioned her. She passed through Immigration and Customs alone by foot, where a new group of agents ordered her to empty the contents of her handbag. She dumped out some makeup, money, and two condoms. The officers feigned outrage and immediately accused her of wanting to go to "John Kay"—the street in Cotonou where sex workers wait for customers. Ironically, this harassment transpired immediately beneath a large roadside billboard sponsored by a public health campaign promoting condom use to avoid transmitting HIV across the border. "They just wanted money," she explained to me afterward, still annoyed. Since she was familiar with the area, Joy understood the allegations and denied them, insulting them for insulting her. Eventually they let her pass.

My luck was not much better. On the way in, Nigerian border agents spent forty-five minutes arguing with and haranguing me, one of them most adamantly insisting that the visa I had been using for a half-year and renewed once already had never been valid and should be promptly torn out of my passport. He instructed an inferior officer to do just that, but said it with a bemused smirk that left me unsure how serious he was. I expected it was mostly a ruse to extract a bribe—to pay a "fee" on the spot or to give him something smaller to look the other way. Eventually other officers intervened and outnumbered him. They agreed to let me go, and off to Cotonou we went.

On my return a few hours later, the NIS officers on the Benin side of the border identified the same discrepancy on my reentry visa, again declaring it invalid and offering, with a smile, to deport me free of charge. They hassled me for presenting a visitors permit within days of expiration, which is of course what necessitated the journey. But the real issue was the validity period of the original reentry visa. The authorization code, they agreed, clearly stated that it was valid for twelve months. However, a few lines below, in the section marked "valid at port of entry within," the New York consulate office had filled in three months. A high-ranking NIS officer I met at the American Embassy had helped me through a previous renewal, and he had explained that this meant I had three months to initiate use of the visa—to arrive physically in Nigeria—and then twelve months to reenter after that. However, no officer at this border would even entertain this idea. They certainly were not about to take my word on it. Instead, they all agreed the consulate had made a mistake in putting different numbers down, that this mistake rendered the visa invalid, and that I could not be allowed reentry without a valid visa. I tried to insist that I should not be punished for their mistake, but they just shrugged and passed me along to the next set of offices for further review.

And so it was that I was escorted from room to room, where official after official would look my over my visa, casually flip through all the other pages, and eventually hand back the passport, shaking his head. I was finally taken to a larger office, where I sat patiently as five more officers passed it around, speaking heatedly in Yoruba. I could not understand them and suspected this was another part of the charade. I knew that the more people they involved in the ploy, the more money they would expect to distribute among them. While driving myself throughout the city, I had learned to "dash" police officers and traffic directors with small bills to avoid tickets, but I could not fathom how much money this kind of bribe would require. So, I continued playing naive to that option, and I tried instead to build rapport in pidgin. I asked the officials about their hometowns and described how I had traveled to see each of those areas, how I shared friends from their villages, and so on, reframing my status from a presumed wealthy foreigner to a familiar and unsalaried student. It all seemed hopeless, until the senior officer in the room finally looked up from the newspaper he was reading and offered to look at the passport. "Ah," he said, "this one, it supersedes this one. New York made a mistake, but this is the most important, so she can go."

I breathed a huge sigh of relief as he sent me down the hall with another officer to the stamp office. The clerk there refused yet again to validate the visa. He had warned me not to go that morning, and here I was, not listening to him. I tried to explain the other officers' conclusions, but he refused, returning me back to them and then arguing some more. Finally, we all collected in the dim breezeway behind his office, the officers for me and the officers against me. I was speaking in pidgin, trying to clarify the technical problem on the visa and the assessment of the senior officer. Their facial expressions suggested some disdain for my claims, but one of them asked me where I learned pidgin, and what else I knew of Nigeria—did I eat the food, see the country, and so on. Intrigued by my responses, the clerk asked if I was married, and when I said no, he asked if I would ever marry a Nigerian. "Yes, I would love to marry a Nigerian!" I affirmed eagerly. Then I risked a joke. "Please, let me marry a Nigerian, so no more visa *wahala*!" This was the Nigerian pidgin word for trouble or hassle. "I'll marry you right now! Just bring the dowry and all of this will be solved. Yes-*o*!" I enthused, desperately. The clerk laughed and at last accepted the other officers' orders to stamp my passport. He came back to hand it over himself, sheepishly explaining that he gave me all he could—ninety days—and hoped that would be okay. "Very okay," I assured him.

These are the same men tasked with identifying the victims who would eventually end up in NAPTIP shelters, and those unwelcome interceptions must be understood within this broader scheme of harassment of women at the border and in state encounters more generally. While the securitization of borders has accelerated in late capitalism, these technologies are built into a long-standing system of authority and abuse that Nigerians know all too well, shaping their desire to migrate, their risk evaluation of informal routes, and their relative acquiescence to corruption and mistreatment at the hands of government officials. Like Joy and Chichi, my travel companions that day, the women at the shelter understand these games to be built into exchanges with the state, even when you are trying (and paying) to do everything right.

In this world of bureaucratic obfuscation, following formalities is not just inconvenient but impossible, blurring the line between regular and irregular movement altogether. Is travel licit when the papers are official but obtained and approved through arbitrary fees? What good are papers if distinguishing between valid and invalid documents required such interpretation and negotiation, as well as flirtation and familiarity? To engage formal routes, as I had insisted on doing, was clearly *less* reliable than crossing by the bush, as most people ordinarily did. As I tried to figure out the correct course of action, in the visa application, at the renewal office, and at the border, I continued to display my own naivety and bias as an American, expecting that such a clear course should exist, be transparent to all, and work in my favor.

These encounters typify many ordinary interactions with state officials in Nigeria, and they share much in common with the experiences of other migrants and travelers around the world. Anthropologist Maybritt Jill Alpes has argued that when you start from an assumption of state closure—that governments will try to stop your travel, rather than facilitate it—migrants' faith in travel brokers and high-risk routes seems a lot more sensible.[2] Consulates are widely known to take your money and still reject your visa. For people without birth certificates, education records, or bank accounts, even truthful claims can require counterfeit documents.

In this context of state closure, the principles of "orderly" movement that are championed in migration management regimes serve to condemn the mobility of ordinary people. Counselors' admonitions for women to go "independently" and signs urging migrants to "use regular routes" or "beware of strangers with attractive offers" are disingenuous. Formal options are closed to most people in

Nigeria, especially without the guidance of a paid broker to help navigate them. Only those with talent and connections can open those doors and only those with luck will pass through them successfully. Dismissing illicit efforts as irrational or irresponsible obscures the fact that no other options are available. In the face of great odds against them, these messages pathologize migrants' determination, resourcefulness, and courage as hazards—hazards to the migrants themselves, and hazards to the nation at large.

TRAFFICKING IN HONOR

From Joy's harassment for carrying condoms to my own facetious promises of marriage, these encounters were also profoundly gendered. The officers approached us not only as women but also specifically as sexually available women, and in return we performed different modes of sexual honor—Joy expressing outrage at the insult to her decency, and I avowing a plan to marry and marry locally. Women traveling alone have long received this kind of unwelcome attention, whether in the guise of protection or intimidation or both. Indeed, the consistency of this kind of harassment suggests it is not an aberration but a feature built into the system, functioning not only to govern international migration but also to police women's mobility and sexuality.

In *Entry Denied*, Eithne Luibhéid describes the US government's history of barring female migrants for reasons related to sexuality, including their being suspected lesbians, prostitutes, pregnant women, and others thought to be "immoral." She describes how the Page Law of 1875 specifically targeted Asian prostitutes but effectively barred all young Chinese women from entering the United States. "Even when these acts had not actually taken place," she observes, "the fear that they might occur was grounds for exclusion."[3] These fears are useful in reminding us that, unlike other state review processes, border inspection is often based on risk and hypothetical harms, rather than actual wrongdoing. Luibhéid argues that these exclusions are not only a practical concern (protecting the men who would be threatened by such women, if not the women themselves) but also a symbolic one—shaping the nation by determining who belongs and why.[4]

Nigeria likewise shares a long history of policing national honor by policing migrant women. In 1939, the leader of a Nigerian diaspora group named Prince Eikineh petitioned the colonial government to address the problem of migrant women "harlots," for fear that they were an embarrassment to the community and all of Nigeria:

> The Gold Coast men and women who have not travelled farther than their area believe that all the Nigerian women are harlots, and that it is a recognised custom of Nigeria. Things have grown to diggy height.

Gold Coast has become a place of Nigerian refuge. Not only grown-up women from Nigeria were to be found here for this nefarious traffic of the flesh but also girls under age are kidnapped and brought here as a training ground.[5]

As in other parts of Africa, groups like this collaborated with the state to deport migrant women who were framed as a threat to the dignity of Nigeria and of other Nigerian migrants.[6] Importantly, these demands arose from within the national community, rather than outside it.

Although catalyzed by a changing European migration agenda and accelerating Italian removal efforts, the deportation crisis in 1999–2001 raised these concerns within Nigeria once again. A renewed sense of patriotism and commitment to international relations under the new democratic regime magnified the stakes of this scourge on the national image. Obasanjo's government responded swiftly by building teams of specialized police forces to manage the return of deportees. These task forces subjected migrant women to a barrage of administrative, medical, and punitive measures to literally and figuratively remove them from society, including, most infamously, parading deportees through the streets of Benin City in ritualized performances of public humiliation.

Nigeria's internal efforts to police migrant women, and thereby manage the reputation crisis it saw as related, happened to coincide with a new global mandate to fight human trafficking, marked by the passage of both the United Nations Palermo Protocol and the US Trafficking Victims Protection Act in the year 2000. This global effort provided new rhetoric toward the same ends. Like much anti-trafficking propaganda, this handbill from the Ministry of Foreign Affairs addresses migrant women directly (see figure 10). "Be a good ambassador of our dear Land ... whenever ... wherever," it reads, suggesting that migrant sex workers and trafficking "victims" are themselves the bad ambassadors.[7] To "say no to trafficking" is to say no to the ostentatious display of the migrant woman's body, represented as scantily dressed and burdened with baggage. In shaming migrant women, the Nigerian government promotes ideas of the nation not only by who it lets in but also by who it lets out. It is only those good citizens, those "good ambassadors" who are qualified to represent the country abroad.

These expectations of good and bad citizenship were also written into Nigeria's original federal anti-trafficking legislation. The 2003 law outlawed human trafficking as well as all "foreign travel that promotes prostitution," with additional penalties for "any Nigerian citizen found guilty in any foreign country of an offence ... who thereby bring the name [of] Nigeria into disrepute."[8] But while written ostensibly to protect the national image, this law has had the ironic

FIGURE 10. "Be a Good Ambassador." Migrant women sex workers represent the poor ambassadors of Nigeria's Fourth Republic. Handbill produced by the Ministry of Foreign Affairs, Nigeria.

effect of further damaging it. It has rarely been enforced in Nigeria but has provided grounds for Nigerian migrants to claim asylum for double jeopardy, itself an embarrassment to the state.[9] Likewise, international reports of police harassment of possible trafficking victims further undermined the Nigeria's reputation as a promising new democracy. The Nigerian government needed new ways to govern the migrants it saw as deviant.

DISCIPLINE AND DESIRE

Those tools arrived in the form of other disciplinary components of the global anti-trafficking apparatus. Discourses of protection and prevention legitimized state interests in stopping women from migrating, and technologies of rescue and sheltering provided a more effective means than arrest and public harassment. As in the more overtly punitive regimes that preceded them, shelter rehabilitation programs still targeted the moral questions of women's mobility, but in the globally sanctioned modes of therapeutic intervention and education. These programs acted not on past traumas but on women's own ambitions, manifested in their desires to migrate again after release. In the name of vulnerability reduction, counselors questioned women's capacity for responsible decision making, dismissed their ambition as greed and materialism, and appropriated divine authority to support their judgments. They defined successful rehabilitation as the refusal of migrant sex work and the professed preference for a more modest life in Nigeria, and they "empowered" women who struck them as most committed to this path.

The idea of human trafficking derives power from the seemingly universal and self-evident abhorrence of the practice: it has been called "a blight on humanity," "a scourge on the nation," and "pure evil in our midst." The category "modern-day slavery" further amplifies these sentiments, inserting the imagery of historic chattel slavery into self-conceptions of liberal modernity.[10] However, the different political agendas present within the counter-trafficking landscape—those of neo-abolitionists, labor rights activists, and, importantly, border security advocates—reveal competing visions of justice and liberation. From the UN's Palermo Protocol to global NGO movements, these contradictions have normalized ambivalence in campaigns like NAPTIP's, where women are treated at once as victims and culprits, as innocent and guilty. These distinctions are further blurred in the shelter, where the risk of recidivism and vulnerability to retrafficking are virtually indistinguishable.

Nigeria's campaign against human trafficking differs from earlier reactions to the deportation crisis, such as parading deportees, publicly listing their HIV status, and shaming them in news media. But there are important continuities as well. The violent practices of arrest and detention were not eliminated but obscured with more publicly palatable rationales.[11] The project of moral correction was not abandoned but strengthened through counseling and vocational training. In short, the anti-trafficking framework levies shame on migrant women in new ways. Whether delivered as enlightenment, empowerment, or rehabilitation, the shelter is used to reform women's ideas of success, dignity, and freedom itself. These strategies are not unique to one shelter in Nigeria nor even to the anti-trafficking apparatus. Rather, they are part and parcel of a global regime of migration management that presents itself as neutral and orderly but in practice serves to police the deviant mobility of already marginalized people around the world—manifested in impossible bureaucracies, harassment at borders, and lauded anti-trafficking schemes alike.

EFFECTS

It is impossible to say whether women like Florence are, in the end, any better off for having been stopped at the Lagos airport or for being put through rehabilitation at the shelter. I think Florence would say it was for the best. During the first week at the shelter, I asked her to tell me about the fiancé she kept mentioning.

"His name is Desmond," she said, smiling softly, "and we will get married when we have the money. He even says that after we marry I can return to school and finish. I will settle down."

"You mean you won't travel?" I asked.

"No, I won't travel. Not after hearing stories like this from Mr. Ben," she said, gesturing to where he had sat across the hall. "They could deceive me, so it is better that I just marry. God will provide."

After she returned home, her days looked much like they did before traveling. Eventually she married Desmond, as she had always planned to do, and they now have two children whom she dotes on endlessly. The four of them live in the same single small room he has rented since Florence first came to the shelter, settled around an open-air courtyard off a busy street in Benin City, with shared cooking space and bathing grounds. Their room is adorned with framed posters of Jay-Z, Beyoncé, and Rihanna; another one features a large American-style mansion with multiple sports cars lined in front. Posed pictures from their traditional wedding, with coral bead crowns and extended family in rows, are pinned to the corners of the frames, next to first-birthday photos of the children and studio family portraits in coordinated polos. Desmond works several informal jobs to try to support the family, and Florence hopes she will get "something going" as soon as her youngest is finished breastfeeding.

They live mostly off money his mother sends from Italy.

Notes

INTRODUCTION

1. All names are pseudonyms and some biographical details have been altered to maintain the anonymity of study participants.

2. Nigerian Pidgin English is a creole language spoken across Nigeria and West Africa, especially in ethnically mixed areas like Benin City. It combines vocabulary and grammatical structures from English and local languages and is understood as an informal language (in pidgin it is called *brokun*, as in broken English). It is also a common tongue for music, comedy, and Nollywood film, and it is increasingly used in dedicated radio and news forums, including a dedicated BBC News channel.

3. William Walters describes this absolutism as "anti-policy"—comparing antitrafficking work to other policy platforms framed as in the negative as uniform prohibitions, such as anticorruption, antiracism, or the War on Poverty. He argues that this single negative framework can disguise the proliferation of policies offered as "anti," obscuring diverse political agendas under the common enemy of a single taken-for-granted bad thing. William Walters, "Anti-Policy and Anti-Politics: Critical Reflections on Certain Schemes to Govern Bad Things," *European Journal of Cultural Studies* 11, no. 3 (2008): 267–288.

4. Kathleen Barry, *Female Sexual Slavery* (New York: New York University Press, 1979); *The Prostitution of Sexuality* (New York: New York University Press, 1995); Sheila Jeffreys, *Anticlimax: A Feminist Perspective on the Sexual Revolution* (New York: New York University Press, 1991); *The Idea of Prostitution* (North Melbourne, Victoria: Spinifex Press, 2008); *The Industrial Vagina: The Political Economy of the Global Sex Trade* (New York: Routledge, 2009).

5. Jo Doezema argues that these relationships reproduce colonial-era projects whereby elite western feminists asserted status and power for themselves by advocating on behalf of the mythical suffering of third world prostitutes, specifically drawing on Victorian campaigns against prostitution in India. "Loose Women or Lost Women? The Re-Emergence of the Myth of White Slavery in Contemporary Discourses of Trafficking in Women," *Gender Issues* 18, no. 1 (1999): 23–50.; "Ouch! Western Feminists' 'Wounded Attachment' to the 'Third World Prostitute,'" *Feminist Review* 67 (2001): 16–38.

6. Jennifer Suchland, *Economies of Violence: Transnational Feminism, Postsocialism, and the Politics of Sex Trafficking* (Durham, NC: Duke University Press, 2016); Anne T. Gallagher, *The International Law of Human Trafficking* (New York: Cambridge University Press, 2010).

7. Kay B. Warren, "The 2000 UN Human Trafficking Protocol: Rights, Enforcement, Vulnerabilities," in *The Practice of Human Rights: Tracking Law between the Global and the Local*, ed. Mark Goodale and Sally Engle Merry (Cambridge: Cambridge University Press, 2007), 242–270.

8. Jo Doezema, "Forced to Choose: Beyond the Voluntary v. Forced Prostitution Dichotomy," in *Global Sex Workers: Rights, Resistance, and Redefinition*, ed. Kamala Kempadoo and Jo Doezema (New York: Routledge, 1998), 34–50; *Sex Slaves and Discourse Masters: The Construction of Trafficking* (New York: Zed Books, 2010).

9. Gretchen Soderlund, "Running from the Rescuers," *NWSA Journal* 17 (2005): 64–87.

10. This interrogation of messy contradictions broadly follows Michel Foucault's emphasis on discontinuities within discursive formations. Foucault, *The Archaeology of Knowledge* (New York: Vintage, 2010).

11. I agree with Jennifer Suchland regarding the harms of a myopic focus on definitions and individual choice in criticisms of anti-trafficking work. She argues, "We do not need a better definition of human trafficking. What we need is a more critical approach to the economic and social dynamics of trafficking as a symptom of—not as distinct from—our political and economic systems." Suchland, *Economies of Violence*, 5.

12. Emily L. Thuma, *All Our Trials: Prisons, Policing, and the Feminist Fight to End Violence* (Urbana: University of Illinois Press, 2019).

13. Kristin Bumiller, *In an Abusive State: How Neoliberalism Appropriated the Feminist Movement against Sexual Violence* (Durham, NC: Duke University Press, 2008).

14. The expanded prosecution of sex crimes and gender violence is, of course, only one part of a globally expanding system of incarceration known as the prison industrial complex. Angela Y. Davis, *Are Prisons Obsolete?* (New York: Seven Stories Press, 2003).

15. Elizabeth Bernstein, *Brokered Subjects: Sex, Trafficking, and the Politics of Freedom* (Chicago: University of Chicago Press, 2018).

16. Suchland, *Economies of Violence*.

17. Jennifer Musto, *Control and Protect: Collaboration, Carceral Protection, and Domestic Sex Trafficking in the United States* (Berkeley: University of California Press, 2016).

18. The human rights approach has also been manipulated for political gain. Jennifer Suchland documents how this critical edge of the human rights framework was weaponized in US political projects after the Cold War. That is, the United States used human trafficking and human rights accusations to suggest that post-Soviet states were economically aberrant parts of the capitalist world order, rather than take responsibility for the same kinds of exploitation seen within US borders. Suchland, *Economies of Violence*.

19. Juliet Stumpf, "The Crimmigration Crisis: Immigrants, Crime, and Sovereign Power," *American University Law Review* 56 (2006): 367–419.

20. Although widely presented as "waves," "floods," and other metaphors of demographic threat, the fears associated with increased migration, during this period and others, are not supported by evidence. Instead of reflecting any harm to receiving communities, these fears tend to reflect the successful consolidation of political power through xenophobia and political scapegoating. Leo R. Chavez, *Covering Immigration: Popular Images and Politics of the Nation* (Berkeley: University of California Press, 2001), and *The Latino Threat: Constructing Immigrants, Citizens, and the Nation* (Stanford: Stanford University Press, 2013); Douglas S. Massey, Jorge Durand, and Nolan J. Malone, *Beyond Smoke and Mirrors: Mexican Immigration in an Era of Economic Integration* (New York: Russell Sage Foundation, 2002); Suchland, *Economies of Violence*.

21. Didier Bigo, "Security and Immigration: Toward a Critique of the Governmentality of Unease," *Alternatives* 27, no. 1 (2002): 63–92.

22. Juliet Stumpf, "Crimmigration Crisis."

23. Jenna M. Loyd and Alison Mountz, *Boats, Borders, and Bases: Race, the Cold War, and the Rise of Migration Detention in the United States* (Oakland: University of California Press, 2018).

24. Gallagher, *International Law of Human Trafficking*.

25. A. W. Neal. "Securitization and Risk at the EU Border: The Origins of FRONTEX," *JCMS: Journal of Common Market Studies* 47 (2009): 333–356.

26. Maurizio Albuhari, *Crimes of Peace: Mediterranean Migrations at the World's Deadliest Border* (Philadelphia: University of Pennsylvania Press, 2015); Jason De Leon,

The Land of Open Graves: Living and Dying on the Migrant Trail (Oakland: University of California Press, 2015).

27. Wendy Chapkis, "Trafficking, Migration, and the Law: Protecting Innocents, Punishing Immigrants," *Gender & Society* 17 no. 6 (2003): 923–937; Hein de Haas, "The Myth of Invasion: The Inconvenient Realities of African Migration to Europe," *Third World Quarterly* 29, no. 7 (2008): 1305–1322; Maybritt Jill Alpes, *Brokering High-Risk Migration and Illegality in West Africa: Abroad at Any Cost* (New York: Routledge, 2016).

28. Wendy Chapkis, "Soft Glove, Punishing Fist: The Trafficking Victims Protection Act of 2000," in *Regulating Sex: The Politics of Intimacy and Identity*, ed. Elizabeth Bernstein and Laurie Schaffner (New York: Routledge, 2005), 51–66.

29. Didier Fassin, "Compassion and Repression: The Moral Economy of Immigration Policies in France, *Cultural Anthropology* 20, no. 3 (2005): 362–387.

30. Didier Fassin, "Policing Borders, Producing Boundaries. The Governmentality of Immigration in Dark Times," *Annual Review of Anthropology* 40, no. 1 (2011): 213–226.

31. Katherine Beckett and Naomi Murakawa, "Mapping the Shadow Carceral State: Toward an Institutionally Capacious Approach to Punishment," *Theoretical Criminology* 16, no. 2 (2012): 221–244.; Kevin Lewis O'Neill and Jatin Dua, "Captivity: A Provocation," *Public Culture* 30, no. 1 (2018): 3–18.

32. The International Organization for Migration (IOM) has developed a range of education campaigns, integration programs, professional trainings, and return recruitment efforts that teach people how to migrate according to established "orderly" state interests. In so doing, these programs render "disorderly" migration as a problem to be solved. Rutvica Andrijasevic and William Walters, "The International Organization for Migration and the International Government of Borders," *Environment and Planning: Society and Space* 28 (2010): 977–999; Martin Geiger and Antoine Pécoud, eds, *Disciplining the Transnational Mobility of People* (New York: Palgrave MacMillan, 2013).

33. Similar protection rhetoric is used to support the criminal prosecution of asylum seekers at the US southern border and the aggressive patrolling of the Mediterranean Sea by the EU agency Frontex. In this way, interventions targeting trafficking victims can resemble police action while also disavowing that likeness. William Walters, "Foucault and Frontiers: Notes on the Birth of the Humanitarian Border," in *Governmentality: Current Issues and Future Challenges*, ed. Ulrich Bröckling et al. (New York: Routledge, 2010), 138–164.

34. This pressure for poor countries to coordinate migration and development policies was made explicit in the European Union's 2002 Seville Summit, just two years after the Palermo Protocol was passed. It explicitly aimed to influence the migration policies of origin and transit countries through bilateral agreements addressing development policy, technical cooperation, and trade. Franck Düvell, "The Globalisation of Migration Control," *Open Democracy*, June 13, 2003.

35. For example, Menjívar argues that "outsourcing [of border controls] involves a series of extraterritorial activities in sending and in transit countries at the request of the more powerful receiving state," in a process that reveals the "buttressing of power imbalances between sending countries, on one hand, and transit and receiving countries, on the other." Cecilia Menjívar, "Immigration Law beyond Borders: Externalizing and Internalizing Border Controls in an Era of Securitization," *Annual Review of Law and Social Science* 10 (2014): 353–369.

36. This approach to reform projects comes from French philosopher Michel Foucault. He uses the term "government" to describe the "conduct of conduct," tracing historical shifts in the arts of governing from emphasizing sovereign power, or the authority to make and impose law, to other ways of influencing behavior. The history of punishment, he argues, evolves from violent acts on the body to more diffuse technologies of control

he calls *discipline*. This is the kind of control we can observe in Nigeria's anti-trafficking schemes. Discipline developed not only in prisons but also in hospitals, schools, factories, and armies, which, like the shelter, are all equipped with their own architecture and rituals of surveillance. They produce docile bodies through the organization of time, space, and reality itself, culminating in the ideal of self-discipline and eliminating the need for external coercion altogether. Michel Foucault, *Discipline and Punish: The Birth of the Prison* (New York: Vintage, 1995).

37. In feminist philosophy, this epistemological claim is called standpoint theory and is associated with Black feminism, whereas anthropologists have variously explored its relevance through subaltern and postcolonial theory. Both traditions interrogate power dynamics between scholars and their interlocutors, questioning claims to objectivity that were historically associated with positions of privilege and instead favoring a politically engaged, socially situated practice of knowledge production.

38. For accounts of migration in the region, see Alpes, *Brokering High-Risk Migration*, and Plambech, "Sex, Deportation, and Rescue."

39. Because Benin City is situated between major Yoruba and Igbo linguistic regions and is home to a number of smaller ethnic groups, Nigerian pidgin is spoken widely as a lingua franca and as a first language in the home. I gained proficiency in pidgin over the course of my research and conducted most interviews in a combination of pidgin and formal English.

40. Chi Adanna Mgbako, *To Live Freely in this World: Sex Worker Activism in Africa* (New York: New York University, 2016); Ntokozo Yingwana, "'We Fit in the Society by Force': Sex Work and Feminism in Africa," *Meridians* 17, no. 2 (2018): 279–295.

41. Simanti Dasgupta, "Sovereign Silence: Immoral Traffic (Prevention) Act and Legalizing Sex Work in Sonagachi," *Political and Legal Anthropology Review* 37, no. 1 (2014): 109–125.

42. Kamala Kempadoo and Jo Doezema, *Global Sex Workers*.

43. Denise Brennan, *Life Interrupted: Trafficking into Forced Labor in the United States* (Durham, NC: Duke University, 2014).

44. I fully expect that some readers will be unsatisfied with this choice, and I refer them to the invaluable scholarship by anthropologists who work in this region and focus on these and other related questions. Alpes, *Brokering High-Risk Migration;* Clementina Osezua, "Changing Status of Women and the Phenomenon Trafficking of Women for Transactional Sex in Nigeria: A Qualitative Analysis," *Journal of International Women's Studies* 14, no. 3 (2013): 14–30; Sine Plambech, "Sex, Deportation and Rescue: Economies of Migration among Nigerian Sex Workers," *Feminist Economics* 23, no. 3 (2017): 134–159.

1. CRISIS

1. "Up against Sexport," *The News* (Lagos), August 8, 2000.

2. Stanley Cohen, *Folk Devils and Moral Panics* (New York: Routledge, 1972).

3. The Kingdom of Benin's trading presence along the West African coastline prompted the naming of the Bight of Benin inside the Gulf of Guinea. This is how the Republic of Benin, the modern-day nation-state and Nigeria's neighbor to the west, gets its name—not to be confused with Benin City or the historical Kingdom of Benin, located in modern-day Nigeria.

4. For example, the Portuguese ship captain Lourenço Pinto provided this account in 1691: "According to the testimony of this captain, Great Benin, where the king resides, is larger than Lisbon; all the streets run straight and as far as the eye can see. The houses are large, especially that of the king, which is richly decorated and has fine columns. The

city is wealthy and industrious. It is so well governed that theft is unknown and the people live in such security that they have no doors on their houses." Quoted in Alan Ryder, *Benin and the Europeans, 1485–1897* (London: Longmans, 1969), 113.

5. For an account of the ongoing barriers to repatriating these items, see Dan Hicks, *The Brutish Museum: The Benin Bronzes, Colonial Violence and Cultural Restitution* (London: Pluto Press, 2020).

6. Etannibi E. O. Alemika, "Policing and Perceptions of Police in Nigeria," *Police Studies: The International Review of Police Development* 11, no. 4 (1988): 161–176, and "Colonialism, State and Policing in Nigeria," *Crime, Law and Social Change* 20 (1993): 187–219.

7. Toyin Falola and Matthew M Heaton, *A History of Nigeria* (New York: Cambridge University Press, 2008).

8. Amina Mama, "Sheroes and Villains: Conceptualizing Colonial and Contemporary Violence against Women in Africa," in *Feminist Genealogies, Colonial Legacies, Democratic Futures*, ed. M. Jacqui Alexander and Chandra Talpade Mohanty (New York: Routledge, 1997); C. Dennis, "Women and the State in Nigeria: The Case of the Federal Military Government," in *Women, State, and Ideology: Studies from Africa and Asia*, ed. Haleh Afshar (London: SUNY Press, 1987), 13–27.

9. Mbembe, *On the Postcolony.*

10. Falola and Heaton, *A History of Nigeria*, 183.

11. Smith, *A Culture of Corruption*, 100.

12. Jean-François Bayart calls this process extraversion; *The State in Africa: The Politics of the Belly* (Cambridge: Polity, 2009).

13. Patience Elabor-Idemudia, "Nigeria: Agricultural Exports and Compensatory Schemes—Rural Women's Production Re-Sources and Quality of Life," in *Mortgaging Women's Lives: Feminist Critiques of Structural Adjustment*, ed. Pamela Sparr (London: Palgrave Macmillan, 1994), 134–164.

14. Amina Mama, "Khaki in the Family: Gender Discourses and Militarism in Nigeria," *African Studies Review* 41, no. 2 (1998): 1–17.

15. Philomina Okeke, "First Lady Syndrome: The (En)Gendering of Bureaucratic Corruption in Nigeria," *Codesria Bulletin* 3, no. 4 (1998): 16–19.

16. Mama, "Khaki in the Family."

17. European beads are known as *ivie ebo* in Edo and were prominently featured in ceremonial dress for the Oba, as well as for other chiefs and wealthy elites; they also decorated many items stolen from the Oba during the punitive mission of 1897. See Barbara Plankensteiner, ed., *Benin Kings and Ritutals: Court Arts from Nigeria* (Ghent: Snoek & Museum für Völkerkunde, 2007); Ryder, *Benin and the Europeans, 1485–1897*, 255, 276; Susan Tontore, "Precious Red Coral: Markets and Meanings," *Beads* 16, no. 4 (2004): 3–16.

18. Jeffrey E. Cole and Sally S. Booth, *Dirty Work: Immigrants, Domestic Service, Agriculture, and Prostitution in Sicily* (Lanham, MD: Lexington Books, 2007); Jørgen Carling, *Migration, Human Smuggling and Trafficking from Nigeria to Europe* (Geneva: International Organization for Migration, 2006).

19. Some reports trace the Italian market demand for African sex workers in the late 1980s to the European HIV crisis, which at the time was associated with local women and drug users. For an overall picture, see C. E. E. Okojie et al., *Report of Field Survey in Edo State, Nigeria* (Torino: United Nations Interregional Crime and Justice Research Institute, 2003).

20. A 1997 news article reported on this trend under the headline, "Executive Prostitutes Storm Edo . . . as AIDS Fear Grips Residents." It detailed how their families were "putting finishing touches to buying up houses and other needed articles to the tune of millions of naira, in preparation for the arrival of their daughters." It reported that "the expected women of easy virtue have been abroad for over a decade now, and

have concluded plan[s] to retire from this profession of old, to return home to enjoy the wealth they have amassed"—up to $3,500 daily, earned in Italy, Belgium, Spain, Portugal, and Thailand, totaling up to 60 million naira in fixed accounts, in addition to exotic cars, "ranging from the Honda Accord series to the Mercedes Benz and BMW ranges." Vincent Adeyoke, *Weekend Third Eye*, February 2, 1997.

21. Adeyoke, *Weekend Third Eye*.

22. Jacqueline Berman, "(Un)Popular Strangers and Crises (Un)Bounded: Discourses of Sex-Trafficking, the European Political Community and the Panicked State of the Modern State," *European Journal of International Relations* 9, no. 1 (2003): 37–86; Rutvica Andrijasevic, *Migration, Agency, and Citizenship in Sex Trafficking* (New York: Palgrave Macmillan, 2010).

23. Hein de Haas, "The Myth of Invasion: The Inconvenient Realities of African Migration to Europe," *Third World Quarterly* 29, no. 7 (2008): 1305–1322.

24. Adrian Favell and Randall Hansen, "Markets against Politics: Migration, EU Enlargement and the Idea of Europe," *Journal of Ethnic and Migration Studies* 28, no. 4 (2002): 581–601.

25. Peter Andreas, "The Escalation of U.S. Immigration Control in the Post-NAFTA Era," *Political Science Quarterly* 113 (1998): 591–601.

26. For example, a December 1999 *Punch News* article reports 64 women deported from Italy in March 1999 (58 from "Bini Kingdom"), 84 deported in October and November (71 from Edo State), and 85 deported in December (61 from Edo State). The article closes with a statement from the Italian ambassador to Nigeria, who "said his country was determined to flush out illegal immigrants especially prostitutes from Italy." Hortatious Egua, "235 Prostitutes Deported from Italy in Nine Months," *Punch*, December 12, 1999.

27. Carling, *Migration, Human Smuggling and Trafficking*.

28. Sine Plambech, "Sex, Deportation and Rescue: Economies of Migration among Nigerian Sex Workers," *Feminist Economics* 23, no. 3 (2017): 134–159.

29. Nicholas De Genova, *Working the Boundaries: Race, Space, and "Illegality" in Mexican Chicago* (Durham, NC: Duke University Press, 2005).

30. Stephen Ellis, "West Africa's International Drug Trade." *African Affairs* 108, no. 431 (2009): 171–196.

31. Based in part on her work in Italy, Attah was named Nigeria's first Minister of Woman Affairs in 1995, and in 1996 she represented Nigeria at the first world congress for sexual exploitation in Stockholm, Sweden. She continued advocating for greater attention to the crisis in trafficking, bringing the concern to the attention of the Nigerian delegation to the 63rd Interpol General Assembly in 1997, where she is said to have "informed them of the nuisance level to which the African women, especially Nigerians, were constituting themselves," urging the police to put in place necessary machinery to tackle the problem back home. Okojie et al., *Report of Field Survey in Edo State*, 15.

32. Duro Ikhazuagbe, "Prostitution: The Scourge of a Nation," *Post Express on Saturday*, December 22, 2001.

33. Samuel Abasilim, "10,000 out of 40,000 Nigerians in Italy Are Prostitutes," *Daily Times*, June 23, 2000.

34. Femi Ojo-Ade, *Death of a Myth: Critical Essays on Nigeria* (Trenton, NJ: Africa World Press, 2001), 37.

35. Daniel Jordan Smith, *A Culture of Corruption: Everyday Deception and Popular Discontent in Nigeria* (Princeton, NJ: Princeton University Press, 2007); Ebenezer Obadare, *Humor, Silence, and Civil Society in Nigeria* (Rochester, NY: University of Rochester Press, 2016).

36. David Fitzgerald, *A Nation of Emigrants: How Mexico Manages Its Migration* (Berkeley: University of California Press, 2008).

37. Taiwo Adisa, "Sex War in Benin," *The News* (Lagos), June 21, 1999.

38. Nira Yuval-Davis, *Gender and Nation* (London: Sage, 1997).

39. Cinzia Solari, "'Prostitutes' and 'Defectors': How the Ukrainian State Constructs Women Emigrants to Italy and the USA," *Journal of Ethnic and Migration Studies* 11, no. 40 (2014): 1817–1835.

40. The first US Trafficking in Persons (TIP) Report, published by the US Department of State in 2001, described these activities approvingly as "facilitating the repatriation" of more than four hundred women in two years.

41. Gabriel Orok and Moses Uchendu, "AIDS Scare at Force CID," *P.M. News* (Lagos), December 17, 1999.

42. Gabriel Orok, "2 Women Deported from Italy Test Positive for HIV Status," *P.M. News* (Lagos), October 4, 2000.

43. Gabriel Orok, "Nigerian Deportees Pregnant in Detention," *P.M. News* (Lagos), April 23, 1999.

44. Gabriel Orok, "Italy Deports More Nigerian Prostitutes" *P.M. News* (Lagos), November 20, 2000.

45. Daniel Jordan Smith, *AIDS Doesn't Show Its Face: Inequality, Morality, and Social Change in Nigeria* (Chicago: University of Chicago, 2014).

46. "Nigerian Authorities Worry over International Prostitution Rings," *All Africa News Agency*, June 5, 2000.

47. Adaeze Onyeka, "Italy Deports 350 Nigerian Girls," *P.M. News (Lagos)*, November 18, 1999.

48. Victor Ofure Osehobo. "New War on Sexport," *Tempo* (Lagos), December 16, 1999.

49. Clementina Osezua, "Changing Status of Women and the Phenomenon of Trafficking of Women for Transactional Sex in Nigeria: A Qualitative Analysis," *Journal of International Women's Studies* 14, no. 3 (2013): 24.

50. Clementina Osezua, "Transmogrified Religious Systems and the Phenomenon of Sex Trafficking among the Benin People of Southern Nigeria," *AFRREV IJAH: An International Journal of Arts and Humanities* 2, no. 3 (2014): 20–35.

51. Abdulmumini A. Oba, "Juju Oaths in Customary Law Arbitration and their Legal Validity in Nigerian Courts," *Journal of African Law* 52 (2008): 139–158.

52. In May 2018, the Oba of Benin placed a curse on all human traffickers, freeing victims from any oaths they may have taken and condemning all forms of illegal migration.

53. Sine Plambech, "God Brought You Home: Deportation as Moral Governance in the Lives of Nigerian Sex Worker Migrants," *Journal of Ethnic and Migration Studies* 43, no. 13 (2017): 2211–2227.

54. Oluwakemi A. Adesina, "Between Culture and Poverty: The Queen Mother Phenomenon and the Edo International Sex Trade," *Humanities Review Journal* 5, no. 1 (2005): 40.

55. Andrew Apter, *The Pan-African Nation: Oil and the Spectacle of Culture in Nigeria* (Chicago: University of Chicago, 2005).

56. "About Our Logo: Rebirth of the Legacy of a Dignified Mother and Queen," http://www.idia-renaissance.org, accessed November 2020.

57. Adesina, "Between Culture and Poverty," 41.

58. The governor of Edo State went even further, threatening to publish the names, birthdates, addresses, and family of known sex workers in the region. Victor Ofure Osehobo. "New War on Sexport," *Tempo* (Lagos), December 16, 1999.

59. "3,000 Prostitutes Await Deportation in Italy," *Pan African News Agency,* September 14, 2000.

60. Taiwo Adisa, "Sex War in Benin," *The News* (Lagos), June 21, 1999.

61. This spectacle again recalls the public performance of state power in chain gangs described by Michel Foucault and in political executions described by Achille Mbembe. Michel Foucault, *Discipline and Punish: The Birth of the Prison* (New York: Vintage, 1995); Achille Mbembe, *On the Postcolony* (Berkeley: University of California Press, 2001).

62. Gabriel Orok, "8 Deportees Test HIV Positive," *P.M. News* (Lagos), April 19, 2001.

63. Dan Ede, "Lending a Helping Hand: The Wives of the President and the Vice President Throw their Weight behind their Spouses through Humanitarian Projects," *Policy* (Nigeria), March 4–10, 2002. Excerpted in Josiah Emerole, ed. *Amazing Crusade: Media Portrait of Titi Atiku Abubakar War against Human Trafficking* (Abuja: Women Trafficking and Child Labour Eradication Foundation, 2002), 76.

64. FGM was not popularly thought of as a significant problem in Nigeria, in part because the majority of women who have experienced FGM were not aware it had been done to them. M. U. Mandera, "Female Genital Mutilation in Nigeria," *International Journal of Gynecology and Obstetrics* 84, no. 3 (2004): 291–298.

65. Jean Comaroff, "Beyond Bare Life: AIDS, (Bio)Politics, and the Neoliberal Order," *Public Culture* 19, no. 1 (2007): 211.

66. Campaigns against FGM catalyzed international funding for women's movements and NGOs across Africa during this time, reflecting increased Western attention a time when the practice was already waning. Saida Hodžić, *The Twilight of Cutting: African Activism and Life after NGOs* (Berkeley: University of California Press, 2016).

67. Pietro Vulpiani, "Migrant and Refugee Women, Scaremongering and Afterthoughts on Female Genital Mutilations," *Gender Forum* 66 (2017): 477–519; Anouk Guiné and Francisco Javier Moreno Fuentes, "Engendering Redistribution, Recognition, and Representation: The Case of Female Genital Mutilation (FGM) in the United Kingdom and France," *Politics & Society* 45, no. 3 (2007): 26–49.

68. "My First Contact with Italo Girls," *Punch* (Lagos), October 20, 2001, reprinted in Emerole, *Amazing Crusade,* 55.

69. "Atiku's Wife Blames Women for Moral Decadence," *Punch* (Lagos), August 13, 1999, reprinted in Emerole, *Amazing Crusade,* 6.

70. Kazeem Ugbodaga and Uyense Thomas, "Atiku's Wife Wants Cultism, Prostitution Stamped Out," reprinted in Emerole, *Amazing Crusade,* 9.

71. Titi Abubakar, "The Role of the Rule of Law in Abolishing Modern Slavery: Controlling the Global Sex Trade," Proceedings from The Rule of Law in the Global Village: Issues of Sovereignty and Universality, Symposium on the occasion of the signing of the UN Convention against Transnational Organised Crime. Palermo, Italy, December 12–14, 2000; see also "Need for Common Response to Transnational Crimes Discussed at Symposium on Rule of Law in Global Village," United Nations Press Release, UNIS/CP/388, December 14, 2000.

72. Abubakar published a collection of press clippings from these efforts titled *Amazing Crusade.* News stories from this publication are cited throughout this chapter.

73. Suleiman Mohammed, "The Face of Human Trafficking," *Daily Trust,* September 5, 2001, reprinted in Emerole, *Amazing Crusade,* 59.

74. Yomi Odunuga, "Human Trafficking: We'll Rescue Nigerian Victims," *Punch,* August 23, 2001, reprinted in Emerole, *Amazing Crusade,* 58.

75. Opportunities for these collaborations grew as wealthier, migrant-receiving governments expanded border control efforts well beyond sites of crossing; these efforts were often facilitated by the International Organization for Migration (IOM) and included human trafficking prevention and anti-smuggling operations. Rutvica Andrijasevic and

William Walters, "The International Organization for Migration and the International Government of Borders," *Environment and Planning: Society and Space* 28 (2010): 977–999; Ruben Andersson, *Illegality, Inc: Clandestine Migration and the Business of Bordering Europe* (Berkeley: University of California, 2014).

76. Chris Anucha, "Why We Treat Deportees as VIPs," *This Day*, August 7, 2002.

77. Chris Anucha, "War against Human Trafficking: The Immigration Imperative," *This Day*, December 2, 2002.

2. DETENTION

1. Trafficking in Persons (Prohibition) Enforcement and Administration Act 2003, Sections 50–51.

2. The 2008 National Policy on Protection and Assistance for Trafficked Persons is even more explicit, stating directly, "A victim shall not be compelled to stay in a shelter to undergo rehabilitation" (22).

3. The full statement ties this mandate directly to victims' resistance to intervention and a necessary therapeutic purpose: "Most of the victims that we receive think we are meddling into their lives. Just a handful of them come back sober. So, what you experience is that you are working for people who [you] think you are trying to help but they end up fighting with you. . . . We thank God that we put in an effort and that is why we insist that victims that come back must stay for at least six weeks in our shelters whether they like or not in order for us to condition their behaviors and to prepare them for their expected new life. When we counsel them and tell them of the experience of some of the unlucky ones, they begin to see reasons with us and are ready to receive our rehabilitation package." *NAPTIP News* 2, no 2 (Aug–Oct 2010).

4. Anne T. Gallagher and Elaine Pearson, "The High Cost of Freedom: A Legal and Policy Analysis of Shelter Detention for Victims of Trafficking," *Human Rights Quarterly* 32, no. 1 (2010): 73–114.

5. Maggy Lee, "Gendered Discipline and Protective Custody of Trafficking Victims in Asia," *Punishment & Society* 16, no. 2 (2014): 206–222.

6. Gretchen Soderlund describes how "shelter escapes" are normalized by both safe house managers and international journalists reporting on human trafficking, who impose assumptions about captivity and freedom that ought to be challenged by women's regular resistance to so-called rescue and rehabilitation. Soderlund, "Running from the Rescuers," *NWSA Journal* 17 (2005): 64–87.

7. According to a report commissioned by USAID, the Nigerian government leased the building at no cost to NAPTIP for ten years. USAID and the Italian government provided funds to renovate the space, and the UN-affiliated International Organization for Migration (IOM) funded initial operation costs. NAPTIP has run the space independently from January 2005 onward. Chemonics International, *Nigeria Anti-Trafficking Assessment, April 11–27, 2005* (Washington DC: USAID).

8. Mike Dottridge, "Trafficking in Children in West and Central Africa," *Gender and Development* 10, no. 1 (2010): 38–42.

9. Liza Buchbinder, "Ranking States: Tracking the State Effect in West African Anti-trafficking Campaigns," in *Trafficking in Slavery's Wake Law and the Experience of Women and Children in Africa*, ed. Benjamin N. Lawrance and Richard L. Roberts (Athens: Ohio University Press, 2012).

10. Anti-trafficking campaigns against child labor invoke different assumptions about labor and freedom than those targeting sex work, but they still obscure the structural causes of inequality and the experiences of child labor migrants. Sam Okyere, "'Shock and Awe': A Critique of the Ghana-Centric Child Trafficking Discourse," *Anti-Trafficking*

Review 9 (2017): 92–105; Jessaca Leinaweaver, *The Circulation of Children: Kinship, Adoption, and Morality in Andean Peru* (Durham, NC: Duke University, 2008).

11. Aderenti Adepoju, "Creating a Borderless West Africa: Constraints and Prospects for Intra-Regional Migration," in *Migration without Borders: Essays on the Free Movement of People*, ed. Antoine Pécoud and Paul de Guchteneire (New York: Bergahn Books, 2007).

12. Charles Piot, "The 'Right' to Be Trafficked," *Indiana Journal of Global Legal Studies* 18, no. 1 (2011): 199–210.

13. My observations are consistent with specific figures and general comments in the US Department of State's annual Trafficking in Persons Reports emphasizing that NAPTIP's shelters were underutilized since 2005.

14. Saheed Aderinto, *When Sex Threatened the State: Illicit Sexuality, Nationalism, and Politics in Colonial Nigeria, 1900–1958* (Chicago: University of Illinois, 2015).

15. "New War on Sexport," *Tempo* (Lagos), December 16, 1999.

16. "Immigration Raises Taskforce On Deportees, Human Trafficking," *This Day*, January 15, 2002.

17. Chris Anucha, "War against Human Trafficking: The Immigration Imperative," *This Day*, December 4, 2002.

18. "Teenagers from Edo State Rescued from Slavery in Mali," *Nigeria News*, October 5, 2010.

19. "Teenagers from Edo State Rescued from Slavery in Mali."

20. Janie Chuang, "The United States as Global Sheriff: Using Unilateral Sanctions to Combat Human Trafficking," *Michigan Journal of International Law* 27 (2006): 437–494.

21. The United States was excluded from the annual reports until the tenth anniversary edition, released in June 2010.

22. Anne T. Gallagher, *The International Law of Human Trafficking* (New York: Cambridge University Press, 2010); Sally Engle Merry, *The Seductions of Quantification: Measuring Human Rights, Gender Violence, and Sex Trafficking* (Chicago: University of Chicago, 2016).

23. As Gallagher and Pearson point out, this does not require open corruption or neglect: "Even absent manipulative intent, human rights can very easily become a casualty of states' eagerness to demonstrate their anti-trafficking credentials to others. In the current international climate, which is largely dominated by an aggressive unilateral monitoring regime, the compulsion to be viewed as doing something about trafficking is strong and universal. Against this backdrop, shelter detention is one of a growing number of potentially problematic practices that are linked to, and justified by, the anti-trafficking imperative." Gallagher and Pearson, "The High Cost of Freedom," 80.

24. Gallagher and Pearson, "The High Cost of Freedom," 80.

25. Because women at the shelter were effectively under investigation by the government, I avoided direct questions about their travel arrangements when they did not independently volunteer such accounts. Anthropologists Plambech and Alpes offer these narratives from women brokering these arrangements in Benin City and in nearby Cameroon, respectively. Sine Plambech, "Sex, Deportation and Rescue: Economies of Migration among Nigerian Sex Workers," *Feminist Economics* 23, no. 3 (2017): 134–159; Maybritt Jill Alpes, *Brokering High-Risk Migration and Illegality in West Africa: Abroad at Any Cost* (New York: Routledge, 2016).

26. Preemptive intervention originates in security technologies that target "pre-crime," as opposed to policing apparatuses that target crimes already committed. These technologies have been especially important in antiterrorism work, and their use accelerated after the 9/11 attacks, spreading from intelligence operations to other kinds of policing, border control, and security efforts. Lucia Zedner, "Pre-Crime and Post-

Criminology?" *Theoretical Criminology* 11, no. 2 (2007); Jude McCulloch and Sharon Pickering, eds., *Borders and Crime: Pre-Crime, Mobility and Serious Harm in an Age of Globalization* (New York: Palgrave Macmillan, 2012).

27. Alpes shows how these starting assumptions about "closure" are embedded in the language used by aspiring migrants, who look for special "openings" or "lines" to overcome closure, a mere chance for success where failure is still accepted as a likely outcome. Alpes, *Brokering High-Risk Migration*, 16.

28. Titi Abubakar, "The Role of the Rule of Law in Abolishing Modern Slavery: Controlling the Global Sex Trade," in *Proceedings from The Rule of Law in the Global Village: Issues of Sovereignty and Universality, Symposium on the Occasion of the Signing of the UN Convention against Transnational Organised Crime*, Palermo, Italy, December 12–14, 2000.

29. Chi Adanna Mgbako, *To Live Freely in this World: Sex Worker Activism in Africa* (New York: New York University, 2016).

30. Article 5 ("Criminalization") of the Palermo Protocol prohibits attempts at trafficking and participating as an accomplice, as follows:

2. Each State Party shall also adopt such legislative and other measures as may be necessary to establish as criminal offences:
(a) Subject to the basic concepts of its legal system, attempting to commit an offence established in accordance with paragraph 1 of this article;
(b) Participating as an accomplice in an offence established in accordance with paragraph 1 of this article; and
(c) Organizing or directing other persons to commit an offence established in accordance with paragraph 1 of this article.

UN General Assembly, Protocol to Prevent, Suppress and Punish Trafficking in Persons, Especially Women and Children, Supplementing the United Nations Convention against Transnational Organized Crime, Resolution 55/25 (November 15, 2000).

31. Victoria Ijeoma Nwogu, "Nigeria," in *Collateral Damage: The Impact of Anti-Trafficking Measures on Human Rights around the World* (Bangkok: Global Alliance against Traffic in Women, 2007), 142.

32. Alpes, *Brokering High-Risk Migration*.

33. Sine Plambech, "Between 'Victims' and 'Criminals': Rescue, Deportation, and Everyday Violence among Nigerian Migrants," *Social Politics* 21, no. 3 (2014): 395.

34. Lise Bjerkan and Linda Dyrlid, "A Sheltered Life," in *A Life of One's Own: Rehabilitation of Victims of Trafficking for Sexual Exploitation*, ed. Lise Bjerkan (Norway: Fafo, 2005); Gallagher and Pearson, "The High Cost of Freedom"; Rebecca Surtees, *Why Shelters? Considering Residential Approaches to Assistance* (Vienna: NEXUS Institute to Combat Human Trafficking, 2008).

35. Daniel Jordan Smith, *A Culture of Corruption: Everyday Deception and Popular Discontent in Nigeria* (Princeton, NJ: Princeton University Press, 2007).

36. Wale Adebanwi, "My Book Should Provoke a Conversation—Chimamanda Ngozi," *News* (Nigeria), January 9, 2007.

37. Ebenezer Obadare and Wale Adebanwi, *Encountering the Nigerian State* (New York: Palgrave Macmillan, 2010).

38. Ruth Marshall, *Political Spiritualities: The Pentecostal Revolution in Nigeria* (Chicago: University of Chicago, 2009), 209.

39. Jørgen Carling, "Migration in the Age of Involuntary Immobility: Theoretical Reflections and Cape Verdean Experiences," *Journal of Ethnic and Migration Studies* 28, no. 1 (2002): 5–42.

3. VULNERABILITY REDUCTION

1. J. Abdulmalik, L. Kola, and O. Gureje, "Mental Health System Governance in Nigeria: Challenges, Opportunities and Strategies for Improvement," *Global Mental Health* 3 (2016): e9.

2. Didier Fassin and Richard Rechtman, *The Empire of Trauma: An Inquiry into the Condition of Victimhood* (Princeton, NJ: Princeton University Press, 2009), 187–188.

3. Ike Anya, "People Don't Get Depressed in Nigeria," *Granta*, September 5, 2012; Bola Ola et al., "The State of Readiness of Lagos State Primary Health Care Physicians to Embrace the Care of Depression in Nigeria," *Community Mental Health* 50 (2014): 239–244.

4. The 2010 US TIP Report made this observation while providing Nigeria a top Tier One ranking overall. It was also consistent with my own observations over the same period. Department of State, US TIP Report, 2010, 257.

5. These differences are exaggerated further in the move toward quantifiable metrics for compliance to international norms, especially figures that dilute complex empirical data and categorical rankings into composite indicators. Comparisons across composite figures are easy to make, but they provide little meaningful insight to multifaceted political realities. Sally Engle Merry, *The Seductions of Quantification: Measuring Human Rights, Gender Violence, and Sex Trafficking* (Chicago: University of Chicago Press, 2016).

6. Andrew M. Jefferson, "Reforming Nigerian Prisons: Rehabilitating a 'Deviant' State," *British Journal of Criminology* 45, no. 4 (2005): 487–503; and "Prison Officer Training and Practice in Nigeria," *Punishment & Society* 9, no. 3 (2007): 253–269.

7. Jefferson, "Prison Officer Training," 254.

8. Anette Brunovskis and Rebecca Surtees, "Agency or Illness—The Conceptualization of Trafficking," *Gender, Technology and Development* 12, no. 1 (2008): 63.

9. Lise Bjerkan and Linda Dyrlid, "A Sheltered Life," in *A Life of One's Own: Rehabilitation of Victims of Trafficking for Sexual Exploitation*, ed. Lise Bjerkan (Norway: Fafo, 2005), 142.

10. Michel Foucault observes a similar evolution in the mission of prison systems from punishment to correction, shifting the focus of punishment from the prior act of the crime to the ongoing question of the prisoner's soul. But where Foucault describes the discursive construction of a "dangerous" individual, the victim is constructed as a "vulnerable" one. Both embody a sense of liability, putting information about past offenses in the service of future risk reduction. Like the penitentiary, rehabilitation is designed as "an art of effects," where retrafficking, like recidivism, serves as the primary motivating logic for intervention. Foucault, *Discipline and Punish: The Birth of the Prison* (New York: Vintage, 1995), 125.

11. Gregory Bankoff points to how discourses of vulnerability and of development specifically have supported images of the world as "disaster prone" and "poverty-stricken," rather than challenging these narratives. Bankoff, "Rendering the World Unsafe: 'Vulnerability' as Western Discourse," *Disasters* 25, no. 1 (2005): 19–35.

12. This is not inherent to the concept of vulnerability but seems to be specific to its use in describing trafficking victims and women in sex work. For example, in India the term is used differently when describing sex trafficking victims in contrast to other forms of labor exploitation. Prahba Kotiswaran, "Vulnerability in Domestic Discourses on Trafficking: Lessons from the Indian Experience," *Feminist Legal Studies* 20, no. 3 (2012): 245–262.

13. Foucault argues that the sense of a problem is made real and reinforced by the very act of intervening on it. Just as the prison failed to eliminate crime but successfully produced the idea of delinquency, so has the shelter perhaps failed to eliminate trafficking but successfully produced the idea of vulnerability—a politically convenient expla-

nation for the persistent and ostensibly embarrassing emigration of young women to European sex industries. Foucault, *Discipline and Punish.*

14. Laura María Agustín, *Sex at the Margins: Migration, Labour Markets and the Rescue Industry* (London: Zed, 2007); Wendy Chapkis, "Trafficking, Migration, and the Law: Protecting Innocents, Punishing Immigrants," *Gender & Society* 17, no. 6 (2003): 923–937; Jo Doezema, "Loose Women or Lost Women? The Re-Emergence of the Myth of White Slavery in Contemporary Discourses of Trafficking in Women," *Gender Issues* 18, no. 1 (1999): 23–50.

15. College graduates in Nigeria are required to spend a year volunteering with the National Youth Corp before they begin full-time employment. They spend most of their time in professional internships, with the exception of one day each week designated for "community development," when some are assigned to a posting with the NAPTIP enlightenment branch.

16. The closest equivalent to a men's reform package is found outside the anti-trafficking apparatus in various programs to "rehabilitate" militants from the Niger Delta by exchanging weapons for amnesty and vocational training. Oluwatoyin O. Oluwaniyi, "Post-Amnesty Programme in the Niger Delta: Challenges and Prospects," *Conflict Trends* 4 (2011): 46–54.

17. Anne T. Gallagher and Elaine Pearson, "The High Cost of Freedom: A Legal and Policy Analysis of Shelter Detention for Victims of Trafficking," *Human Rights Quarterly* 32, no. 1 (2010): 78.

18. Benjamin Essang and Dele Okanlawon, "Dealing with Victims Is Very Challenging," *NAPTIP News* 2, no. 2 (August–October 2010), 39.

19. Ilana Feldman and Miriam Ticktin, eds, *In the Name of Humanity: The Government of Threat and Care* (Durham, NC: Duke University Press, 2010); Miriam Ticktin, *Casualties of Care: Immigration and the Politics of Humanitarianism in France* (Berkeley: University of California Press, 2011); Fassin and Rechtman, *The Empire of Trauma.*

20. Jo Doezema, *Sex Slaves and Discourse Masters: The Construction of Trafficking* (New York: Zed Books, 2010); Bridget Anderson and Rutvica Andrijasevic. "Sex, Slaves and Citizens: The Politics of Anti-Trafficking," *Soundings* 40 (2008): 135–145; Rutvica Andrijasevic, *Migration, Agency, and Citizenship in Sex Trafficking* (New York: Palgrave Macmillan, 2010); Denise Brennan, "Competing Claims of Victimhood? Foreign and Domestic Victims of Trafficking in the United States," *Sexuality Research and Social Policy* 5, no. 4 (2008): 45–61; Kamala Kempadoo, ed., *Trafficking and Prostitution Reconsidered: New Perspectives on Migration, Sex Work, and Human Rights* (Boulder: Paradigm, 2005).

21. Sine Plambech, "Between 'Victims' and 'Criminals': Rescue, Deportation, and Everyday Violence among Nigerian Migrants," *Social Politics* 21, no. 3 (2014): 390.

22. As a condition of my access to the rehabilitation shelter, I did not observe or participate in investigation and prosecution processes.

23. Foucault argues that there is historically a dual purpose to confession that applies here as well. First, it "signed the truth of the preliminary investigation"—justifying everything that had come before it. Second, it showed that "the accused committed himself to the procedure." Foucault, *Discipline and Punish*, 39.

24. Zain R. Mian, "No Country for Yes Men," *Africa Is a Country*, July 9, 2018. https://africasacountry.com/2018/07/no-country-for-yes-men.

25. Simanti Dasgupta, "Sovereign Silence: Immoral Traffic (Prevention) Act and Legalizing Sex Work in Sonagachi," *Political and Legal Anthropology Review* 37, no. 1 (2014): 109–125.

26. Liza Buchbinder, "Ranking States: Tracking the State Effect in West African Antitrafficking Campaigns," in *Trafficking in Slavery's Wake Law and the Experience of*

Women and Children in Africa, ed. Benjamin N Lawrance and Richard L. Roberts (Athens: Ohio University Press, 2012), 233.

27. Jefferson, "Reforming Nigerian Prisons."

4. RISK ASSESSMENT

1. María Hernández-Carretero and Jørgen Carling, "Beyond 'Kamikaze Migrants': Risk Taking in West African Boat Migration to Europe," *Human Organization* 70, no. 4 (2012): 407–416.

2. Céline Nieuwenhuys and Antoine Pécoud, "Human Trafficking, Information Campaigns, and Strategies of Migration Control," *American Behavioral Scientist* 50, no. 12 (2007): 1674–1695.

3. Publicity vans describes roaming branded vehicles, typically with rooftop audio speakers disseminating information or advertising events. Town criers are designated community figures who share news and religious observations each morning. These items and other listed strategies have been adapted for clarity from the original for clarity. "Departments: Public Enlightenment," NAPTIP, https://www.naptip.gov.ng/?page _id=136.

4. Nieuwenhuys and Pécoud, "Human Trafficking," 1677.

5. Nieuwenhuys and Pécoud, "Human Trafficking," 1684.

6. James Ferguson, *The Anti-Politics Machine: 'Development,' Depoliticization, and Bureaucratic Power in Lesotho* (Cambridge: Cambridge University Press, 1994).

7. F. E. Okonofua et al. "Knowledge, Attitudes and Experiences of Sex Trafficking by Young Women in Benin City, South-South Nigeria." *Social Science & Medicine* 59, no. 6 (2004): 1315–1327.

8. Sine Plambech, dir. *Becky's Journey* (Danish Film Institute, 2014), 24 min.

9. Sine Plambech, "Becky Is Dead," *Beyond Trafficking and Slavery,* openDemocracy, https://www.opendemocracy.net/en/beyond-trafficking-and-slavery/becky-is-dead.

10. Susan Bibler Coutin, *Legalizing Moves: Salvadoran Immigrants' Struggle for U.S. Residency* (Ann Arbor: University of Michigan Press, 2000); Nicholas De Genova, *Working the Boundaries: Race, Space, and "Illegality" in Mexican Chicago* (Durham, NC: Duke University Press, 2005); Nicholas De Genova and Nathalie Peutz, eds., *The Deportation Regime: Sovereignty, Space, and the Freedom of Movement* (Durham, NC: Duke University Press, 2010).

11. Toyin Falola and Matthew M. Heaton, *A History of Nigeria* (New York: Cambridge University Press, 2008).

12. Ferguson, *The Anti-Politics Machine*; Dambisa Moyo, *Dead Aid: Why Aid Is Not Working and How There Is a Better Way for Africa* (New York: Macmillan, 2009).

13. James Ferguson, "Seeing like an Oil Company: Space, Security, and Global Capital in Neoliberal Africa," *American Anthropologist* 107, no. 3 (2005): 377–382.

14. James Ferguson, *Global Shadows: Africa in the Neoliberal World Order* (Durham, NC: Duke University Press, 2006).

15. James Ferguson, *Expectations of Modernity: Myths and Meanings of Urban Life on the Zambian Copperbelt* (Berkeley: University of California Press, 1999), 237–238.

16. News features replicated this index of national worth, for example, when Kim Kardashian's paid visit to Nigeria began with this patriotic declaration: "Despite what is considered as Nigeria's many drawbacks, the nation remains yet a destination point to several international personages, including entertainment celebrities, music stars and exponents." Alexander Abad-Santos, "Nigeria Is Not Impressed by Kim Kardashian," *The Wire,* February 18, 2012.

17. Ferguson, *Global Shadows,* 174.

18. Neli Esipova, Julie Ray, and Anita Pugliese, "Number of Potential Migrants Worldwide Tops 700 Million," *Gallup*, June 8, 2017.

19. Charles Piot, *Nostalgia for the Future: West Africa after the Cold War* (Chicago: University of Chicago Press, 2010).

20. Julie Y. Chu, *Cosmologies of Credit: Transnational Mobility and the Politics of Destination in China* (Durham, NC: Duke University Press, 2010).

21. United Nations Development Programme, *Annual Report: UNDP Nigeria* (Abuja: UNDP Nigeria, 2016).

22. Susanna Fioratta, "Beyond Remittance: Evading Uselessness and Seeking Personhood in Fouta Djallon, Guinea," *American Ethnologist* 42, no. 2 (2015): 295–308.

23. Sine Plambech, "Sex, Deportation and Rescue: Economies of Migration among Nigerian Sex Workers," *Feminist Economics* 23 no. 3 (2017): 134–159.

24. A round-trip airline ticket to Europe from Nigeria usually costs around $1,000, but loan totals escalate because they include illicit travel documents, which vary in cost according to the quality of the product and range between a total of $6,500 to $12,000. That debt increases up to $50,000 with interest, though many migrants eventually pay back much less than that; Plambech, "Sex, Deportation and Rescue."

25. De Genova, *Working the Boundaries*.

26. Nigeria issued a new passport regime with electronic chip technology in 2007 to combat rampant problems with passport fraud and duplication.

27. David Fitzgerald, *A Nation of Emigrants: How Mexico Manages Its Migration* (Berkeley: University of California Press, 2008).

28. Alesha E. Doan and Jean Calterone Williams, *The Politics of Virginity: Abstinence in Sex Education* (Westport, CT: Praeger, 2008).

29. This list is modeled after similar comparisons drawn by Jørgen Carling, distinguishing between Escalation and Illusion; Necessity and Experience; Sacrifice and Betrayal; Capeverdeanity as leaving and Capeverdeanity as Staying. Jørgen Carling, "Migration in the Age of Involuntary Immobility: Theoretical Reflections and Cape Verdean Experiences," *Journal of Ethnic and Migration Studies* 28, no. 1 (2002): 21.

5. SEXUAL AMBITION

1. As discussed in earlier chapters, I am certain this disposition reflects as much the specific relationships I developed with women at the shelter as it proves anything definitive about their feelings toward sex work. As an educated, white, and comparatively wealthy American, I occupied a position of status and privilege by default.

2. Kamala Kempadoo and Jo Doezema, eds., *Global Sex Workers: Rights, Resistance, and Redefinition* (New York: Routledge, 1998); Kamala Kempadoo, ed., *Trafficking and Prostitution Reconsidered: New Perspectives on Migration, Sex Work, and Human Rights* (Boulder: Paradigm, 2005); Chi Adanna Mgbako, *To Live Freely in this World: Sex Worker Activism in Africa* (New York: New York University, 2016).

3. Sine Plambech, "God Brought You Home: Deportation as Moral Governance in the Lives of Nigerian Sex Worker Migrants," *Journal of Ethnic and Migration Studies* 43, no. 13 (2017): 2211–2227; and "Sex, Deportation and Rescue: Economies of Migration among Nigerian Sex Workers," *Feminist Economics* 23 no. 3 (2017): 134–159.

4. Plambech, "Sex, Deportation and Rescue," 145.

5. James Ferguson, *Expectations of Modernity: Myths and Meanings of Urban Life on the Zambian Copperbelt* (Berkeley: University of California Press, 1999); Kenneth Little, *African Women in Towns: An Aspect of Africa's Social Revolution* (Cambridge: Cambridge University Press, 1973); Luise White, *The Comforts of Home: Prostitution in Colonial Nairobi* (Chicago: University of Chicago Press, 1990).

6. Denise Brennan, *What's Love Got to Do with It? Transnational Desires and Sex Tourism in the Dominican Republic* (Durham, NC: Duke University Press, 2004); John M. Chernoff, *Hustling Is Not Stealing: Stories of An African Bar Girl* (Chicago: University of Chicago Press, 2003); Jennifer Cole, *Sex and Salvation: Imagining the Future in Madagascar* (Chicago: University of Chicago Press, 2010).

7. Battabox Media, "How Many Boyfriends Can a Girl Have?" released August 28, 2012, http://battabox.com/2012/08/28/nigeria-dating-boyfriends-nigeria-girls-video/.

8. Jennifer Cole and Lynn M. Thomas, *Love in Africa* (Chicago: University of Chicago Press, 2009); Daniel Jordan Smith, "Contradictions in Nigeria's Fertility Transition: The Burdens and Benefits of Having People," *Population and Development Review* 30, no. 2 (2004): 221–238.

9. Brook Bocast, "Declarations of Promiscuity: 'Housing,' Autonomy, and Urban Female Friendship in Uganda," *City & Society* 29, no. 3 (2017): 370–392.

10. The vague language of "outside" can sound ominous, although practically speaking migrants often have little say in choosing their destination, not because they are victims but because opportunities for visas (fraudulent and otherwise) are so fleeting and variable. Brokers typically pursue multiple channels and ultimately provide customers the most viable option. Maybritt Jill Alpes, *Brokering High-Risk Migration and Illegality in West Africa: Abroad at Any Cost* (New York: Routledge, 2016).

11. Didier Fassin and Richard Rechtman, *The Empire of Trauma: An Inquiry into the Condition of Victimhood* (Princeton, NJ: Princeton University Press, 2009).

12. As a condition of my access to the rehabilitation process, I did not observe or participate in the investigation process. However, these interviews are well documented elsewhere, particularly in studies of Nigerian women seeking migration papers in Europe. Cristiana Giordano, "Practices of Translation and the Making of Migrant Subjectivities in Contemporary Italy," *American Ethnologist* 35, no. 4 (2008): 588–606; Nicola Mai, dir. *Travel* (Royal Anthropological Institute, 2016), 63 min.

13. 1 Corinthians 6:12–20.

14. That Lagos sex workers were also forcibly removed and returned to their home states demonstrates that even sex work within Nigeria is understood and policed as a migration problem, with (internal) deportation as a solution.

15. Indeed, sex workers in Nigeria are more likely to describe unsafe sex as unpaid sex, rather than cite risks of client violence and coercion. Chimaraoke Otutubikey Izugbara, "'Ashawo Suppose Shine Her Eyes': Female Sex Workers and Sex Work Risks in Nigeria," *Health, Risk & Society* 7, no. 2 (2005): 141–159; and "Constituting the Unsafe: Nigerian Sex Workers' Notions of Unsafe Sexual Conduct," *African Studies Review* 50, no. 3 (2007): 29–49.

16. Ishaya Bako, dir. *Silent Tears* (Open Society Initiative for West Africa, 2016).

6. GOD'S PLAN

1. A previous version of this chapter was published as a journal article. Stacey Vanderhurst, "Governing with God: Religion, Resistance, and the State in Nigeria's Counter-Trafficking Programs," *Political and Legal Anthropology Review* 40, no. 2 (2017): 194–209.

2. Ruth Marshall, *Political Spiritualities: The Pentecostal Revolution in Nigeria* (Chicago: University of Chicago Press, 2009); Ebenezer Obadare, *Pentecostal Republic: Religion and the Struggle for State Power in Nigeria* (Chicago: University of Chicago Press, 2018).

3. Brenda Chalfin, *Neoliberal Frontiers: An Ethnography of Sovereignty in West Africa* (Chicago: University of Chicago Press, 2010).

4. Rick Warren, *The Purpose Driven Life: What on Earth Am I Here For?* (Grand Rapids, MI: Zondervan, 2003).

5. In insisting that even corrupt or irreligious officials may be carrying out God's plan, Ben's rhetorical strategy differs from that seen in other political spaces. Nigerian politicians regularly offer declarations of personal devotion to solicit confidence from their constituents, especially allying themselves with prominent Pentecostal leaders. Ebenezer Obadare, *Pentecostal Republic*.

6. Achille Mbembe names this shift in *l' état de religion*, calling forth a contrast with Michel Foucault's original *l' état du droit*, or governmentality by rule of law. Mbembe, "African Modes of Self-Writing," *Public Culture* 14, no. 1 (2002): 239–273.

7. Marshall, *Political Spiritualities*.

8. Fulani is one of the major tribes in Nigeria, residing primarily in the northern part of the country.

9. Marshall, *Political Spiritualities*.

10. As discussed in the following chapter, although all rehabilitated victims were promised some form of support during rehabilitation, available funds limited disbursement to only a fraction of those eligible.

11. Adejumo Gbadebo Olubunmi, E. Olu-Owolabi Fadeke, and O. Fayomi Oluyemi, "Perceived Satisfaction and Effectiveness of Rehabilitation of Victims of Human Trafficking in Nigeria: Implications for Political and Psychological Interventions," *Journal of Education, Society and Behavioural Science* 6, no. 3 (2015): 218–226; Nnenna Okoli and Uwafiokun Idemudia, "Survivor's Perceptions of Human Trafficking Rehabilitation Programs in Nigeria: Empowerment or Disempowerment?," *Journal of Human Trafficking* (2020): 1–19.

12. Vinh-Kim Nguyen, *The Republic of Therapy: Triage and Sovereignty in West Africa's Time of AIDS* (Durham, NC: Duke University Press, 2010).

13. Didier Fassin and Richard Rechtman, *The Empire of Trauma: An Inquiry into the Condition of Victimhood* (Princeton, NJ: Princeton University Press, 2009); Cristiana Giordano, "Practices of Translation and the Making of Migrant Subjectivities in Contemporary Italy," *American Ethnologist* 35, no. 4 (2008): 588–606; Simanti Dasgupta, "Sovereign Silence: Immoral Traffic (Prevention) Act and Legalizing Sex Work in Sonagachi," *Political and Legal Anthropology Review* 37, no. 1 (2014): 109–125.

14. Liza Buchbinder, "Ranking States: Tracking the State Effect in West African Antitrafficking Campaigns," in *Trafficking in Slavery's Wake Law and the Experience of Women and Children in Africa,* ed. Benjamin N. Lawrance and Richard L. Roberts (Athens: Ohio University Press, 2012): 221–240; Sine Plambech, "Between 'Victims' and 'Criminals': Rescue, Deportation, and Everyday Violence among Nigerian Migrants," *Social Politics* 21, no. 3 (2014): 382–402.

15. Anette Brunovskis and Rebecca Surtees, "Agency or Illness—The Conceptualization of Trafficking," *Gender, Technology and Development* 12, no. 1 (2008): 53–76.

16. Ebenezer Obadare and Wale Adebanwi, *Encountering the Nigerian State* (New York: Palgrave Macmillan, 2010), 10.

17. Marshall, *Political Spiritualities*, 129.

18. This shift shows how Mbembe's *l'état de religion* does not necessarily elide state power but can be appropriated within it. Mbembe, "African Modes of Self-Writing."

CONCLUSION

1. John Friedmann, *Empowerment: The Politics of Alternative Development* (Cambridge, MA: Blackwell; Andrea Cornwall, Andrea and Jenny Edwards, "Introduction: Negotiating Empowerment," *IDS Bulletin* 41, no. 2 (2010): 1–9; Nnenna Okoli and Uwafiokun Idemudia, "Survivor's Perceptions of Human Trafficking Rehabilitation Programs in Nigeria: Empowerment or Disempowerment?" *Journal of Human Trafficking* (2020): 1–19.

2. "NAPTIP Rehabilitating, Empowering, Reuniting Victims with Families," *Leadership* (Abuja), October 15, 2015.

3. That these practices can seem self-evidently rational and necessary can obscure their cultural and political consequences, generating new forms of social relations and sovereignty. Vinh-Kim Nguyen, *The Republic of Therapy: Triage and Sovereignty in West Africa's Time of AIDS* (Durham, NC: Duke University Press, 2010).

4. Scholarships allocated in this way are likewise taken for granted as rational and necessary, but they shape terms of public belonging and inclusion far beyond their economic impact. This is demonstrated in the experiences of undocumented students in the United States, who are unable to access federal financial aid. Andrea Flores, "Forms of Exclusion: Undocumented Students Navigating Financial Aid and Inclusion in the United States," *American Ethnologist* 43, no 3 (2016): 540–554.

5. Michel Foucault argues that penitentiaries divide prisoners into two different groups. Whereas some prisoners are redeemable, others are deemed to be without hope for reform, based not on their individual crimes but "according to the dispositions they revealed." Foucault, *Discipline and Punish: The Birth of the Prison* (New York: Vintage, 1995), 126.

6. Brenda Chalfin, *Neoliberal Frontiers: An Ethnography of Sovereignty in West Africa* (Chicago: University of Chicago Press, 2010).

7. Daniel Jordan Smith, *A Culture of Corruption: Everyday Deception and Popular Discontent in Nigeria* (Princeton, NJ: Princeton University Press, 2007).

8. In addition to personal financial hardships, these delays also contribute to strained social relations that migrants face on returning to their community. Erlend Paasche, May-Len Skilbrei, and Sine Plambech, "Vulnerable Here or There? Examining the Vulnerability of Victims of Human Trafficking Before and After Return," *Anti-Trafficking Review* 10 (2018): 34–51.

EPILOGUE

1. Daniel Jordan Smith, *A Culture of Corruption: Everyday Deception and Popular Discontent in Nigeria* (Princeton, NJ: Princeton University Press, 2007).

2. Maybritt Jill Alpes, *Brokering High-Risk Migration and Illegality in West Africa: Abroad at Any Cost* (New York: Routledge, 2016).

3. Eithne Luibhéid, *Entry Denied: Controlling Sexuality at the Border* (Minneapolis: University of Minnesota Press, 2002), xv.

4. Similar inspections have been documented in Britain in the 1970s, with parallels in the treatment of human trafficking victims as well. Marinella Marmo and Evan Smith, "Female Migrants: Sex, Value and Credibility in Immigration Control," in *Borders and Crime: Pre-Crime, Mobility and Serious Harm in an Age of Globalization*, ed. Jude McCulloch and Sharon Pickering (New York: Palgrave Macmillan, 2012): 54–71.

5. Saheed Aderinto, *When Sex Threatened the State: Illicit Sexuality, Nationalism, and Politics in Colonial Nigeria, 1900–1958* (Chicago: University of Illinois Press, 2015); Benedict B. Naanen, "'Itinerant Gold Mines': Prostitution in the Cross River Basin of Nigeria, 1930–1950," *African Studies Review* 34 (1991): 57–79.

6. Kenneth Little, *African Women in Towns: An Aspect of Africa's Social Revolution* (Cambridge: Cambridge University Press, 1973), 96–102; Luise White, *The Comforts of Home: Prostitution in Colonial Nairobi* (Chicago: University of Chicago Press, 1990), 190–194; Aderinto, *When Sex Threatened the State*.

7. Pauline Gardiner Barber, "The Ideal Immigrant? Gendered Class Subjects in Philippine-Canada Migration," *Third World Quarterly* 29, no. 7 (2008): 1265–1285; Robyn M. Rodriguez and Helen Schwenken, "Becoming a Migrant at Home: Subjecti-

vation Processes in Migrant-Sending Countries Prior to Departure," *Population, Space, and Place* 19 (2013): 375–388.

8. The additional penalties for "bringing the name of Nigeria into disrepute" are reproduced exactly from a 1990 military law known as Decree 33 that targeted Nigerian drug traffickers abroad. These provisions may have been incorporated in part to demonstrate that Nigeria's penalties against human trafficking were at least as stiff as those lobbied against drug trafficking, while recognizing that both activities have national consequences.

9. Investigation into these grounds for asylum claims is evident in the reports of European so-called fact-finding missions conducted in the years immediately after the NAPTIP law was passed. Danish Immigration Service (DIS), Report on Human Rights Issues in Nigeria, 1/2005 ENG (2005); Geir Skogseth, Fact-Finding Trip to Nigeria (Abuja, Lagos and Benin City), 12–26 March. Landinfo—The Country of Origin Information Centre, https://landinfo.no/asset/491/1/491_1.pdf (2006).

10. Ironically, while many advocates against "modern-day slavery" readily point out how forced labor is embedded in mainstream capitalist economies, they offer little in the way of systemic solutions such as labor protections and regulation. Instead, they identify individual criminals as the main culprits while supporting consumerist solutions in fair-trade options and charitable giving. Jennifer Lynn Musto, "What's in a Name? Conflations and Contradictions in Contemporary U.S. Discourses of Human Trafficking," *Women's Studies International Forum* 32, no. 4 (2009): 281–287.

11. Foucault argued that this transformation in governance—from sovereign authority of the law to more diffuse modes of discipline—was essential to the liberal era. However, these regimes do not replace each other but coexist. He called this relationship the "sovereignty-discipline-government" triangle, with "its primary target the population and as its essential mechanism the apparatuses of security." Michel Foucault, "Governmentality," in *The Foucault Effect: Studies in Governmentality*, ed. Graham Burchell, Colin Gordon, and Peter Miller (Chicago: University of Chicago Press, 1991), 102.

Bibliography

Abdulmalik, J., L. Kola, and O. Gureje. "Mental Health System Governance in Nigeria: Challenges, Opportunities and Strategies for Improvement." *Global Mental Health* 3 (2016): e9.

Adebanwi, Wale. "My Book Should Provoke a Conversation—Chimamanda Ngozi." *News (Nigeria)*, January 9, 2007.

Adepoju, Aderenti. "Creating a Borderless West Africa: Constraints and Prospects for Intra-Regional Migration." In *Migration without Borders: Essays on the Free Movement of People*, edited by Antoine Pécoud and Paul de Guchteneire, 161–174. New York: Berghahn Books, 2007.

Aderinto, Saheed. *When Sex Threatened the State: Illicit Sexuality, Nationalism, and Politics in Colonial Nigeria, 1900–1958.* Chicago: University of Illinois Press, 2015.

Adesina, Oluwakemi A. "Between Culture and Poverty: The Queen Mother Phenomenon and the Edo International Sex Trade." *Humanities Review Journal* 5, no. 1 (2005): 28–46.

Agustín, Laura María. *Sex at the Margins: Migration, Labour Markets and the Rescue Industry.* London: Zed Books, 2007.

Albuhari, Maurizio. *Crimes of Peace: Mediterranean Migrations at the World's Deadliest Border.* Philadelphia: University of Pennsylvania Press, 2015.

Alemika, Etannibi E. O. "Colonialism, State and Policing in Nigeria." *Crime, Law and Social Change* 20 (1993): 187–219.

——. "Policing and Perceptions of Police in Nigeria." *Police Studies: The International Review of Police Development* 11, no. 4 (1988): 161–176.

Alpes, Maybritt Jill. *Brokering High-Risk Migration and Illegality in West Africa: Abroad at Any Cost.* New York: Routledge, 2016.

Anderson, Bridget, and Rutvica Andrijasevic. "Sex, Slaves and Citizens: The Politics of Anti-Trafficking." *Soundings* 40 (2008): 135–145.

Andersson, Ruben. *Illegality, Inc: Clandestine Migration and the Business of Bordering Europe.* Berkeley: University of California Press, 2014.

Andreas, Peter. "The Escalation of U.S. Immigration Control in the Post-NAFTA Era." *Political Science Quarterly* 113 (1998): 591–601.

Andrijasevic, Rutvica. *Migration, Agency, and Citizenship in Sex Trafficking.* New York: Palgrave Macmillan, 2010.

Andrijasevic, Rutvica, and William Walters. "The International Organization for Migration and the International Government of Borders." *Environment and Planning: Society and Space* 28 (2010): 977–999.

Anya, Ike. "People Don't Get Depressed in Nigeria." *Granta,* September 5, 2012.

Apter, Andrew. *The Pan-African Nation: Oil and the Spectacle of Culture in Nigeria.* Chicago: University of Chicago Press, 2005.

Barry, Kathleen. *Female Sexual Slavery.* New York: New York University Press, 1979.

——. *The Prostitution of Sexuality.* New York: New York University Press, 1995.

Bankoff, Gregory. "Rendering the World Unsafe: 'Vulnerability' as Western Discourse." *Disasters* 25, no. 1 (2001): 19–35.

Bayart, Jean-François. *The State in Africa: The Politics of the Belly*. Cambridge: Polity, 2009.

Beckett, Katherine, and Naomi Murakawa. "Mapping the Shadow Carceral State: Toward an Institutionally Capacious Approach to Punishment." *Theoretical Criminology* 16, no. 2 (2012): 221–244.

Berman, Jacqueline. "(Un)Popular Strangers and Crises (Un)Bounded: Discourses of Sex-Trafficking, the European Political Community and the Panicked State of the Modern State." *European Journal of International Relations* 9, no. 1 (2003): 37–86.

Bernstein, Elizabeth. *Brokered Subjects: Sex, Trafficking, and the Politics of Freedom*. Chicago: University of Chicago Press, 2018.

Bigo, Didier. "Security and Immigration: Toward a Critique of the Governmentality of Unease." *Alternatives* 27, no. 1 (2002): 63–92.

Bjerkan, Lise, and Linda Dyrlid. "A Sheltered Life." In *A Life of One's Own: Rehabilitation of Victims of Trafficking for Sexual Exploitation*, edited by Lise Bjerkan, 121–153. Oslo: Fafo, 2005.

Bocast, Brook. "Declarations of Promiscuity: 'Housing,' Autonomy, and Urban Female Friendship in Uganda." *City & Society* 29, no. 3 (2017): 370–392.

Bola Ola, Jim Crabb, Abiodun Adewuya, Femi Olugbile, and Olayinka A. Abosede. "The State of Readiness of Lagos State Primary Health Care Physicians to Embrace the Care of Depression in Nigeria." *Community Mental Health* 50 (2014): 239–244.

Brennan, Denise. "Competing Claims of Victimhood? Foreign and Domestic Victims of Trafficking in the United States." *Sexuality Research and Social Policy: Journal of NSRC* 5, no. 4 (2008): 45–61.

——. *Life Interrupted: Trafficking into Forced Labor in the United States*. Durham, NC: Duke University Press, 2014.

——. *What's Love Got to Do with It? Transnational Desires and Sex Tourism in the Dominican Republic*. Durham, NC: Duke University Press, 2004.

Brunovskis, Anette, and Rebecca Surtees. "Agency or Illness—The Conceptualization of Trafficking." *Gender, Technology and Development* 12, no. 1 (2008): 53–76.

Buchbinder, Liza. "Ranking States: Tracking the State Effect in West African Antitrafficking Campaigns." In *Trafficking in Slavery's Wake: Law and the Experience of Women and Children in Africa*, edited by Benjamin N. Lawrance and Richard L. Roberts, 221–240. Athens: Ohio University Press, 2012.

Carling, Jørgen. *Migration, Human Smuggling and Trafficking from Nigeria to Europe*. Geneva: International Organization for Migration, 2006.

——. "Migration in the Age of Involuntary Immobility: Theoretical Reflections and Cape Verdean Experiences." *Journal of Ethnic and Migration Studies* 28, no. 1 (2002): 5–42.

Chalfin, Brenda. *Neoliberal Frontiers: An Ethnography of Sovereignty in West Africa*. Chicago: University of Chicago Press, 2010.

Chapkis, Wendy. "Soft Glove, Punishing Fist: The Trafficking Victims Protection Act of 2000." In *Regulating Sex: The Politics of Intimacy and Identity*, edited by Elizabeth Bernstein and Laurie Schaffner, 51–66. New York: Routledge, 2005.

——. "Trafficking, Migration, and the Law: Protecting Innocents, Punishing Immigrants." *Gender & Society* 17, no. 6 (2003): 923–937.

Chavez, Leo R. *Covering Immigration: Popular Images and the Politics of the Nation*. Berkeley: University of California Press, 2001.

——. *The Latino Threat: Constructing Immigrants, Citizens, and the Nation*. Stanford: Stanford University Press, 2008.

Chernoff, John Miller. *Hustling Is Not Stealing: Stories of An African Bar Girl*. Chicago: University of Chicago Press, 2003.

Chu, Julie Y. *Cosmologies of Credit: Transnational Mobility and the Politics of Destination in China.* Durham, NC: Duke University Press, 2010.

Chuang, Janie. "The United States as Global Sheriff: Using Unilateral Sanctions to Combat Human Trafficking." *Michigan Journal of International Law* 27 (2006): 437–494.

Cohen, Stanley. *Folk Devils and Moral Panics.* New York: Routledge, 1972.

Cole, Jeffrey E., and Sally S. Booth. *Dirty Work: Immigrants, Domestic Service, Agriculture, and Prostitution in Sicily.* Lanham, MD: Lexington Books, 2007.

Cole, Jennifer. *Sex and Salvation: Imagining the Future in Madagascar.* Chicago: University of Chicago Press, 2010.

Cole, Jennifer, and Lynn M. Thomas, eds. *Love in Africa.* Chicago: University of Chicago Press, 2009.

Comaroff, Jean. "Beyond Bare Life: AIDS, (Bio)Politics, and the Neoliberal Order." *Public Culture* 19, no. 1 (2007): 197–219.

Cornwall, Andrea, and Jenny Edwards. "Introduction: Negotiating Empowerment." *IDS Bulletin* 41, no. 2 (2010): 1–9.

Coutin, Susan Bibler. *Legalizing Moves: Salvadoran Immigrants' Struggle for U.S. Residency.* Ann Arbor: University of Michigan Press, 2000.

Dasgupta, Simanti. "Sovereign Silence: Immoral Traffic (Prevention) Act and Legalizing Sex Work in Sonagachi." *Political and Legal Anthropology Review* 37, no. 1 (2014): 109–125.

De Genova, Nicholas P. *Working the Boundaries: Race, Space, and "Illegality" in Mexican Chicago.* Durham, NC: Duke University Press, 2005.

De Genova, Nicholas P., and Nathalie Peutz, eds. *The Deportation Regime: Sovereignty, Space, and the Freedom of Movement.* Durham, NC: Duke University Press, 2010.

De Haas, Hein. "The Myth of Invasion: The Inconvenient Realities of African Migration to Europe." *Third World Quarterly* 29, no. 7 (2008): 1305–1322.

Dennis, C. "Women and the State in Nigeria: The Case of the Federal Military Government." In *Women, State, and Ideology: Studies from Africa and Asia,* edited by Haleh Afshar, 13–27. London: SUNY Press, 1987.

Doan, Alesha E., and Jean Calterone Williams. *The Politics of Virginity: Abstinence in Sex Education.* Westport, CT: Praeger, 2008.

Doezema, Jo. "Forced to Choose: Beyond the Voluntary v. Forced Prostitution Dichotomy." In *Global Sex Workers: Rights, Resistance, and Redefinition,* edited by Kamala Kempadoo and Jo Doezema, 34–50. New York: Routledge, 1998.

——. "Loose Women or Lost Women? The Re-Emergence of the Myth of White Slavery in Contemporary Discourses of Trafficking in Women." *Gender Issues* 18, no. 1 (1999): 23–50.

——. "Ouch!: Western Feminists' 'Wounded Attachment' to the 'Third World Prostitute.'" *Feminist Review* 67 (2001): 16–38.

——. *Sex Slaves and Discourse Masters: The Construction of Trafficking.* New York: Zed Books, 2010.

Dottridge, Mike. "Trafficking in Children in West and Central Africa." *Gender and Development* 10, no. 1 (2010): 38–42.

Düvell, Franck. "The Globalisation of Migration Control." *Open Democracy,* June 13, 2003.

Elabor-Idemudia, Patience. "Nigeria: Agricultural Exports and Compensatory Schemes— Rural Women's Production Resources and Quality of Life." In *Mortgaging Women's Lives: Feminist Critiques of Structural Adjustment,* edited by Pamela Sparr, 134–164. London: Palgrave Macmillan, 1994.

Ellis, Stephen. "West Africa's International Drug Trade." *African Affairs* 108, no. 431 (2009): 171–196.

Emerole, Josiah, ed. *Amazing Crusade: Media Portrait of Titi Atiku Abubakar War against Human Trafficking*. Abuja: Women Trafficking and Child Labour Eradication Foundation, 2002.

Falola, Toyin, and Matthew M Heaton. *A History of Nigeria*. New York: Cambridge University Press, 2008.

Fassin, Didier. "Compassion and Repression: The Moral Economy of Immigration Policies in France." *Cultural Anthropology* 20, no. 3 (2005): 362–387.

——. "Policing Borders, Producing Boundaries: The Governmentality of Immigration in Dark Times." *Annual Review of Anthropology* 40, no. 1 (2011): 213–226.

Fassin, Didier, and Richard Rechtman. *The Empire of Trauma: An Inquiry into the Condition of Victimhood*. Princeton, NJ: Princeton University Press, 2009.

Favell, Adrian, and Randall Hansen. "Markets against Politics: Migration, EU Enlargement and the Idea of Europe." *Journal of Ethnic and Migration Studies* 28, no. 4 (2002): 581–601.

Feldman, Ilana, and Miriam Iris Ticktin, eds. *In the Name of Humanity: The Government of Threat and Care*. Durham, NC: Duke University Press, 2010.

Ferguson, James. *The Anti-Politics Machine: "Development," Depoliticization, and Bureaucratic Power in Lesotho*. Cambridge: Cambridge University Press, 1994.

——. *Expectations of Modernity: Myths and Meanings of Urban Life on the Zambian Copperbelt*. Berkeley: University of California Press, 1999.

——. *Global Shadows: Africa in the Neoliberal World Order*. Durham, NC: Duke University Press, 2006.

——. "Seeing like an Oil Company: Space, Security, and Global Capital in Neoliberal Africa." *American Anthropologist* 107, no. 3 (2005): 377–382.

Fioratta, Susanna. "Beyond Remittance: Evading Uselessness and Seeking Personhood in Fouta Djallon, Guinea." *American Ethnologist* 42, no. 2 (2015): 295–308.

Fitzgerald, David. *A Nation of Emigrants: How Mexico Manages Its Migration*. Berkeley: University of California Press, 2008.

Flores, Andrea. "Forms of Exclusion: Undocumented Students Navigating Financial Aid and Inclusion in the United States." *American Ethnologist* 43, no 3 (2016): 540–554.

Foucault, Michel. *The Archaeology of Knowledge*. New York: Vintage, 2010.

——. *Discipline and Punish: The Birth of the Prison*. New York: Vintage, 1995.

——. "Governmentality." In *The Foucault Effect: Studies in Governmentality*, edited by Graham Burchell, Colin Gordon, and Peter Miller, 87–104. Chicago: University of Chicago Press, 1991.

Friedmann, John. *Empowerment: The Politics of Alternative Development*. Cambridge, MA: Blackwell, 1992.

Gallagher, Anne T. *The International Law of Human Trafficking*. New York: Cambridge University Press, 2010.

Gallagher, Anne T., and Elaine Pearson. "The High Cost of Freedom: A Legal and Policy Analysis of Shelter Detention for Victims of Trafficking." *Human Rights Quarterly* 32, no. 1 (2010): 73–114.

Gardiner Barber, Pauline. "The Ideal Immigrant? Gendered Class Subjects in Philippine-Canada Migration." *Third World Quarterly* 29, no. 7 (2008): 1265–1285.

Geiger, Martin, and Antoine Pécoud, eds. *Disciplining the Transnational Mobility of People*. New York: Palgrave MacMillan, 2013.

Giordano, Cristiana. "Practices of Translation and the Making of Migrant Subjectivities in Contemporary Italy." *American Ethnologist* 35, no. 4 (2008): 588–606.

Guiné, Anouk, and Francisco Javier Moreno Fuentes. "Engendering Redistribution, Recognition, and Representation: The Case of Female Genital Mutilation (FGM) in the United Kingdom and France." *Politics & Society* 35, no. 3 (2007): 477–519.

Hernández-Carretero, María, and Jørgen Carling. "Beyond 'Kamikaze Migrants': Risk Taking in West African Boat Migration to Europe." *Human Organization* 70, no. 4 (2012): 407–416.

Hicks, Dan. *The Brutish Museum: The Benin Bronzes, Colonial Violence and Cultural Restitution*. London: Pluto Press, 2020.

Hodžić, Saida. *The Twilight of Cutting: African Activism and Life after NGOs*. Berkeley: University of California Press, 2016.

Izugbara, Chimaraoke Otutubikey. "'Ashawo Suppose Shine Her Eyes': Female Sex Workers and Sex Work Risks in Nigeria." *Health, Risk & Society* 7, no. 2 (2005): 141–159.

——. "Constituting the Unsafe: Nigerian Sex Workers' Notions of Unsafe Sexual Conduct." *African Studies Review* 50, no. 3 (2007): 29–49.

Jefferson, Andrew M. "Prison Officer Training and Practice in Nigeria." *Punishment & Society* 9, no. 3 (2007): 253–269.

——. "Reforming Nigerian Prisons: Rehabilitating a 'Deviant' State." *British Journal of Criminology* 45, no. 4 (2005): 487–503.

Jeffreys, Sheila. *Anticlimax: A Feminist Perspective on the Sexual Revolution*. New York: New York University Press, 1991.

——. *The Idea of Prostitution*. Melbourne: Spinifex Press, 2008.

——. *The Industrial Vagina: The Political Economy of the Global Sex Trade*. New York: Routledge, 2009.

Kempadoo, Kamala. *Trafficking and Prostitution Reconsidered: New Perspectives on Migration, Sex Work, and Human Rights*. Boulder: Paradigm, 2005.

Kempadoo, Kamala, and Jo Doezema, eds. *Global Sex Workers: Rights, Resistance, and Redefinition*. New York: Routledge, 1998.

Kotiswaran, Prabha. "Vulnerability in Domestic Discourses on Trafficking: Lessons from the Indian Experience." *Feminist Legal Studies* 20, no. 3 (2012): 245–262.

Lee, Maggy. "Gendered Discipline and Protective Custody of Trafficking Victims in Asia." *Punishment & Society* 16, no. 2 (2014): 206–222.

Leinaweaver, Jessaca. *The Circulation of Children: Kinship, Adoption, and Morality in Andean Peru*. Durham, NC: Duke University, 2008.

Little, Kenneth Lindsay. *African Women in Towns: An Aspect of Africa's Social Revolution*. New York: Cambridge University Press, 1973.

Loyd, Jenna M., and Alison Mountz. *Boats, Borders, and Bases: Race, the Cold War, and the Rise of Migration Detention in the United States*. Oakland: University of California Press, 2018.

Luibhéid, Eithne. *Entry Denied: Controlling Sexuality at the Border*. Minneapolis: University of Minnesota Press, 2002.

Mama, Amina. "Khaki in the Family: Gender Discourses and Militarism in Nigeria." *African Studies Review* 41, no. 2 (1998): 1–17.

——. "Sheroes and Villains: Conceptualizing Colonial and Contemporary Violence against Women in Africa." In *Feminist Genealogies, Colonial Legacies, Democratic Futures*, edited by M. Jacqui Alexander and Chandra Talpade Mohanty, 46–62. New York: Routledge, 1997.

Mandera, M. U. "Female Genital Mutilation in Nigeria." *International Journal of Gynecology and Obstetrics* 84, no. 3 (2004): 291–298.

Marmo, Marinella, and Evan Smith. "Female Migrants: Sex, Value and Credibility in Immigration Control." In *Borders and Crime: Pre-Crime, Mobility and Serious Harm in an Age of Globalization*, edited by Jude McCulloch and Sharon Pickering, 54–71. New York: Palgrave Macmillan, 2012.

Marshall, Ruth. *Political Spiritualities: The Pentecostal Revolution in Nigeria*. Chicago: University of Chicago Press, 2009.

Massey, Douglas S., Jorge Durand, and Nolan J. Malone. *Beyond Smoke and Mirrors: Mexican Immigration in an Era of Economic Integration*. New York: Russell Sage Foundation, 2002.

Mbembe, Achile. "African Modes of Self-Writing." *Public Culture* 14, no. 1 (2002): 239–273.

———. *On the Postcolony*. Berkeley: University of California Press, 2001.

McCulloch, Jude, and Sharon Pickering, eds. *Borders and Crime: Pre-Crime, Mobility and Serious Harm in an Age of Globalization*. New York: Palgrave Macmillan, 2012.

Menjívar, Cecilia. "Immigration Law beyond Borders: Externalizing and Internalizing Border Controls in an Era of Securitization." *Annual Review of Law and Social Science* 10 (2014): 353–369.

Merry, Sally Engle. *The Seductions of Quantification: Measuring Human Rights, Gender Violence, and Sex Trafficking*. Chicago: University of Chicago Press, 2016.

Mgbako, Chi Adanna. *To Live Freely in this World: Sex Worker Activism in Africa*. New York: New York University Press, 2016.

Mian, Zain R. "No Country for Yes Men." *Africa Is a Country*, July 9, 2018. https://africasacountry.com/2018/07/no-country-for-yes-men.

Moyo, Dambisa. *Dead Aid: Why Aid Is Not Working and How There Is a Better Way for Africa*. New York: Macmillan, 2009.

Musto, Jennifer. *Control and Protect: Collaboration, Carceral Protection, and Domestic Sex Trafficking in the United States*. Berkeley: University of California Press, 2016.

———. "What's in a Name? Conflations and Contradictions in Contemporary U.S. Discourses of Human Trafficking." *Women's Studies International Forum* 32, no. 4 (2009): 281–287.

Naanen, Benedict B. "'Itinerant Gold Mines': Prostitution in the Cross River Basin of Nigeria, 1930–1950." *African Studies Review* 34 (1991): 57.

Neal, A. W. "Securitization and Risk at the EU Border: The Origins of FRONTEX." *JCMS: Journal of Common Market Studies* 47 (2009): 333–356.

Nguyen, Vinh-Kim. *The Republic of Therapy: Triage and Sovereignty in West Africa's Time of AIDS*. Durham, NC: Duke University Press, 2010.

Nieuwenhuys, Céline, and Antoine Pécoud. "Human Trafficking, Information Campaigns, and Strategies of Migration Control." *American Behavioral Scientist* 50, no. 12 (2007): 1674–1695.

Nwogu, Victoria Ijeoma. "Nigeria." In *Collateral Damage: The Impact of Anti-Trafficking Measures on Human Rights around the World*, 142–170. Bangkok: Global Alliance against Traffic in Women, 2007.

Oba, Abdulmumini A. "Juju Oaths in Customary Law Arbitration and their Legal Validity in Nigerian Courts." *Journal of African Law* 52 (2008): 139–158.

Obadare, Ebenezer. *Humor, Silence, and Civil Society in Nigeria*. Rochester, NY: University of Rochester Press, 2016.

———. *Pentecostal Republic: Religion and the Struggle for State Power in Nigeria*. Chicago: University of Chicago Press, 2018.

Obadare, Ebenezer, and Wale Adebanwi. *Encountering the Nigerian State*. London: Palgrave Macmillan, 2010.

Ojo-Ade, Femi. *Death of a Myth: Critical Essays on Nigeria*. Trenton, NJ: Africa World Press, 2001.

Okeke, Philomina. "First Lady Syndrome: The (En)Gendering of Bureaucratic Corruption in Nigeria." *Codesria Bulletin* 3, no. 4 (1998): 16–19.

Okojie, C. E. E., O. Okojie, K. Eghafona, G. Vincent-Osaghae, and V. Kalu. *Report of Field Survey in Edo State, Nigeria*. Torino: United Nations Interregional Crime and Justice Research Institute, 2003.

Okoli, Nnenna, and Uwafiokun Idemudia, "Survivor's Perceptions of Human Trafficking Rehabilitation Programs in Nigeria: Empowerment or Disempowerment?" *Journal of Human Trafficking* (2020): 1–19.

Okonofua, F. E., S. M. Ogbomwan, A. N. Alutu, Okop Kufre, and Aghahowa Eghosa. "Knowledge, Attitudes and Experiences of Sex Trafficking by Young Women in Benin City, South-South Nigeria." *Social Science & Medicine* 59, no. 6 (2004): 1315–1327.

Okyere, Sam. "Shock and Awe": A Critique of the Ghana-Centric Child Trafficking Discourse." *Anti-Trafficking Review* 9 (2017): 92–105.

Olubunmi, Adejumo Gbadebo, E. Olu-Owolabi Fadeke, and O. Fayomi Oluyemi. "Perceived Satisfaction and Effectiveness of Rehabilitation of Victims of Human Trafficking in Nigeria: Implications for Political and Psychological Interventions." *Journal of Education, Society and Behavioural Science* 6, no. 3 (2015): 218–226.

Oluwaniyi, Oluwatoyin O. "Post-Amnesty Programme in the Niger Delta: Challenges and Prospects." *Conflict Trends* 4 (2017): 46–54.

O'Neill, Kevin Lewis, and Jatin Dua. "Captivity: A Provocation." *Public Culture* 30, no. 1 (2018): 3–18.

Osezua, Clementina. "Changing Status of Women and the Phenomenon of Trafficking of Women for Transactional Sex in Nigeria: A Qualitative Analysis." *Journal of International Women's Studies* 14, no. 3 (2013): 14–30.

——. "Transmogrified Religious Systems and the Phenomenon of Sex Trafficking among the Benin People of Southern Nigeria." *AFRREV IJAH: An International Journal of Arts and Humanities* 2, no. 3 (2014): 20–35.

Paasche, Erlend, May-Len Skilbrei, and Sine Plambech. "Vulnerable Here or There? Examining the Vulnerability of Victims of Human Trafficking before and after Return." *Anti-Trafficking Review* 10 (2018): 34–51.

Piot, Charles. *Nostalgia for the Future: West Africa after the Cold War*. Chicago: University of Chicago Press, 2010.

——."The 'Right" to Be Trafficked." *Indiana Journal of Global Legal Studies* 18, no. 1 (2011): 199–210.

Plambech, Sine. "Becky Is Dead." *Beyond Trafficking and Slavery*, openDemocracy. October 10, 2016, https://www.opendemocracy.net/en/beyond-trafficking-and-slavery/becky-is-dead/.

——. "Between 'Victims' and 'Criminals': Rescue, Deportation, and Everyday Violence Among Nigerian Migrants." *Social Politics* 21, no. 3 (2014): 382–402.

——. "God Brought You Home: Deportation as Moral Governance in the Lives of Nigerian Sex Worker Migrants." *Journal of Ethnic and Migration Studies* 43, no. 13 (2017): 2211–2227.

——. "Sex, Deportation and Rescue: Economies of Migration among Nigerian Sex Workers." *Feminist Economics* 23, no. 3 (2017): 134–159.

Plankensteiner, Barbara, ed. *Benin Kings and Rituals: Court Arts from Nigeria*. Ghent: Snoek & Museum für Völkerkunde, 2007.

Rodriguez, Robyn M., and Helen Schwenken. "Becoming a Migrant at Home: Subjectivation Processes in Migrant-Sending Countries prior to Departure." *Population, Space, and Place* 19 (2013): 375–388.

Ryder, Alan. F. C. *Benin and the Europeans, 1485–1897*. London: Longmans, 1969.

Smith, Daniel Jordan. *AIDS Doesn't Show Its Face: Inequality, Morality, and Social Change in Nigeria*. Chicago: University of Chicago Press, 2014.

——. "Contradictions in Nigeria's Fertility Transition: The Burdens and Benefits of Having People." *Population and Development Review* 30, no. 2 (2004): 221–238.

——. *A Culture of Corruption: Everyday Deception and Popular Discontent in Nigeria.* Princeton, NJ: Princeton University Press, 2007.

Soderlund, Gretchen. "Running from the Rescuers." *NWSA Journal* 17 (2005): 64–87.

Solari, Cinzia. "'Prostitutes' and 'Defectors': How the Ukrainian State Constructs Women Emigrants to Italy and the USA." *Journal of Ethnic and Migration Studies* 11, no. 40 (2014): 1817–1835.

Suchland, Jennifer. *Economies of Violence: Transnational Feminism, Postsocialism, and the Politics of Sex Trafficking.* Durham, NC: Duke University Press, 2016.

Stumpf, Juliet. "The Crimmigration Crisis: Immigrants, Crime, and Sovereign Power." *American University Law Review* 56 (2006): 367–419.

Surtees, Rebecca. *Why Shelters? Considering Residential Approaches to Assistance.* Washington, DC: NEXUS Institute to Combat Human Trafficking, 2008.

Ticktin, Miriam. *Casualties of Care: Immigration and the Politics of Humanitarianism in France.* Berkeley: University of California Press, 2011.

Tontore, Susan. "Precious Red Coral: Markets and Meanings." *Beads: Journal of the Society of Bead Researchers* 16, no. 4 (2004): 3–16.

Vanderhurst, Stacey. "Governing with God: Religion, Resistance, and the State in Nigeria's Counter-Trafficking Programs." *Political and Legal Anthropology Review* 40, no. 2 (2017): 194–209.

Vulpiani, Pietro. "Migrant and Refugee Women, Scaremongering and Afterthoughts on Female Genital Mutilations." *Gender Forum* 66 (2017): 26–49.

Warren, Kay B. "The 2000 U.N. Human Trafficking Protocol: Rights, Enforcement, Vulnerabilities." In *The Practice of Human Rights: Tracking Law between the Global and the Local,* edited by Mark Goodale and Sally Engle Merry, 242–270. New York: Cambridge University Press, 2007.

Walters, William. "Anti-Policy and Anti-Politics: Critical Reflections on Certain Schemes to Govern Bad Things." *European Journal of Cultural Studies* 11, no. 3 (2008): 267–288.

——. "Foucault and Frontiers: Notes on the Birth of the Humanitarian Border." In *Governmentality: Current Issues and Future Challenges,* edited by Ulrich Bröckling, Susanne Krasmann, and Thomas Lemke, 138–164. New York: Routledge, 2010.

White, Luise. *The Comforts of Home: Prostitution in Colonial Nairobi.* Chicago: University of Chicago Press, 1990.

Yingwana, Ntokozo. "'We Fit in the Society by Force': Sex Work and Feminism in Africa." *Meridians* 17, no. 2 (2018): 279–295.

Yuval-Davis, Nira. *Gender and Nation.* London: Sage, 1997.

Zedner, Lucia. "Pre-Crime and Post-Criminology?" *Theoretical Criminology* 11, no. 2 (2007): 261–281.

Zolberg, Aristide R. "The Exit Revolution." In *Citizenship and Those Who Leave: The Politics of Emigration and Expatriation,* edited by Nancy L. Green and François Weil, 33–61. Urbana: University of Illinois Press, 2007.

Index

Abacha, Maryam, 22. *See also* First Ladies' Syndrome
Abacha, Sani, 22, 25
abjection, 89
Abubakar, Titi. *See also* First Ladies' Syndrome
Abuja, 38, 110, 120, 158
agency. *See* rescue narratives; resistance of migrant women; sex workers
Alpes, Maybritt Jill, 161, 176n25, 177n28, 182n9
ambition, 26–27, 66–68, 91–92, 100, 102–3, 106–7
arrests of sex workers, 25, 38, 48, 117, 120
ashawo, 116, 117. *See also* sex workers
assisted voluntary return, 57, 174n75
asylum seekers, 36, 164, 169n33, 185n9
Attah, Judith, 25
author, positionality of, 14, 88, 158

Babangida, Ibrahim "IBB," 21–22
Babangida, Maryam, 22. *See also* First Ladies' Syndrome
Becky's Journey (film), 86–87
belonging, 11, 89–90, 100, 162
Benin Bronzes, 20
Benin City: history of, 20–21, 32; sex work in, 107–8. *See also* Edo women
Benin Republic, 158–59, 170
Better Life for Rural Women organization (BLP), 22
Bini ethnic group, 19, 30–31. *See also* Edo women
Black feminism, 11, 170n37
Blessing (woman), 74–75, 91, 93–97, 107–8, 134, 148
borders: interceptions at, 37–39, 47–50, 53, 55–56; securitization of, 8–11, 24, 99. *See also* passport control
Buhari, Muhamadu, 21

carceral feminism, 6–7
carceral protection, 3–4, 7–10, 57–60. *See also* crimmigration; detention
chain migration, 23. *See also* migration
Child Care Trust (CCT), 35

child trafficking, 47, 91
churches, 31, 113, 124, 128. *See also* Pentecostal Christianity; religious authority
claims on state resources, 35–36, 72, 135–39, 145–47
Coalition against Trafficking in Women (CATW), 4–5. *See also* neo-abolitionism
coercion, 5, 9, 20, 115, 118–20. *See also* deception
Comaroff, Jean, 36
commercial sex. *See* sex workers; sex work industry
confession, 14, 111–23, 133–35, 179n23
consent, 7, 37, 54, 106, 114
"convincing victims," 4, 56–59, 63, 68–73, 113, 138, 147
coral trade, 23
corruption: of border agents, 3, 53, 97, 158–62; of government, 21–23, 60, 88; NAPTIP and, 43, 65, 76–77, 97, 125–30, 139, 145; of social institutions, 20, 31, 113
counselors, 45–46, 64–67. *See also* group therapy; psychiatry
criminalization, 6, 8–9, 37–39. *See also* Palermo Protocol (2000)
crimmigration, 8–9, 11. *See also* carceral protection; migration
culpability, 64, 68–70, 84

deception, 5, 13, 49, 78–79, 81, 110, 119. *See also* coercion; naivety
democratic transition. *See* political transitions
Department of Public Enlightenment, 39, 46, 80–81. *See also* education campaigns; NAPTIP
Department of Counseling and Rehabilitation, 46, 80. *See also* NAPTIP; psychiatry
deportation, 15–16, 24–25, 27–28, 163, 182n14. *See also* passport control
detention: at borders, 3, 9, 55–56; escapes from, 44, 59–60; individual resistance to, 3, 16, 42–43, 56–58; as protection, 38–39, 43, 58–59, 61; release from, 144–45, 149–50; TIP Report on, 51. *See also* carceral protection; criminalization

disease. *See* HIV/AIDS
Doezema, Jo, 167n5
drug trafficking, 25, 38, 96, 185n8
Dubai, 110, 158

economic opportunity: in Gambia, 93–94;
through debt migration, 14, 30–31, 89–90,
95–97; through sex work, 106–7, 108–10.
See also poverty; sexual exchange
Edo women: Queen Idia, 32–33; reputation of,
19–20. *See also* Benin City
education campaigns, 10, 39, 46, 80–85, 100
Eikineh, Prince, 162–63
emigration. *See* migrant-sending states;
migration
empowerment, 39, 106, 140–42, 145–47,
151–56. *See also* rehabilitation
Entry Denied (Luibhéid), 162
European Union (EU): delegations from, 57,
76, 114; as Fortress Europe, 8, 24; as migrant
destination, 23–25, 36, 86–87, 89–90

fact-finding missions, 57, 76, 114, 185n9
Falola, Toyin, 21
Famakin, Joseph, 141
families of migrant women, 28, 30–33, 49–50,
58, 69, 134
female genital mutilation (FGM), 35–36,
174n64, 174n66
Ferguson, James, 89
FESTAC '77 (festival), 32
financial independence. *See* economic
opportunity
First Ladies' Syndrome, 22–23, 30,
35–37
Florence, 1–2; detention life of, 45, 74–75; on
migration, 91–94, 122–23; migration
attempt and interception of, 2–3, 42,
78–79; passport of, 98–99; post-detention
life of, 150–51, 166; on sex work, 107–10,
111–12
Force Criminal Investigation Department,
27–28
Foucault, Michel, 169n36, 178n10, 178n13,
179n23, 183n6, 184n5, 185n11

Global Alliance against Trafficking in Women
(GAATW), 5
God. *See* churches; Pentecostal Christianity;
religious authority
GONGOs, 22
governmentality. *See* Foucault, Michel
government NGOs (GONGOs), 22

group therapy, 43, 68, 74, 78, 91–92, 102–105,
110, 127, 144, 146. *See also* counselors;
psychiatry
Grupo Beto, 99

harassment. *See* corruption; retaliation;
shaming of women
HIV/AIDS, 25, 28–29, 35, 46, 137
human rights, 8–10, 22, 38, 65, 111
human trafficking: as contested, 3–5, 14, 78,
86, 95, 106, 118; criminalization of, 6, 8–9,
37–39; definitions of, 6–7, 50–51, 106, 165,
168n11; types of, 46–48. *See also* deception;
sex work industry; traffickers

IBB. *See* Babangida, Ibrahim "IBB"
Idia (queen), 32–33
Idia Renaissance, 32, 33, 38
Igbinedion, Eki, 30, 33
illegality, 23–24, 88, 96. *See also* passport
control; smuggling
information campaigns, 10, 39, 46, 80–85,
100
innocence, 14, 72–73, 105–6, 110–12, 118
interception. *See* borders; preemptive
interceptions; rescue narratives
International Organization for Migration
(IOM), 46, 84, 96, 169n32, 174n75, 175n7
introspection, 66–68, 124, 139. *See also* group
therapy; "opening up"
investigation, 27–28, 39, 73–75, 98–99, 106,
182n12
Italy: deportation campaigns in, 15–16, 24–25,
27–28; sex industry of, 23; trade and chain
migration to, 23

Jefferson, Andrew, 65
juju, 31, 49

Kingdom of Great Benin, 20, 32–33
Kuti, Fela, 128

labor rights activism, 5–6, 165
labor trafficking and exploitation, 47, 70, 79,
87–88
Lagos Zonal Shelter (NAPTIP). *See* detention;
NAPTIP
Libya, 112–15, 122

Marshall, Ruth, 60, 138–39
media representations, 18–19, 24–26, 28–31,
34, 49
Mexico, 9, 99

CPSIA information can be obtained
at www.ICGtesting.com
Printed in the USA
LVHW042309260522
719869LV00003B/507